WI'

UT:

Addiction and the Medical Complications of Drug Abuse

Addiction and the
Medical Complications
of Drug Abuse

Edited by
Steven B. Karch, MD, FFFLM

Consultant Pathologist and Toxicologist
Berkeley, California

CRC Press
Taylor & Francis Group
Boca Raton   London   New York

CRC Press is an imprint of the
Taylor & Francis Group, an informa business

CRC Press
Taylor & Francis Group
6000 Broken Sound Parkway NW, Suite 300
Boca Raton, FL 33487-2742

© 2008 by Taylor & Francis Group, LLC
CRC Press is an imprint of Taylor & Francis Group, an Informa business

No claim to original U.S. Government works
Printed in the United States of America on acid-free paper
10 9 8 7 6 5 4 3 2 1

International Standard Book Number-13: 978-1-4200-5443-9 (Hardcover)

Visit the Taylor & Francis Web site at
http://www.taylorandfrancis.com

and the CRC Press Web site at
http://www.crcpress.com

Contents

Preface

Substance misuse is often considered to be an unpopular subject with many doctors, partly because of the frequent relapse experienced by addicts and partly because of the behavioral problems that can occur when drug users interact with substance misuse treatment services.

Many clinical drug treatment services are dominated by the prescribing of methadone to those dependent on heroin (diacetylmorphine). Methadone maintenance treatment (MMT) has been the most rapidly expanding treatment for heroin dependence over the last 30 years with increasingly large numbers of countries providing such treatment for extensive treatment populations. Even more recently buprenorphine, a partial agonist, has been introduced into drug treatment services and has provided an alternative to methadone. Many doctors involved with addiction problems will see themselves as having only a prescribing role whereas specialists in the field will, in addition, require a repertoire of psychotherapy skills.

Prescribing for patients who may have a dependence on a number of drugs, who may wish to conceal the extent of their substance use, and who may have a marked tolerance to some classes of drug is discussed in order to help inform the practitioner.

The first six chapters of this volume provide an overview, primarily for the nonspecialist. Topics discussed in detail include the psychology of addiction, substitute prescribing, and the identification and management of withdrawal symptoms, both sedative and stimulant. Chapter 7 is a brief discussion of toxicological testing, primarily for the purpose of assessing compliance. Chapters 8 and 9 examine the specific clinical syndromes associated with drugs of abuse.

The Editor

Steven B. Karch, M.D., FFFLM, received his undergraduate degree from Brown University. He attended graduate school in anatomy and cell biology at Stanford University. He received his medical degree from Tulane University School of Medicine. Dr. Karch did postgraduate training in neuropathology at the Royal London Hospital and in cardiac pathology at Stanford University. For many years he was a consultant cardiac pathologist to San Francisco's Chief Medical Examiner.

In the U.K., Dr. Karch served as a consultant to the Crown and helped prepare the cases against serial murderer Dr. Harold Shipman, who was subsequently convicted of murdering 248 of his patients. He has testified on drug abuse–related matters in courts around the world. He has a special interest in cases of alleged euthanasia, and in episodes where mothers are accused of murdering their children by the transference of drugs, either *in utero* or by breast feeding.

Dr. Karch is the author of nearly 100 papers and book chapters, most of which are concerned with the effects of drug abuse on the heart. He has published seven books. He is currently completing the fourth edition of *Pathology of Drug Abuse*, a widely used textbook. He is also working on a popular history of Napoleon and his doctors.

Dr. Karch is forensic science editor for Humana Press, and he serves on the editorial boards of the *Journal of Cardiovascular Toxicology*, the *Journal of Clinical Forensic Medicine* (London), *Forensic Science, Medicine and Pathology*, and *Clarke's Analysis of Drugs and Poisons*.

Dr. Karch was elected a fellow of the Faculty of Legal and Forensic Medicine, Royal College of Physicians (London) in 2006. He is also a fellow of the American Academy of Forensic Sciences, the Society of Forensic Toxicologists (SOFT), the National Association of Medical Examiners (NAME), the Royal Society of Medicine in London, and the Forensic Science Society of the U.K. He is a member of The International Association of Forensic Toxicologists (TIAFT).

Contributors

Joanna Banbery, M.B.B.S.
The Leeds Addiction Unit
Leeds, U.K.

Neal L. Benowitz, M.D.
Division of Clinical Pharmacology and
  Experimental Therapeutics
University of California
San Francisco, California

Nick Lintzeris, M.B.B.S., Ph.D.
National Addiction Centre
South London and Maudsley NHS Trust
London, U.K.

Kent R. Olson, M.D.
Division of Clinical Pharmacology and
  Experimental Therapeutics
University of California
San Francisco, California

Duncan Raistrick, M.B.B.S.
The Leeds Addiction Unit
Leeds, U.K.

Brett A. Roth, M.D.
University of Texas Southwestern Medical
  Center
Dallas, Texas

Kim Wolff, Ph.D.
King's College London
Institute of Psychiatry
National Addiction Centre
London, U.K.

Shoshana Zevin, M.D.
Department of Internal Medicine
Shaare Zedek Medical Center
Jerusalem, Israel

CHAPTER 1

The Principles of Addiction Medicine

Duncan Raistrick, M.B.B.S.
The Leeds Addiction Unit, Leeds, U.K.

CONTENTS

Many doctors involved with addiction problems will see themselves as having only a prescribing role whereas specialists in the field will, in addition, require a repertoire of psychotherapy skills. Prescribing for patients who may have a dependence on a number of drugs, who may wish to conceal the extent of their substance use, and who may have a marked tolerance to some classes of drug presents difficulties for the unwary or ill-informed doctor. In order to prescribe safely and effectively doctors must:

1. Understand the nature of dependence
2. Understand the dependence-forming potential of drugs
3. Understand the importance of motivation

1.1 UNDERSTANDING THE NATURE OF DEPENDENCE

In the U.K. and North America, the understanding of addiction has been dominated by the disease theory and the social learning theory. Heather[1] succinctly describes the history and development of thinking underpinning these theories. Other theories or, perhaps more correctly, models of addiction have been popular in particular cultures or where partial explanations have utility; for example, psychoanalytical interpretations of addictive behavior are common in some European countries, and equally, religious or moral failures are attractive reasons to account for addictive behavior where spiritual values are important as in many Asian and Indian communities.

The important implications of the disease theory depend on the notion that addiction is caused by some irreversible deficiency or pathology and that treatment is, therefore, primarily a medical concern. Certain conclusions inevitably follow from such a premise: (1) abstinence is the only treatment goal, (2) loss of control is the hallmark feature, (3) patients are not responsible for their illness, (4) therapists tend to be medical practitioners, and, finally, (5) community-based prevention will be ineffective.

In formulating a description of alcohol and later other drug dependence, Edwards and Gross[2] argued against the disease model in favor of a biopsychosocial construction of dependence, which was identified as belonging to a separate dimension from substance-related harms. This formulation has been adopted in the International Classification of Diseases, ICD-10.[3] The important implications of social learning theory are: a range of treatment goals is possible, the ability to control substance use is emphasized, users are active participants in treatment, therapists tend to be nonmedical, and fiscal and other control measures will be effective.

The biopsychosocial description of dependence has been criticized for placing unwarranted emphasis on withdrawal symptoms. While the anticipation or experience of withdrawal may indeed be a potent source of negative reinforcement for drinking, it is not the only source of reinforcement, and it may be that the positive reinforcement of a pharmacological (drug) effect is more important whether or not an individual also experiences withdrawal. To take account of this, Raistrick et al.[4] have proposed a modified description of the dependence syndrome and developed the idea of substance dependence as a purely psychological phenomenon where tolerance and withdrawal are understood as consequences of regular drinking, rather than being a part of dependence. The withdrawal symptoms themselves are one step removed from the cognitive response to the symptoms, which may or may not include thoughts about drinking. If withdrawal symptoms were themselves a defining element of dependence, then different drugs would be associated with different kinds of dependence, but this is not a widely held view. Rather, it is believed that dependence can readily shift from one substance to another.[5] The markers of substance dependence translate the neuroadaptive elements of the biopsychosocial description of dependence into cues that condition cognitions and behaviors and are therefore of more universal application. There are ten markers of substance dependence:

1. Preoccupation with drinking or taking drugs
2. Salience of substance use behavior
3. Compulsion to start using alcohol or drugs
4. Planning alcohol- or drug-related behaviors
5. Maximizing the substance effect
6. Narrowing of substance use repertoire
7. Compulsion to continue using alcohol and drugs
8. Primacy of psychoactive effect
9. Maintaining a constant state (of intoxication)
10. Expectations of need for substance use

In summary, the most complete account of addictive behaviors comes from a synthesis of physiology, pharmacology, psychology, sociology, and social learning. Dependence exists along a continuum of severity implying the need for different treatments and outcome goals. Substance-related harms in physical, psychological, and social spheres belong to a separate domain. *Addiction* has become a term without precise meaning, but is generally taken to include dependence, problem use, and any related harms. While social learning allows that anyone may become dependent on psychoactive substances and may also unlearn their dependence, it does not preclude the possibility that substance use may cause deficiencies of endogenous neurotransmitters, which are usually reversible, or permanent damage to receptor structure and connectivity. Indeed, it is likely that such changes occur.

1.2 UNDERSTANDING THE DEPENDENCE-FORMING POTENTIAL OF DRUGS

1.2.1 Potency of Psychoactive Effect

In humans, the reinforcing properties of psychoactive substances, which combine to generate the umbrella construct dependence, are complex: a prominent view attaches importance to the positive reinforcing effects of inducing pleasurable mood states and the negative reinforcement of avoiding painful affects. Pervin[5] explores this very issue in a study of four polydrug users: subjects were asked to describe situations (1) where they wanted to use drugs, (2) after they had used drugs, (3) where they wanted to use drugs but could not, and (4) unrelated to drug use, and then to associate affects from a prepared list with the four situations they described. A factor analysis produced three factors accounting for 44% of the variance: the first factor, Wish, was characterized as being tense, helpless, jittery, lonely; the second factor, After Drugs, was characterized as lonely, empty, inhibited, angry; and the third factor, Taking Drugs, included confidence, relaxed, high, secure, strong, satisfied. The results also indicated that subjects discriminated between drugs suited to dealing with different effects.

In two complementary reports, Johanson and Uhlenbuth[6,7] compared changes in mood among normal volunteers in a choice experiment between placebo, diazepam, and amphetamine. Amphetamine 5 mg was chosen significantly more often than placebo, 81% of possible choices, with increased scores for vigor, friendliness, elation, arousal, positive mood, and decreased scores for confusion. In contrast, diazepam 5 and 10 mg were chosen significantly less often than placebo, 28 and 27% of choices, respectively, with decreased scores on vigor and arousal and increased scores on confusion and fatigue. The point to underline here is that normal subjects are likely to have different effects from patient groups and the reinforcing potential of different substances will therefore vary between such groups: within matched subjects the reinforcing properties of different substances will also vary in strength.

At a clinical level, most doctors are wary of addictive drugs: for example, long-term methadone prescribing is intended to achieve pharmacological stability, at least partially block the effect of other opioids, and prevent withdrawal symptoms. However, Bickel et al.[8] suggest that, although methadone is seen as a low tariff drug, treatment retention is, in part, associated with its reinforcing properties. Using a choice paradigm, subjects maintained on methadone 50 mg daily, identified to subjects as capsule A, had the option of taking capsule B, which, in different trials, contained either methadone 50, 60, 70, or 100 mg, in place of capsule A. Capsule B was chosen on 50, 73, 87, and 97%, respectively, of occasions: at the highest dose, subjects identified an opioid effect and a liking for the drug but no high or withdrawal was reported. The clinical implications are quantified by McGlothlin and Anglin[9] in a 7-year follow-up of patients attending high- vs. low-dose methadone maintenance programs: the high-dose program performed better in terms of retention, significantly fewer arrests and periods of incarceration, less criminal activity, and less supplementary drug use. In a similar type of study, Hartnoll et al.[10] followed up addicts randomly allocated to an injectable heroin or oral methadone program: at 1-year follow-up, 74% of the heroin group against 29% of the methadone group were still in treatment but only 10% against 30% had achieved abstinence from illicit drugs. So, the dilemma is that prescriptions most liked by addicts, namely, those that are more reinforcing, achieve good program retention and a degree of stability, but at the cost of slowing movement away from substance use and the associated subculture.

The potency of psychoactive effect is not simply a function of dose or plasma level, but also depends on receptor uptake characteristics. For example, Chiang and Barnett[11] have shown that immediately after intravenous tetrahydrocannabinal a rising plasma concentration of approximately

45 ng/ml relates to a subjective high of 10% whereas the same falling plasma concentration 15 min later relates to a high of nearly 80% on a self-rating 0 to 100% scale. This phenomenon is accounted for by a slow uptake of THC at the receptors. Active metabolites may spuriously suggest the same phenomenon.

Similarly, the partial agonist buprenorphine has a high, but slow, binding affinity at the opiate mu receptor: it has the potential to act as antagonist against pure opioid agonists and itself appears to have a ceiling effect at about 1 mg subcutaneously for subjective response. Although addicts identify buprenorphine as having an opioid effect and therefore potential for misuse, its binding affinity at the mu receptor and antagonist activity confer a quite different reinforcement profile to pure agonists such as diamorphine (heroin).

The clinical significance is demonstrated by Johnson et al.[12] who substituted heroin for buprenorphine in ascending daily doses of 2, 4, and 8 mg: using this regimen, diamorphine withdrawal symptoms were avoided and, overall, subjects reported a feeling of well-being. Withdrawal from buprenorphine 8 mg daily does not precipitate an opiate withdrawal syndrome.

1.2.2 Pharmacokinetics

The previous section argued that the mood-altering effects of psychoactive drugs may, depending on the pre-drug mental state, have both positive and negative reinforcing properties. Psychoactive effect alone is insufficient explanation of within-drug-group differences of dependence forming potential: different pharmacokinetics is important. The benzodiazepines and opioids are the most fruitful source of investigation here because both drug groups contain many different compounds that are widely used and misused. However, it is difficult to conduct studies that control for confounding factors such as absorption rate, potency, purity, half-life, or street availability (and likelihood of supplementing). It is perhaps not surprising that researchers are parsimonious with conclusions.

There are ethical problems in conducting laboratory experiments with potent drugs such as heroin and to avoid this problem Mello et al.[13] investigated the reinforcing efficacy in primates for three opioids: they found buprenorphine and methadone to have similar strength but heroin to be more powerful. Equally in humans heroin is preferred to other opiates including morphine.[14] Since heroin is converted to morphine within the central nervous system (CNS), it can be concluded that its faster rate of CNS availability accounts for the difference. Absorption rate and, therefore, immediacy of effect have similarly been shown to be important for benzodiazepines. Funderburk et al.[15] compared the effects of equipotent oral doses of lorazepam (0, 1.5, 3, and 6 mg) and diazepam (0, 10, 20, and 40 mg) in recreational benzodiazepine users: the drug liking ratings were similar for both drugs, suggesting that the absorption rate, which is similar for the two drugs, is more important than the elimination half-life, which is much shorter for lorazepam even though subjective ratings of effect persist much longer for this compound. Learning theory predicts the importance of absorption rate in that the most immediate positive consequence of a behavior (drug taking) is the most reinforcing. While potency and the speed of onset of effect are particularly important for initiating dependence, elimination rate assumes greater importance in building and maintaining dependence. As a rule, the more quickly a drug is metabolized, the sooner the user experiences a loss of effect and possibly also withdrawal symptoms. Both of these consequences become cues for further drug use.

1.2.3 Plasticity

Plasticity is defined as the degree to which the effect of a drug is independent of internal environment (e.g., mood, thirst) and external environment (e.g., with friends, comfort). Edwards[16] has described substances as existing along a continuum: highly plastic substances, that is, those where the content of the effect is markedly influenced by environment, exist at one end (e.g., solvents, LSD), and substances with very predictable content (e.g., heroin, cocaine) exist at the opposite end. Plasticity has a bearing on the dependence-forming potential of substances; where the content of a drug effect is uncertain, repeated use is unlikely. In contrast, a very predictable effect may not suit the variety of uses demanded of a recreational substance, but yet be powerfully reinforcing, that is, addictive. It is interesting that the most popular recreational drugs, alcohol and cannabis, fall around the middle of the plasticity continuum, perhaps signaling a point that allows an agreeable interaction between drug and expectation effects. In summary, the dependence-forming potential of a drug is a function of:

1. Potency of effect
2. Speed of entering the CNS
3. Speed of joining with receptors
4. Elimination rate
5. Predictability of effect

1.3 UNDERSTANDING THE IMPORTANCE OF MOTIVATION

The measurement of dependence and the identification of substance-related problems tell the clinician what outcome goals are likely to be successful and how much treatment is needed; alongside this an understanding of motivation informs what kind of treatment is needed. The Model of Change described by Prochaska and DiClemente[17] is a motivational model widely used in the addiction field. The purpose of using the model is twofold: first, to understand what is going on for a patient at a given time; second, to inform the patient of the choice of interventions. People who are not motivated to change their substance use are said to be at the pre-contemplation stage, which is characterized by denial and rationalization of substance use and its consequences. There are two strands to treatment strategy at this stage: one is to minimize harm without expecting to change the substance use behavior (for example, by giving nutritional supplements or substitute prescribing). The second is to introduce conflict about the substance use (for example, by making links with untoward life events and thereby creating motivation for change). The temptation is to offer treatments aimed at changing substance use behavior before the patient is ready to change. In such circumstances the treatment will always fail.

The experience of significant conflict about substance use (for example, when an arrest is felt to be incompatible with a self-image of being a sensible and responsible person) or when the cost of substance use is causing family hardship indicates movement into the contemplation stage. At this stage, motivational interventions, which may involve the use of simple clinical tools (for example, the decision matrix), or may draw on more sophisticated skills (for example, motivational interviewing),[18] are indicated. At this stage substitute prescribing or agonist prescribing may be helpful.

The action stage is reached when conflict is resolved and there is a commitment to change. A number of things will have happened at a psychological level: the person will believe that life will be better on stopping or controlling their substance use (positive outcome expectancy), they are able to change (self-efficacy), and they will know how to change (skills learning). Elective detoxification is the most common medical intervention at the action stage.

The maintenance stage follows behavioral change. This is the achievement of abstinence or controlled substance use. Maintenance of behavior change for alcohol misuse may be assisted by prescribing a sensitizing agent such as disulfiram or, for opiate misuse, prescribing an antagonist such as naltrexone. Pharmacological interventions are no more than an adjunct to the main task of achieving lifestyle change. Successful exit from the maintenance stage, recovery, requires that the patient has confidence and skills to deal with substance use cues. Achieving the right mix of pharmacology and psychology is more art than science, but an understanding of the underlying brain mechanisms, reviewed for clinicians by Nutt,[19] and a parallel understanding of motivation will help achieve safe and effective prescribing.

1.4 PRESCRIBING IN CONTEXT

Addiction problems are everyone's business: the sociologist, the politician, the biochemist, the doctor, the police officer, the parent, the pharmacist, the taxpayer, the drug dealer, and the public. The list is long; such is the diversity of interests vested in substance use and misuse. Everyone will have opinions about addiction including opinions about what doctors should prescribe. Doctors should seek the widest possible clinical freedom to manage addiction patients and to secure this freedom. It follows that prescribers must be sensitive to the prevailing medicopolitical views on what constitutes good practice. People who misuse substances, particularly illicit substances, may have particularly forceful views about what doctors should prescribe, but these views are likely to change depending on where a person is within his or her addiction career. It follows that prescribers must have an understanding of addictive behaviors and characteristics of addictive substances. The Model of Change (described above) is a simple, commonly used tool that offers a framework for prescribing and other interventions.

For most people who have developed a moderate or severe dependence, pharmacotherapy will, at some time, be an important part of treatment. However, prescribing alone will never be sufficient. It follows that prescribers must have a repertoire of skills, including behavior therapy and psychotherapy or, alternatively, must work with a co-therapist. When working with a co-therapist, the doctor must be satisfied with the reasons for prescribing and take responsibility for the prescription given.

1.5 GENERAL PRECAUTIONS

Doctors who are inexperienced in the field of addiction often feel pressured to prescribe beyond their knowledge and skills, and as a result may issue inappropriate prescriptions. In contrast, specialists are likely to be circumspect about the place of pharmacotherapy and especially so when this means prescribing addictive drugs.[20] The precautions listed below are applicable to any prescribing; however, patients who misuse both prescribed and illicit drugs are especially at risk, not least because prescriptions are often for potent preparations in doses higher than normally recommended. Doctors may be required to justify their prescribing to a variety of authorities and are more likely to fall afoul of legal action or audit because of precipitate rather than delayed prescribing. Having established the appropriateness of prescribing, the following checklist will ensure the safety of a prescription:

Prescribe drugs with low dependence-forming potential.
Prescribe drugs with low injection potential.
Prescribe drugs with low "street value."
Prescribe inherently stabilizing drugs.
Assess:
    Risk of overdose by patient
    Risk of overdose by others living with patient
    Risk of diversion for profit or misuse
    Risk of failing to control use as prescribed
Assess tolerance before prescribing potentially lethal doses.
Check other prescribed medication.
Check on co-existing medical conditions.
Monitor compliance.

Safety of prescribing needs to be balanced against a regimen that is convenient for the patient and which will therefore achieve the best results in terms of retention and compliance.[21,22] Before finally giving a prescription, it is crucial to ensure that both the doctor and the patient understand the purpose of the prescription.[23] There should be agreement on how to monitor whether or not the intended purpose is being achieved; if the purpose is not achieved then the prescription should be reviewed and possibly discontinued. This does not imply an end to therapy but rather consideration of a shift to an alternative, possibly nonpharmacological treatment.

REFERENCES

1. Heather, N. and Robertson, I., *Problem Drinkers,* Oxford: Oxford University Press, 1989.
2. Edwards, G. and Gross, M.M., Alcohol dependence: provisional description of a clinical syndrome, *Br. Med. J.,* 1, 1058, 1976.
3. World Health Organisation, *The ICD-10 Classification of Mental and Behavioural Disorders: Clinical Descriptions and Diagnostic Guidelines,* Geneva: World Health Organisation, 1992.
4. Raistrick, D.S., Bradshaw, J., Tober, G., Weiner, J., Allison, J., and Healey, C., Development of the Leeds Dependence Questionnaire, *Addiction,* 89, 563, 1994.
5. Pervin, L.A., Affect and addiction, *Addict. Behav.,* 13, 83, 1988.
6. Johanson, C.E. and Uhlenhuth, E.H., Drug preference and mood in humans: diazepam, *Psychopharmacology,* 71, 269, 1980.
7. Johanson, C.E. and Uhlenhuth, E.H., Drug preference and mood in humans: d-amphetamine, *Psychopharmacology,* 71, 275, 1980.
8. Bickel, W.K., Higgins, S.T., and Stitzer, M.L., Choice of blind methadone dose increases by methadone maintenance patients, *Drug Alcohol Depend.,* 18, 165, 1986.
9. McGlothlin, W.H. and Anglin, D., Long-term follow-up of clients of high and low-dose methadone programs, *Arch. Gen. Psychiatry,* 38, 1055, 1981.
10. Hartnoll, R.L., Mitcheson, M.C., Battersby, A., Brown, G., Ellis, M., Fleming, P., and Hedley, N., Evaluation of heroin maintenance in controlled trial, *Arch. Gen. Psychiatry,* 37, 877, 1980.
11. Chiang, C.W. and Barnett, G., Marijuana effect and delta-9-tetrahydrocannabinol plasma levels, *Clin. Pharmacol. Ther.,* 36, 234, 1984.
12. Johnson, R.E., Cone, E.J., Henningfield, J.E., and Fudala, P.J., Use of buprenorphine in the treatment of opiate addiction. I. Physiologic and behavioural effects during a rapid dose induction, *Clin. Pharmacol. Ther.,* 46, 335, 1989.
13. Mello, N.K., Lukas, S.E., Bree, M.P., and Mendekson, J.H., Progressive ration performance maintained by buprenorphine, heroin and methadone in macaque monkeys, *Drug Alcohol Depend.,* 21, 81, 1988.
14. Stimson, G.V. and Oppenheimer, E., *Heroin Addiction: Treatment and Control in Britain,* London: Tavistock Publications, 1982.
15. Funderburk, F.R., Griffiths, R.R., McLeod, D.R., Bigelow, G.E., Mackenzi, A., Liebson, I.A., and Nemeth-Coslett, R., Relative abuse liability of lorazepam and diazepam: an evaluation in "recreational" drug users, *Drug Alcohol Depend.,* 22, 215, 1988.
16. Edwards, G., Drug dependence and plasticity, *Q. J. Stud. Alcohol,* 35, 176, 1974.
17. Prochaska, J.O. and DiClemente, C.C., *The Transtheoretical Approach: Crossing Traditional Boundaries of Therapy,* Homewood, IL: Dow Jones-Irwin, 1984.
18. Tober, G., Motivational interviewing with young people, in Miller, W. and Rollnick, S., Eds., *Motivational Interviewing: Preparing People to Change*, New York: Guildford, 1991.
19. Nutt, D.J., Addiction: brain mechanisms and their treatment implications, *Lancet,* 347, 31, 1996.
20. Finn, P., Program administrator and medical staff attitudes toward six hypothetical medications for substance abuse treatment, *J. Psychoactive Drugs,* 28, 161, 1996.
21. Pani, P.P., Piratsu, R., Ricci, A., and Gessa, G.L., Prohibition of take-home dosages: negative consequences on methadone maintenance treatment, *Drug Alcohol Depend.,* 41, 81, 1996.
22. Greenfield, L., Brady, J.V., Besteman, K.J., and De Smet, A., Patient retention in mobile and fixed-site methadone maintenance treatment, *Drug Alcohol Depend.,* 42, 125, 1996.
23. Department of Health. *Drug Misuse and Dependence: Guidelines in Clinical Management.* London: HMSO, 1999.

CHAPTER 2

Substitute Prescribing: Opioid-Specific Prescribing

Kim Wolff, Ph.D.
King's College London, Institute of Psychiatry, National Addiction Centre, London, U.K.

CONTENTS

Substitute prescribing is the prescription of the main drug of misuse or a drug from the same pharmacological group but of lower dependence potential to a dependent individual. The main purpose of substitute prescribing is to stabilize a person's substance use and offer a period of time to work on non-drug-focused interventions. Slow reduction or detoxification can occur at any time during substitute prescribing. Recipients of substitute prescribing may fall into one or more of the following categories:

1. Diagnosis of opioid, cocaine, amphetamine, or benzodiazepine dependence
2. Minimum 6-month history of regular use
3. Regular injecting, especially if high risk, of whatever duration
4. Failed attempts to achieve abstinence
5. At time of initial assessment, likely to be at the pre-contemplation or contemplation stage of change

Evidenced-based guidelines for providing substitute treatment for drug misusers have been reported[1-3] and, in brief, aim to bring about:

Short term:
    Attract patients into treatment
    Relieve withdrawal symptoms
Long term:
    Retain in treatment

Reduce injecting behavior
Stabilize drug use
Stabilize lifestyle
Reduce criminal behavior
Reduce human immunodeficiency virus (HIV), HBV, and HBC transmission
Reduce death rate

2.1 OPIOID-SPECIFIC PRESCRIBING

Maintenance prescribing differs from substitute prescribing only in that there is no active effort to bring about change in a person's drug use or psychological state. The majority of clinical drug misuse services are concerned principally with the prescription of methadone to heroin users. American reviews tend to cite methadone as a direct pharmacological treatment in the way that insulin is used for diabetes. Many Europeans, however, would view methadone more as a substitute treatment whereby the improvements that are seen result from removing individuals from the process of using street drugs.[2]

2.1.1 Methadone Maintenance Prescribing

Methadone, a synthetic opioid first reported as a maintenance (long-term, fixed-dose) treatment for opiate dependence by Dole and Nyswander,[4] is the most widely used pharmacological treatment for this type of addiction in Britain and North America. Methadone first appeared in Europe in the late 1960s in response to an emerging use of heroin and was officially introduced into Britain in 1968.[5] Today methadone remains the preferred drug of choice for the treatment of heroin dependence,[6] dominating the substitute prescribing market.[7]

Substantial evidence exists in the international literature to support the effectiveness of methadone maintenance treatment (MMT), particularly with regard to reduction in intravenous drug misuse,[8,9] less crime,[10,11] reemployment,[12] social rehabilitation,[13] overall health status,[12] improved quality of lifestyle,[14] and safety and cost effectiveness compared to other (drug-free) alternatives.[15] The National Treatment Outcome Research Study (NTORS) reported similar findings in Britain.[16] Retention in treatment is the key, however, and discernible treatment effects are only seen when patients remain in treatment for longer than 1 year.[17] The available evidence indicates that it is methadone per se that retains patients in treatment.[18]

Following a move toward a harm minimization (rather than abstinence) in response to the perceived threat from the HIV, there was a rapid expansion of methadone treatment in Britain, the U.S., and Australia.[19] Methadone treatment continues to play an important role in the prevention of the transmission of HIV infection among injectors of heroin.[20,21]

2.1.2 Treatment Compliance

Studies of treatment response have shown that patients who comply with the recommended course of treatment have favorable outcomes during treatment and longer-lasting post-treatment benefits. Thus, it is discouraging for many practitioners that opiate users are frequently poorly compliant or noncompliant and subsequently resume substance use.[22] Insufficient methadone dose has been identified as a major cause of therapeutic failure and relapse to re-abuse drugs,[18] affecting behavior above and beyond individual differences in motivation and severity of drug dependence.

Despite more than 35 years of clinical use of methadone for the treatment of heroin dependence, appropriate dosing remains controversial. However, a consistent relationship between higher doses of the drug, less illicit opioid use, and retention in treatment has been frequently observed.[23–29] Previous research indicates that an insufficient dose (inadequate for the prevention of withdrawal symptoms for the total duration of the dosing interval, 24 h) is a major problem for opioid users during treatment.[30] Unfortunately, the likelihood of success is offset by the fact that many patients do not remain in treatment until they are rehabilitated, and those who drop out usually return (relapse) to drug misuse.[31]

2.1.3 Therapeutic Drug Monitoring for Methadone

Many different parameters have been investigated to help assess the efficacy of methadone maintenance treatment. Randomized controlled trials to investigate methadone treatment have been advocated recently.[10] A randomized controlled trial of methadone maintenance treatment in 593 Australian prisoners indicated that heroin use was significantly lower among treated prisoners than control subjects at follow up.[32,33]

The usual procedure for assessing opioid users at clinics involves urinalysis screening for drugs of abuse (see Chapter 7). Urinalysis drug screening is an important way of assessing drug misuse by patients undergoing methadone treatment, but sheds no light on patient compliance, i.e., whether the patient is taking medication as prescribed. It is essential to know if a patient is taking all of their medication (at the correct time and in the correct amount) and to find out whether the patient is using extra methadone (obtained illicitly) or selling some of the prescription, perhaps to other users. Urinalysis will only indicate whether or not a patient has taken some of the medication. Dosage alterations based on interpretation of plasma measurements may help more patients do well on methadone.[34-36]

Scientific measurements, in addition to urinalysis and report systems, are clearly needed to evaluate patients. It was found that plasma measurements of methadone filled the gap and provided much needed evidence on compliance. Compliance in methadone maintenance patients has been measured using a pharmacological indicator to "estimate" plasma methadone concentrations. The study showed that many patients took their medication haphazardly (incorrect self-administration), whereas others supplemented their dose with illicit methadone.[37]

The success or failure of patients in methadone treatment may be related to the determination of an appropriate daily oral dose,[38] identifying patients who respond poorly to treatment,[39] and ensuring compliance to the dosage regimen. Such tasks are difficult as clinicians are currently without an accurate, convenient, and objective therapeutic tool for therapeutic drug monitoring.

Blood is the primary biological sample for pharmacokinetic analyses, as both parent and metabolite concentrations can be quantified and samples cannot be adulterated by the donor.[40] Methadone plasma concentration has been correlated to oral dose when compliance is good[39,41,42] and plasma methadone concentration can be used to determine an appropriate oral dose.

Studies have reported that there is a robust linear relationship between plasma methadone concentration and oral dose, when patients are on a constant dose, and compliance is good.[42,43] This relationship can be demonstrated over a wide range of dosages (3 to 100 mg), and the correlation has been reported at $r = 0.89$.[42]

2.1.4 Indications for Plasma Methadone Monitoring

Take-home methadone: Initially attendance at a methadone dispensing clinic is required on a daily basis to consume medication under staff supervision. This requirement becomes impractical when the patient is assuming responsibility and trying to engage in work, rehabilitation, education programs, or responsible homemaking. Shared-care may be a sensible solution. A collaborative relationship between the prescribing doctor, community pharmacist, and specialist drug treatment center has been advocated as good practice as a means to allow flexibility with prescribing. Unfortunately, the practice of permitting take-home supplies for unsupervised self-administration has contributed problems, including:[44]

1. Accidental ingestion of methadone by nontolerant persons, especially children
2. Methadone toxic reactions

3. Overdose fatalities
4. Diversion for illicit sale
5. Redistribution to other heroin users suffering from withdrawal symptoms
6. Redistribution to drug users seeking a new euphoriant

Monitoring the concentration of methadone in patients who take the drug away from the clinic is advisable to confirm that the prescribed dose is being consumed in the correct amount and at the correct time.

Methadone is metabolized by a specific cytochrome P450 pathway, but as a predominantly oral drug absorption is a prerequisite for its activity. The absorption process is affected by many factors, not least the degree of intestinal first-pass metabolism, which occurs by cytochrome P4503A (CYP3A) and the active extrusion of absorbed drug by the multidrug efflux pump, *P*-glycoprotein (P-gr).

Measuring *N*-demethylation activity or depletion in human liver microsomes and recombinant P450 isoform showed the highest contribution for CYP3A4.[45,46] However, the metabolism of methadone is complex and has been shown to be subject to *N*-demethylation by CYP2B6, 2CI9, 2D6, and 2C9.[47] Accordingly, CYP3A4 selective inhibitors or monoclonal human anti-CYP3A4 antibodies are able to inhibit the foundation of the main metabolic product EDDP by up to 80%,[48] and CYP3A4 inducers produce a similar reaction in the opposite direction.

Hence many compounds may affect methadone kinetics. Concomitant administration of enzyme-inducing (or inhibiting) drugs is said to be a factor influencing methadone kinetics. Reports suggest that rifampicin,[49,50] phenytoin,[51] barbiturates,[52] and disulfiram[53] are associated with unexpectedly low plasma methadone concentrations. Similar affects have been reported with zidovudine (azidothymidine; AZT), fucidic acid,[54] and amitriptyline,[55] which are not known enzyme inducers. Reports of the effect of drug inhibitors on the kinetics of methadone are less apparent clinically, but the effect has been demonstrated for fluconazole.[56] Diazepam appears to inhibit the metabolism of methadone,[57] but not with therapeutic (<40 mg\day diazepam\day) dosing.[58] Interaction between methadone and medications used to treat HIV infection are other examples.[59]

Physiological state: Other factors said to influence the clearance of methadone include excessive alcohol consumption[60] and physiological states such as pregnancy.[61] To conclude, when compliance is good, plasma methadone concentrations can be used to validate dosing regimes. Conversely, plasma methadone measurements can also be used to assess compliance.

REFERENCES

1. Department of Health. *Drug Misuse and Dependence: Guidelines in Clinical Management.* London: HMSO, 1999.
2. Seivewright, N.A. and Greenwood, J., What is important in drug misuse treatment. *Lancet,* 347, 373, 1996.
3. Lingford-Hughes, A.R., Welch, S., and Nutt, D.J., Evidence-based guidelines for the pharmacological management of substance misuse addiction and co-morbidity: recommendations from the British Association for Psychopharmacology, *J. Psychopharmacol.,* 18, 293, 2004.
4. Dole, V.P. and Nyswander, M., A medical treatment for diacetylmorphine (heroin) addiction, *J. Am. Med. Assoc.,* 193, 80, 1965.
5. Solberg, U., Burkhaut, G., and Nilson, M., An overview of opiate substitution treatment in the European Union and Norway. *Int. J. Drug Policy,* 8, 575, 2002.
6. Verster, A. and Buning, E., *European Methadone Guidelines,* Amsterdam, the Netherlands: Euro-Methwork, 2000.
7. Corkery, J.M., Schifano, F., Ghodse, A.H., and Oyefeso, A., The effects of methadone and its role in fatalities. *Hum. Psychopharmacol. Clin. Exp.,* 19, 565, 2004.

8. Schuster, C.R., The National Institute on Drug Abuse and methadone maintenance treatment, *J. Psychoactive Drugs*, 23, 111, 1991.

9. Gossop, M., Marsden, J., Stewart, D., and Kidd, T., Reduction or cessation of injecting behaviours? Treatment outcomes at 1 year follow-up, *Addict. Behav.*, 28, 785, 2003.

10. Hall, W., Bell, J., and Carless, J., Crime and drug use among applicants for methadone maintenance, *Drug Alcohol Depend.*, 31, 123, 1993.

11. Gossop, M., Marsden, J., and Stewart, D., NTORS after five years: changes in substance use, health and criminal behaviour during the five years after intake, London: Department of Health, 2001.

12. Ball, J.C., Lange, W.R., Myers, C.P., and Friedman, S.R., Reducing the risk of AIDS through methadone maintenance treatment, *J. Health Social Behav.*, 29, 214, 1988.

13. Ward, J., Mattick, R., and Hall, W., *Key Issues in Methadone Maintenance Treatment,* University of New South Wales Press, Sydney, Australia, 1992.

14. Reno, R.R. and Aiken, L.S., Life activities and life quality of heroin addicts in and out of treatment, *Int. J. Addict.*, 28, 211, 1993.

15. Glass, R.M., Methadone maintenance: new research on a controversial treatment [editorial], *J. Am. Med. Assoc.*, 269, 1995, 1993.

16. Gossop, M., Marsden, J., Edwards, C., Stewart, D., Wilson, A., Segar, G., and Lehmann, P., *The National Treatment Outcome Study (NTORS): Summary of the Project, the Clients, and Preliminary Findings,* London: Department of Health, 1996.

17. D'Aunno, T. and Vaughn, T.E., Variations in methadone treatment practice, *J. Am. Med. Assoc.*, 267, 253, 1992.

18. Caplehorn, J.R.M., Bell, J., Kleinbaum, D.G., and Gebski, V.J., Methadone dose and heroin use during maintenance treatment, *Addiction*, 88, 119, 1993.

19. Kang, S.-Y. and De Leon, G., Correlates of drug injection behaviours among methadone outpatients, *Am. J. Drug Alcohol Abuse*, 19, 107, 1993.

20. Thiede, H., Hagan, H., and Murrill, C.S., Methadone treatment and HIV and Hepatitis B and C: risk reduction in the Seattle area, *J. Urban Health*, 77, 331, 2000.

21. Wong, K.H., Lee, S.S., Lim, W.I., and Low, H.K., Adherence to methadone is associated with a lower level of HIV related risk behaviour in drug users, *J. Subst. Abuse Treat.*, 24, 233, 2003.

22. Wolff, K., Hay, A., Raistrick, D., Calvert, R., and Feely, M., Measuring compliance in methadone maintenance patients: use of pharmacological indicator to "estimate" methadone plasma levels, *Clin. Pharmacol. Ther.*, 50, 199, 1991.

23. Gerstein, D.R., The effectiveness of drug treatment, in *Addictive States*, O'Brien, C.P. and Jaffe, J.H., Eds., New York: Raven Press, 1992, 235.

24. Strain, E.C., Bigelow, G.E., Liebson, I.A., and Stitzer, M.L., Moderate versus high dose methadone in the treatment of opioid dependence; a randomized trial, *J. Am. Med. Assoc.*, 281, 1000, 1999.

25. Faggiano, F., Vigana-Tagliati, F.E., and Lemma, P., Methadone Maintenance at Different Doses, The Cochrane Library, Chichester, U.K.: John Wiley & Sons, 1, 37, 2004.

26. Wolff, K., Hay, A.W.M., and Raistrick, D., Plasma methadone measurements and their role in methadone detoxification programmes, *Clin. Chem.*, 38, 420, 1992.

27. Ball, J.C. and Ross, A., *The Effectiveness of Methadone Maintenance Treatment*, New York: Springer, 1991.

28. Ling, W. and Wessan, D.R., Methadyl acetate and methadone as maintenance treatments for heroin addicts. A Veterans Administration cooperative study, *Arch. Gen. Psychiatry*, 232, 149, 2003.

29. Barnett, P.G., Rodgers, J.H., and Bloch, D.A., A meta analysis comparing buprenorphine to methadone for treatment of opiate dependence, *Addiction*, 96, 683, 2001.

30. Wolff, K. and Hay, A.W.M., Plasma methadone monitoring with methadone maintenance treatment, *Drug Alcohol Depend.*, 36, 69, 1994.

31. Wolff, K., Sanderson, M., and Hay, A.W.M., Methadone concentrations in plasma and their relationship to drug dosage, *Clin. Chem.*, 37, 205, 1991.

32. Wolff, K., Hay, A.W.M., Raistrick, D., and Calvert, R., Steady state pharmacokinetics of methadone in opioid addicts, *Eur. J. Clin. Pharmacol.*, 44, 189, 1993.

33. Kreek, M.J., Gutjahr, C.R., Garfield, J.W., Bowen, D.V., and Field, F.H., Drug interactions with methadone, *Ann. N.Y. Acad. Sci.*, 281, 350, 1976.

34. Liu, S.J. and Wang, R.I.H., Case report of barbiturate-induced enhancement of methadone metabolism and withdrawal syndrome, *Am. J. Psychiatry,* 141, 1287, 1984.

35. Dole, V.P., Implications of methadone maintenance for theories of narcotic addiction, *J. Am. Med. Assoc.,* 260, 3025, 1988.

36. Blaine, J.D., Renault, P.F., Levine, G.L., and Whysner, J.A., Clinical use of LAAM, *Ann. N.Y. Acad. Sci.,* 311, 214, 1978.

37. Kreek, M.J., Garfield, J.N., Gutjahr, C.L., and Giusti, L.M., Rifampicin induced methadone withdrawal, *N. Engl. J. Med.,* 294, 1104, 1976.

38. Caplehorn, J., Bell, J., Kleinbaum, D., and Gebski, V., Methadone dose and heroin use during maintenance treatment, *Addiction,* 88, 119, 1993.

39. Dyer, K.R., Foster, D.J.R., White, J.M., Somogyi, A.A., Menelaou, A., and Bochner, F., Steady-state pharmacokinetics and pharmacodynamics in methadone maintenance patients: comparison of those who do and do not experience withdrawal and concentration-effect relationships, *Clin. Pharmacol. Ther.,* 65, 685, 1999.

40. Fishman, S.M., Wilsey, B., Yang, J., Reisfield, G.M., Bandman, T.B., and Borsook, D., Adherence monitoring and drug surveillance in chronic opioid therapy, *J. Pain Sympt. Manage.,* 20, 293, 2000.

41. Eap, C.B., On the usefulness of therapeutic drug monitoring of methadone, *Eur. Addict. Res.,* 6, 31, 2000.

42. Wolff, K., Hay, A., Raistrick, D., Calvert, R., and Feely, M., Measuring compliance in methadone maintenance patients: use of a pharmacologic indicator to "estimate" methadone plasma levels, *Clin. Pharmacol. Ther.,* 50, 199, 1999.

43. Torrens, M., Castillo, C., San, L., del Moral, E., González, M.L., and de la Torre, R., Plasma methadone concentrations as an indicator of opioid withdrawal symptoms and heroin use in a methadone maintenance program, *Drug Alcohol Depend.,* 52, 193, 1998.

44. Wolff, K., Rostami-Hodjegan, A., Hay, A.W., Raistrick, D., and Tucker, G., Population-based pharmacokinetic approach for methadone monitoring of opiate addicts: potential clinical utility, *Addiction,* 95, 1771, 2000.

45. Foster, D.J., Somogyi, A.A., White, J.M., and Bochner, F., Population pharmacokinetics of (R)-, (S)- and rac-methadone in methadone maintenance patients, *Br. J. Clin. Pharmacol.,* 57, 742, 2004.

46. Iribarne, C., Berthou, F., Baird, S., Dreano, Y., Picart, D., Bail, J.P., Beaune, P., and Menez, J., Involvement of cytochrome P450 3A4 enzyme in the N-demethylation of methadone in human liver microsomes, *Chem. Res. Toxicol.,* 9, 365, 1996.

47. Gerber, J.G., Rosenkraz, S., Segal, Y., Aberg, J., D'Amico, R., Mildvan, D., Gulick, R., Hughes, V., Vlexner, C., Aweeka, F., Hsu, A., Gal, J., and ACTG 401 Study Team, Effect of ritonavir/saquinavir on stereoselective pharmacokinetics of methadone: results of AIDS Clinical Trials Group (ACTG) 401, *J. Acquir. Immune Defic. Syndr.,* 27, 153, 2001.

48. Foster, D.J., Somogyi, A.A., and Bochner, F., Methadone N-demethylation in human liver microsomes: lack of stereoselectivity and involvement of CYP3A4, *Br. J. Clin. Pharmacol.,* 47, 403, 1999.

49. Raistrick, D., Hay, A., and Wolff, K., Methadone maintenance and tuberculosis treatment, *Br. Med. J.,* 313, 925, 1996.

50. Tong, T.G., Pond, S.M., Kreek, M.J., Jaffery, N.F., and Benowitz, N.L., Phenytoin induced methadone withdrawal, *Ann. Intern. Med.,* 94, 349, 1981.

51. Liu, S.-J. and Wang, R.I.H., Case report of barbiturate-induced enhancement of methadone metabolism and withdrawal syndrome, *Am. J. Psychiatry,* 141, 1287, 1984.

52. Tong, T.G., Benowitz, N.N.L., and Kreek, M.J., Methadone-disulfiram interaction during methadone maintenance, *J. Clin. Pharmacol.,* 10, 506, 1980.

53. Mertins, L., Brockmeyer, N.H., Daecke, C., and Goos, M., Pharmacokinetic interaction of antimicrobial agents with levomethadon (L) elimination in drug addicted AIDS patients [abstr.], presented at 2nd European Conference on Clinical Aspects of HIV Infection, March 8/9, 1990.

54. Plummer, J.L., Gourlay, G.K., Cousins, C., and Cousins, M.J., Estimation of methadone clearance: application in the management of cancer pain, *Pain,* 33, 313, 1988.

55. Spaulding T.C., Minimum, L., Kotake, A.N., and Takemori, A.E., The effects of diazepam on the metabolism of methadone by the liver of methadone dependent rats, *Drug Metab. Dispos.,* 2, 458, 1974.

56. Pond, S.M., Tong, T.G., Benowitz, N.L., Jacob, P., and Rigod, J., Lack of effect of diazepam on methadone metabolism in methadone maintained addicts, *Clin. Pharmacol. Ther.,* 31, 139, 1982.

57. Nilsson, M.-I., Grönbladh, L., Widerlöv, E., and Ånggård, E., Pharmacokinetics of methadone in methadone maintenance treatment: characterization of therapeutic failures, *Eur. J. Clin. Pharmacol.*, 25, 497, 1983.

58. Perret, G., Deglon, J.J., Kreek, M.J., Ho, A., and La Harpe, R., Lethal methadone intoxications in Geneva, Switzerland, from 1994 to 1998, *Addiction*, 95, 1647, 2000.

59. Gourevitch, M.N. and Friedland, G.H., Interactions between methadone and medications used to treat HIV infection: a review, *Mt. Sinai J. Med.*, 67, 429, 2000.

60. Kreek, M.J., Metabolic interactions between opiates and alcohol, *Ann. N.Y. Acad. Sci.*, 362, 36, 1981.

61. Wolff, K., Boys, A., Hay, A.W.M., and Raistrick, D., Methadone kinetics in pregnancy, *Eur. J. Clin. Pharmacol.*, 61, 763, 2005.

CHAPTER 3

Substitute Prescribing: Buprenorphine Maintenance Prescribing

Nick Lintzeris, M.B.B.S., Ph.D.
National Addiction Centre, South London and Maudsley NHS Trust, London, U.K.

CONTENTS

Generally, the more efficacious the drug is at producing its pharmacological effect, the greater the addiction potential and value as an illicit drug. Drugs with lower efficacy are called partial agonists. Buprenorphine (BPN) is a partial agonist for opioid receptors. The pharmacological profile of partial agonists is such that they are useful in substitution therapy because they provide some reinforcement of the opiate effect but should also reduce illicit heroin use.

BPN, a derivative of the morphine alkaloid thebaine, is a partial agonist at the μ opiate receptor, resulting in milder, less euphoric, and less sedating opiate effects than full opioid agonists such as heroin, morphine, or methadone. In adequate doses, BPN exerts sufficient opiate effects to diminish cravings for heroin and prevent opiate withdrawal features. BPN also has a high affinity for μ receptors, binding more tightly than full agonists such as heroin or methadone, and through this mechanism reduces the effects of any additional heroin (or other opiate) use.

BPN is also an antagonist at the κ opiate receptor, which may be associated with some antidysphoric[1-3] and antipsychotic properties[4] in certain individuals. Further research is required in this area, and BPN is not currently indicated for these conditions.

3.1 PHARMACOKINETICS

BPN undergoes extensive first-pass metabolism when taken orally and has more potent effects when injected or taken sublingually. Contemporary preparations in addiction treatment utilize sublingual tablets.* Peak plasma concentrations are achieved 1 to 2 h after sublingual administration. BPN is principally metabolized by two hepatic pathways: conjugation with glucuronic acid and N-dealkylation by the CP450 3A4 enzyme system to nor-BPN, an active metabolite that appears not to cross the blood–brain barrier and therefore is of minor clinical importance. Metabolites are excreted in the biliary system with enterohepatic cycling, and the majority of the drug is excreted in feces and urine.

BPN has a relatively short half-life, however, and can exert a considerably longer duration of action, due to its high affinity for μ opiate receptors and its high lipophilicity (accumulation in fat with chronic dosing). Peak effects are described within 1 to 4 h after sublingual administration, with continued effects for up to 12 h at low doses (e.g., 2 mg) to as long as 72 h at higher doses (such as 16 or 32 mg).[5] The prolonged duration at high doses enables alternate-day, 3-day, and even 4-day dispensing regimens in many patients.[6,7]

BPN has an advantageous safety profile due to ceiling dose–response effects, such that high doses (16 mg or more) do not produce substantially greater peak opiate effects than lower doses (8 or 12 mg)[8] and do not result in significant respiratory depression even in non-opiate-dependent individuals. As with methadone, there are concerns regarding the safety of BPN in combination with other sedatives (alcohol, benzodiazepines), and a number of deaths have occurred under such circumstances. Many patients describe less sedation with BPN than methadone. As with other opiates, constipation, disturbed sleep, drowsiness, headaches, sweating, and nausea are the more common side effects[5] with most side effects subsiding as tolerance develops.

The partial agonist properties of BPN and prolonged duration of action are thought to account for a milder opiate withdrawal syndrome following the cessation of BPN compared to heroin, morphine, or methadone.[9] The cessation of long-term BPN results in opiate withdrawal peaking 3 to 14 days after cessation, with mild symptoms persisting for weeks. Cessation of short BPN courses (e.g., 1 to 2 weeks) appears to be associated with only minor withdrawal discomfort of several days duration.

Precipitated withdrawal is caused by the high affinity of BPN displacing other opiates (e.g., methadone, heroin) from opiate receptors, but having less opiate activity (partial agonist). This rapid reduction in opiate effects can be experienced as precipitated withdrawal, typically occurring within 1 to 3 h after the first BPN dose, peaking in severity over the first 3 to 6 h, and then subsiding. Precipitated withdrawal is of concern if a patient has recently used heroin (e.g., <6 h previously) or methadone (<24 h previously) prior to his or her BPN dose. Transferring from high-dose methadone (e.g., above 60 mg) to BPN increases the risk of precipitated withdrawal, due to methadone's long duration of action (Table 3.1).

Table 3.1   Pharmacological Properties and Clinical Implications of BPN

Pharmacological Property	Clinical Implication
Partial agonist producing mild opiate effects	Reduces cravings for heroin and increases treatment retention
	Less sedating than full agonists (heroin, morphine, or methadone)
Alleviates opiate withdrawal	Can be used for maintenance or detoxification
High receptor affinity diminishes the effects of additional opiate use	Diminishes heroin use
	Complicates attempts at analgesia with other opioids (e.g., morphine)
Long duration of action	Allows for once-a-day, to three times a week dosing schedules
Ceiling dose–response effects	Safer in overdose
Sublingual preparation	More time involved in supervised dispensing
Comparable affinity for mu receptors to opioid antagonists	Treatment with naltrexone can be commenced within 24 h of BPN
Side-effect profile similar to other opiates	Generally well tolerated by heroin users, with most side effects transient

---

* Most studies using sublingual buprenorphine have used a liquid solution in 30% aqueous ethanol. However, commercial sublingual preparations (e.g., Subutex, Suboxone) are tablets with approximately 50% bioavailability of the ethanol solution.

Objectively, there was no significant difference between the two groups on measures of opiate withdrawal symptoms. The group receiving alternate-day treatment reported subtle withdrawal symptoms subjectively whereas the daily treatment group reported no such problems.[10] A 24-h dosage interval is most commonly recommended. Opiate-dependent subjects find BPN an acceptable treatment for their dependence and report a "morphine-like" effect. It is possible to convert people from heroin or methadone to BPN with minimal withdrawal problems.[11]

Due to its wide therapeutic index, BPN is relatively safe in overdose. It has been shown that there is a ceiling effect at higher doses of BPN. This is due to its intrinsic opiate antagonist activity and means that it is possible for a nondependent person to tolerate a single dose of BPN up to 70 times the recommended analgesic dose without life-threatening consequences.[12] Sublingual preparations have been shown to be as effective as subcutaneous preparations and to have a similar profile of effects in opiate-dependent subjects.[13]

As with methadone, effective BPN maintenance treatment requires regular monitoring and review, structured dispensing arrangements, access to psychosocial services, and long-term treatment retention. A key goal during BPN induction is to prevent precipitated withdrawal, which can usually be achieved by patient education; delaying the first BPN dose until the patient is in mild opiate withdrawal; and commencing with a low first BPN dose (e.g., 4 mg). After ensuring precipitated withdrawal has been averted, the BPN dose should be rapidly titrated upwards, achieving effective doses (e.g., 12 to 24 mg for most patients) within 3 days of commencing treatment. Maintenance BPN doses should be titrated against treatment objectives for each patient. Doses of between 12 and 24 mg/day are often required in order for patients to cease unsanctioned opiate use. Low doses (less than 8 mg/day) are more commonly associated with ongoing heroin use. In treatment settings where BPN dosing is predominately supervised, the frequency of dispensing (and hence inconvenience and costs) can be reduced for most patients by alternate- and 3-day dosing. A dose intended for a 48-h interval is approximately twice a daily dose, and a 3-day dose is approximately 2.5 to 3 times a daily dose. Withdrawal from BPN maintenance treatment should only be recommended for stable patients who have ceased substance abuse, are medically, socially, and psychiatrically stable, and who wish to withdraw from maintenance treatment. A gradual reduction over weeks is usually recommended, with 2 mg dose reductions every 2 to 4 weeks as tolerated.

3.2 STIMULANT SPECIFIC

Substitute prescribing for amphetamine usually takes the form of dexamphetamine sulfate tablets whereas there is no obvious alternative for cocaine dependence. However, prescriptions of this kind are only appropriate for a very small minority of patients. It is more likely to be the case that prescribing for stimulant dependence takes the form of an agonist of a different pharmacological group to the main drug of misuse but having its action at the same receptors or in the same neurochemical pathways (replacement prescribing). Typically these agents are used to reduce cravings associated with the cessation of stimulant use. Replacement prescribing is addressed in detail in Chapter 5.

3.3 BENZODIAZEPINE SPECIFIC

Little attention has thus far been paid to the extent to which benzodiazepines are abused primarily as the drug of choice. It seems that benzodiazepines are frequently abused on the illicit drug scene in combination with other drugs, particularly alcohol,[14] stimulants,[15] and opiates.[16] However, there appear to be a number of features that indicate benzodiazepine abuse: two key factors appear to be supra therapeutic dosage to extremely high levels and intermittent binge usage.

Substitution prescribing usually takes the form of a long-acting alternative, most commonly diazepam, which has the effect of stabilizing drug use. More recently, chlordiazepoxide has been used to substitute for the benzodiazepine of choice because of its low abuse potential, low street value, and long elimination half-life.

3.4 OUTCOMES FOR SUBSTITUTE PRESCRIBING

The Department of Health[17] has selected hierarchies of outcomes for substitute prescribing in the areas of drug use, physical and psychological health, and social functioning, as follows:

Drug use:
1. Abstinence from drugs
2. Near abstinence from drugs
3. Reduction in the quantity of drugs consumed
4. Abstinence from street drugs
5. Reduced use of street drugs
6. Change in drug taking behavior from injecting to oral consumption
7. Reduction in the frequency of injecting

Physical and psychological health:
1. Improvement in physical health
2. No deterioration in physical health
3. Improvement in psychological health
4. Reduction in sharing injection equipment
5. Reduction in sexual risk-taking behavior

Social functioning and life context:
1. Reduction in criminal activity
2. Improvement in employment status
3. Fewer working/school days missed
4. Improved family relationships
5. Improved personal relationships
6. Domiciliary stability/improvement

REFERENCES

1. Emrich, H.M., Vogt, P., and Herz, A., Possible antidepressant effects of opioids: action of buprenorphine, *Ann. N.Y. Acad. Sci.,* 398, 108, 1982.
2. Kosten, T.R., Morgan, C., and Kosten, T.A., Depressive symptoms during buprenorphine treatment of opioid abusers, *J. Subst. Abuse Treat.,* 7, 51, 1990.
3. Groves, S. and Nutt, D.J. Buprenorphine and schizophrenia, *Hum. Psychopharmacol.,* 6, 71, 1991.
4. Kosten, T., Krystal, J.H., Charney, D.S., Price, L.H., Morgan, C.H., and Kleber, H.D., Opioid antagonist challenges in buprenorphine maintained patients, *Drug Alcohol Depend.,* 25, 73, 1990.
5. Walsh, S.L., Preston, K.L., Stitzer, M.L., Cone, E.J., and Bigelow, G.E., Clinical pharmacology of buprenorphine: ceiling effects at high doses, *Clin. Pharmacol. Ther.,* 55, 569, 1994.
6. Johnson, R.E., Cone, E.J., Henningfield, J.E., and Fudala, P.J., Use of buprenorphine in the treatment of opiate addiction. I. Physiologic and behaviour effects during a rapid dose induction, *Clin. Pharmacol. Ther.,* 46, 335, 1989.
7. Cowan, A., Lewis, J.W., and MacFarlane, I.R., Agonist and antagonist properties of buprenorphine, *Br. J. Pharmacol.,* 60, 537, 1977.
8. Amass, L., Bickel, W.K., Higgins, S.T., and Badger, G.J., Alternate day dosing during buprenorphine treatment of opioid dependence, *Br. J. Pharmacol.,* 60, 537, 1994.
9. Jasinski, D.R., Fudala, P.J., and Johnson, R.E., Sublingual versus subcutaneous buprenorphine in opiate abusers, *Clin. Pharmacol. Ther.,* 45, 513, 1989.

10. Perera, K.M.H., Tulley, M., and Jenner, F.A., The use of benzodiazepines among drug addicts, *Br. J. Addict.,* 82, 511, 1987.

11. Strang, J., Seivewright, N., and Farrell, M., Oral and intravenous abuse of benzodiazepines, in *Benzodiazepine Dependence*, Hallstrom, C., Ed. Oxford: Oxford Medical Publications, 1993, 9.

12. Busto, U., Sellers, E.M., Naranjo, C.A., Kappell, H.D., Sanchez-Craig, M., and Simpkins, J., Patterns of benzodiazepine abuse and dependence, *Br. J. Addict.,* 81, 87, 1986.

13. Johnson, S.M. and Fleming, W.W., Mechanisms of cellular adaptive sensitivity changes: applications to opioid tolerance and dependence, *Pharmacol. Rev.,* 41, 435, 1989.

14. Foy, A., Drug withdrawal: a selective review, *Drug Alcohol Rev.,* 10, 203, 1991.

15. Paulos, C.X. and Cappell, H., Conditioned tolerance to the hypothermic effect of ethyl alcohol, *Science*, 206, 1109, 1979.

16. Whitfield, C.L. et al., Detoxification of 1,024 alcoholic patients without psychoactive drugs, *JAMA,* 239, 1409, 1974.

17. Department of Health. *Drug Misuse and Dependence: Guidelines in Clinical Management.* London: HMSO, 1999.

CHAPTER 4

Treatment of Withdrawal Syndromes

Joanna Banbery, M.B.B.S.
The Leeds Addiction Unit, Leeds, U.K.

CONTENTS

4.1 UNDERSTANDING WITHDRAWAL SYNDROMES

A withdrawal syndrome is the constellation of physiological and behavioral changes that are directly related to the sudden cessation (or reduction in use) of a psychoactive drug to which the body has become adapted. The *Diagnostic and Statistical Manual of the American Psychiatric Association* in its revised fourth edition (DSM-IV-R)[1] requires three criteria to be fulfilled before a diagnosis of substance withdrawal can be made. For each drug or group of drugs it lists the symptoms and signs that must be present:

Criterion 1: The development of a syndrome (which is substance specific) due to the cessation of or reduction in substance use. The substance use must be heavy and prolonged.
Criterion 2: The withdrawal syndrome must cause clinically significant distress or impairment in social and/or occupational functioning.
Criterion 3: The symptoms caused must not be due to any other medical or mental condition.

Dependence has been discussed in Chapter 1. Withdrawal symptoms were described as a consequence of regular drug use rather than as a fundamental element. On a cellular level, dependent use of a drug will cause a state of adaptation in which the presence of the drug is necessary for normal functioning and in which the removal of the drug will cause some abnormality of function.[2] Drug-induced alterations to function include alteration of the fluidity of the cell membrane, or alteration in neurotransmitters and receptor changes. Each group of drugs will produce its own characteristic withdrawal syndrome, which will be dependent on specific alterations to the above systems. These have already been well reviewed.[3]

Although the basis of withdrawal lies in the cellular and receptor changes, it is important not to forget that there is a significant psychological component. Changes at the tissue level give rise to symptoms and signs. These are then interpreted in a way that will depend on a person's situation and expectations about withdrawal together with his or her emotional state. These reactions then feed back and may magnify the original changes or help to reduce them. Psychologists have found that withdrawal symptoms will behave as conditioned responses. They will develop more quickly if associated with a cue and can be evoked by environmental stimuli when the drug has not been used for some time.[4] This helps to explain why the clinical symptoms presented by patients are very variable both from time to time and place to place. The time it takes to develop a withdrawal effect will depend on the pharmacokinetics of the drug, so that withdrawal from methadone, which has a long half-life, will not become evident for 24 to 36 h, whereas withdrawal from heroin, with a shorter half-life, will occur within 6 to 8 h of the last dose. This is of clinical importance in planning a detoxification.

4.1.1 Detoxification

When drug use ceases, the nervous system will begin to undergo a return to normal functioning. During this time, abnormal responses will be evident in the form of withdrawal symptoms, and the patient will be vulnerable both physically and psychologically. Detoxification is the process of rapidly and successfully achieving a drug-free state and will usually involve both the prescription of drugs to attenuate withdrawal symptoms and attention to the relief of other stressors.

It is an appropriate intervention for those patients who are at the "action" stage of change,[5] that is, those patients who have demonstrated a commitment to change their substance use, believe they are able to change, and have acquired the necessary skills to enable them to sustain change. Detoxification will also be necessary for other patients as an expedience in situations such as emergency hospitalization or rapidly deteriorating mental or physical health.

The goal of achieving abstinence with the minimum amount of discomfort should be agreed upon with the patient. Adequate preparation is essential; the patient must be informed of the expected symptoms, their likely duration, medication that will be used to relieve symptoms and its likely effects. Consideration should be given to the setting for the detoxification. Home, outpatient, or inpatient facilities may all be suitable. The physician and the patient will need to agree upon an environment that is comfortable, nonthreatening, and safe. If the detoxification is to be undertaken at home, there must be confidence that any withdrawal symptoms will not be severe and that adequate support is available.

The appearance of withdrawal symptoms should be carefully monitored with consideration being given to the use of assessment scales.[6] If an outpatient detoxification is being performed the patient may attend on a daily basis for an objective assessment of withdrawal symptoms to be made. The severity of the syndrome will influence the dosage and frequency of medication given to alleviate them. Physicians should have an awareness of which drugs will cause severe or dangerous withdrawal symptoms and may require particularly careful assessment. Increasingly, patients present with polydrug use, which requires extra vigilance and may require adaptations of usual prescribing regimens.

Patients who are to be detoxified will require a thorough medical examination usually with routine blood tests. These patients are at high risk of an underlying medical problem related either to specific drug-related harm, e.g., intravenous users at risk of abscesses, endocarditis, etc., or related to lifestyle, such as malnutrition or tuberculosis. An assessment of mental state is important and this should be monitored during detoxification. Patients may present, for example, with confusion or lowering of mood with suicidal ideation. These symptoms usually do not require anything beyond symptomatic relief and resolve as withdrawal progresses; however, the appropriate level of nursing care and support must be assessed.

Other therapies play an important role in detoxification and can minimize the need for medication. Relaxation training has been said to be a useful way to reduce stress particularly in benzodiazepine withdrawal, and complementary therapies such as massage have also been used to reduce discomfort. Controlled studies of their efficacy are awaited. Competent nursing care is also important. The patient's condition should be assessed accurately, and it has been shown that this can in itself reduce withdrawal symptom scores.[7] Reassurance and attention to nutrition and sleeping patterns also play their part. Any medication prescribed will either substitute for the drug that has been withdrawn or treat the symptoms of the withdrawal syndrome. Consideration must be given to the dosage and the length of time of prescribing.

It has been said that the three most common errors in the management of withdrawal syndromes are (1) failure to diagnose, (2) prescription of too much for too long, and (3) failure to use psychological means to abate withdrawal.[8] The physician must have adequate knowledge of the symptoms, signs, and duration of the common withdrawal syndrome and of their treatment to guard against all of these.

4.2 OPIATE-SPECIFIC WITHDRAWAL SYNDROME

DSM-IV-R[1] describes opioid withdrawal following cessation or reduction in heavy and prolonged use of either illicit drugs or prescribed medication. The syndrome described consists of craving for the drug and three or more of the following symptoms: dysphoric mood, nausea or vomiting, lachrymation and rhinnarhea, muscle aches, pupillary dilatation, piloerection, diarrhea, yawning, or insomnia. The signs and symptoms should develop acutely within days of cessation of drug use and be severe enough to impair a patient's functioning. In addition to this, body temperature and blood pressure may be slightly elevated with a variable effect on pulse. As discussed earlier, the onset of a withdrawal syndrome will depend on the quantity of the drug used and the route of administration,[9] as well as the frequency of usage, and the half-life of the drug. Heroin withdrawal normally begins 6 to 8 h after last use, symptoms peak at 2 to 3 days, and have usually resolved within a week. Withdrawal from other opiates is similar but will exhibit different time scales and intensities, e.g., methadone withdrawal may last for several weeks and not commence for 36 to 48 h. Opioid withdrawal can also be precipitated by an antagonist such as naloxone, which will produce a severe withdrawal with peak intensity about 30 min from administration.

The opiate withdrawal syndrome is very rarely life-threatening and has been described as being similar to having influenza. It is, however, experienced as sufficiently unpleasant for it to be avoided whenever possible by users and for its successful negotiation to be the necessary first step toward abstinence. For this reason it is important that it is properly managed by the clinician.

The essential judgment in a planned detoxification is about its speed. A rapid detoxification will produce more severe withdrawal symptoms than a slower one, but it may be easier to maintain motivation. There are a number of different pharmacological approaches that may be used and tailored to the individual's requirements. A brief review of the use of methadone, alpha-2 agonists, and buprenorphine in detoxification is given.

4.2.1 Detoxification Using Methadone

A wide variety of different regimens has been used and there is some lack of clarity between those that are long-term slow reductions and merge with methadone maintenance therapy (MMT) and those that are short term and aimed at immediate abstinence. In clinical practice patients who are on methadone maintenance treatment will usually have their methadone dose reduced gradually, commonly at a rate of 5 mg every 2 weeks to a daily dose of 20 to 30 mg. Reductions then occur in smaller increments to zero. In the U.K. there is no recommended time for this process of reduction to continue. In the U.S. the FDA regulations permit extended opioid detoxification for up to 6 months.

Various time scales for withdrawal have been studied.[10] It is important to inform patients about what to expect during detoxification as almost everyone undergoing methadone reduction will experience withdrawal symptoms. These have been shown to be a major factor in precipitating relapse. However, data from the literature are hardly comparable; programs vary widely with regard to duration,[10] design,[11] and treatment objectives, impairing the application of meta-analysis. A recent review by Amato[6] confirmed that slow tapering with temporary substitution of long-acting opioids (methadone), accompanied by medical supervision and ancillary medications can reduce withdrawal severity. Nevertheless the majority of patients relapsed to heroin use.

Negotiation between prescriber and patient about rates of reduction together with the understanding that extra psychological support will be available during detoxification are also important. The setting for detoxification should be given consideration.[12] Opioid users are likely to live in environments with other drug users, which makes abstinence difficult to achieve. It may be appropriate to consider the initial reductions of methadone as an outpatient and then admit the patient to finally achieve a drug-free state.

Methadone reduction regimens have been de rigueur in many clinical settings but in practice it is often difficult to achieve abstinence by this method, with patients often becoming "stuck" when low doses of methadone (15 mg/day) are reached. Indeed it has been said that "most methadone treatment is maintenance treatment because most patients fail detoxification."[13] Although it is a common clinical problem, the cause is not clear. It may be that the withdrawal symptoms become intolerable. Another explanation is that the drug user wants to seek a drug effect which is lost at lower dosages. Current practice suggests that methadone reduction should be attempted in combination with other psychological interventions and other pharmacological agents (buprenorphine).

4.2.2   Detoxification Using Buprenorphine

There is an emerging evidence base for the use of buprenorphine (BPN) in detoxification regimens. For detoxification, most comparative randomized trials have been against symptomatic medications (e.g., clonidine, benzodiazepines). The evidence suggests that BPN is more effective in reducing withdrawal severity, increasing detoxification completion rates, and increasing uptake of post-detoxification (e.g., naltrexone maintenance) treatment. There is less research directly comparing BPN and methadone reductions, although the evidence suggests there is less "rebound" withdrawal (symptoms after stopping medication) following short courses of BPN compared to methadone.

BPN can be used in brief detoxification regimens over 1 to 2 weeks in inpatient or outpatient settings to assist individuals detoxifying from heroin; or in more gradual outpatient reduction regimens lasting several weeks to months. Longer-term reduction regimens appear to be associated with more "rebound withdrawal," but do allow a greater opportunity for the patient to "stabilize" while in treatment. As in any detoxification program, a key aspect is to facilitate patients continuing in ongoing treatment for their dependence. This may entail naltrexone treatment, counseling, or rehabilitation programs for those aiming to achieve abstinence, or continuing in maintenance BPN treatment for those unable to immediately achieve long-term abstinence.

The milder withdrawal syndrome associated with BPN compared with methadone suggests that transfer to BPN may be one option for stable patients who are ready to cease maintenance substitution treatment, but are experiencing difficulties withdrawing from methadone.[14] There have been a number of fixed-dose and flexible-dose Phase III randomized trials comparing BPN to

Table 4.1   Selecting Medications: Advantages and Disadvantages of BPN Compared to Methadone

Advantages	Disadvantages
Greater blockade of heroin use	Blockade not desired by some patients
Smoother opiate effect and less sedating than methadone	Some patients do better with sedating effects of high-dose methadone
Safer in overdose than methadone	Tablets easily abused if not supervised
	Safety in pregnancy not yet established
Milder withdrawal than methadone	Mild withdrawal may make it too easy to "jump off"
3 or 4 times a week supervised dosing possible for most clients (~66%)	Supervised dispensing more time-consuming
Some clients prefer BPN	Some clients prefer methadone

methadone maintenance treatment, recently reviewed in a systematic Cochrane review.[15] Fixed dose studies suggest comparable efficacy when used in equivalent doses (low dose, 20 to 35 mg, methadone is broadly equivalent to low dose, 2 to 4 mg, BPN), although to date there have been no trials comparing "gold standard" high dose (e.g., 80 to 120 mg) methadone to high dose (e.g., 16 to 32 mg) BPN treatment. Flexible dosing studies have identified greater early treatment dropout among BPN patients, which may reflect the slow BPN induction regimens used in these trials.

The increased range of opioid pharmacotherapies potentially allows for better tailoring of medications to suit the patient's treatment objectives. While research suggests comparable efficacy between the two medications, it has yet to provide a clear indication of which individuals will benefit most from maintenance treatment with either BPN or methadone. Without a clear evidence base, clients and clinicians must consider a range of factors when selecting a pharmacotherapy, including a patient's past history of response to a medication, individual variation in pharmacokinetics (e.g., rapid methadone metabolizers), adverse events, logistics of participating in treatment (such as costs, accessibility of services), and patient (and clinician) expectancy. Particular issues in selecting BPN and methadone are shown in Table 4.1.

Substitution treatment (such as methadone) has historically been confined to specialist clinic-based programs. Recent decades have seen the expansion of substitution maintenance and detoxification treatment into primary care (general practice and community pharmacy) settings in many countries in order to "normalize" addiction treatment, reduce treatment costs, and increase the accessibility of services. This trend has extended to the U.S., where trained and accredited physicians can deliver BPN treatment outside of clinic settings ("office based prescribing"). Increasingly, the role of specialist services is to target patients with more complex treatment needs (e.g., polydrug dependence, severe social dysfunction, or medical or psychiatric comorbidity).

A number of studies have examined the acceptability and effectiveness of BPN in the treatment of opiate dependence. It has been shown that BPN treatment is as effective as methadone in the detoxification of heroin users.[16] BPN has been shown to attenuate self-administration of illicit opiates in opiate-dependent individuals. The study used a daily dose of 8 mg of subcutaneous BPN and recorded a 69 to 98% suppression of heroin self-administration, which compares favorably to the opiate antagonist naltrexone.[17] Treatment with opiate antagonists (e.g., naltrexone) can be commenced as soon as 24 h after the cessation of BPN without precipitating severe opiate withdrawal; in comparison, naltrexone usually precipitates severe withdrawal if initiated within days of heroin or methadone use.

There are a number of different pharmacological options available for the treatment of opiate withdrawal and it is important to tailor detoxification to suit each individual. As Seivewright and Greenwood[18] point out, a 17-year-old who has been using heroin for 6 months with few social problems will require treatment different from a 35-year-old injector of heroin with a long history of dependence and failed previous detoxifications. The first patient may do best being detoxified using lofexidine; the second may need a long-term methadone reduction program. There is a need for further research to establish precisely which group of patients is likely to do best with which treatment.

4.2.3 Detoxification Using Adrenergic Agonists

A subgroup of the adrenergic agonists are the alpha-2 agonists clonidine and lofexidine, which are being increasingly used in opiate detoxification. Chronic administration of opiate drugs results in tolerance to the effects mediated by opiate receptors such as euphoria, and tolerance to the effects of opiates on the automatic nervous system, which is mediated by noradrenergic pathways. The locus coeruleus in the dorsal pons is the origin of much of the central nervous system noradrenergic activity. It is associated with opiate and presynaptic alpha-2-noradrenergic receptors, which are inhibiting.

Chronic opiate intake leads to tolerance and to stimulation of the opiate receptors. Abrupt withdrawal leads to an escape from this inhibition and a rebound rapid firing of the neurons. A "noradrenergic storm" results and is responsible for many of the opiate withdrawal symptoms.[19] Clonidine and lofexidine act as presynaptic alpha-2-adrenergic agonists, which inhibit this and therefore are able to attenuate symptoms. However, those experiencing the most severe withdrawal symptoms are not well controlled by clonidine and the symptoms of arthralgia, myalgia, anergia, and insomnia were not alleviated. Its use has also been limited because of its potentially serious side effects, which include hypotension, sedation, and psychiatric symptoms in those who are vulnerable.

Lofexidine is a newer alpha-2-adrenergic agonist (licensed in the U.K. since 1992), which appears not to have the same problems with side effects and which has gained in popularity as a non-opiate for use in detoxification in a variety of settings. Lofexidine when used to withdraw patients from methadone demonstrated good completion rates, and there were no reports of significant lowering of blood pressure or sedation. However, residual withdrawal symptoms, with insomnia, lethargy, and bone pain mentioned, were observed in users stabilized on relatively low doses of methadone.

Bearn et al.[9] conducted the first randomized double-blind study comparing methadone and lofexidine detoxification in 86 polydrug-abusing opioid addicts. The lofexidine group experienced more severe symptoms from day 3 to day 7 and by day 20 both groups showed a similar progressive decline in symptoms. The two treatments had similar effects on blood pressure and treatment completion.

4.2.4 Naltrexone-Assisted Detoxification

In an attempt to reduce the duration of the opiate withdrawal syndrome, particularly from long-acting opioids such as methadone, combinations of compounds have been used. A rapid process using scopolamine with naltrexone and naloxone has been reported.[20]

More recently interest has been shown in very rapid (<48 h) opiate detoxification, using opiate antagonists and general anesthesia. However, this method is expensive and adds a risk of death to a nonfatal condition. Reports of delirium from rapid opioid detoxification have also emerged.[21]

The addition of other medications to lofexidine in detoxification (such as hypnotics, muscle relaxants, and antidiarrheal medication) may need to be considered on an individual basis. Other short-acting opioids such as dihydrocodeine have been used in detoxification regimens although there is little evidence for their efficacy. One regimen employed involves a crossover period from low dose (30 mg or less) methadone to the equivalent dose of dihydrocodeine over 7 to 10 days and then a reduction of dihydrocodeine over the following 7 days.[22]

4.3 STIMULANT-SPECIFIC WITHDRAWAL SYNDROME

Withdrawal symptoms of these drugs, manifest in broad terms as the inverse of the stimulant effects, can be explained by the neurochemical changes that they induce. The existence of a withdrawal syndrome was for some time controversial because of the lack of physical withdrawal symptoms and signs. During the 1980s, the use of cocaine in the form of crack increased dramatically in North America and this has led to an increase in clinical and research evidence about its dependence-forming properties and withdrawal syndrome. DSM-IV-R[1] defines both amphetamine and cocaine withdrawal in the same way.

The symptoms are characterized by a constellation of signs and symptoms that appear within a few hours to several days after either cessation or reduction in heavy or prolonged use of the drugs. The symptoms must not be due to another medical or mental disorder and must cause impairment of functioning. It is described as consisting of dysphoric mood and two or more of the following: fatigue, vivid and unpleasant dreams, insomnia or hypersomnia, increased appetite, and either psychomotor retardation or agitation. Drug craving and anhedonia may also be present. Cocaine withdrawal has been reported to reach its peak in 2 to 4 days, with symptoms such as lowering of mood, fatigue, and general malaise lasting for several weeks. Amphetamine withdrawal is also reported to peak within 2 to 4 days with the most characteristic symptoms being lowering of mood and associated suicidal ideation.

Most of the recent studies looking at stimulant withdrawal have investigated cocaine. However, given the different pharmacokinetics of amphetamine and cocaine it would be reasonable to expect quite different time courses for the appearance, peak, and duration of the respective withdrawal syndromes. The half-life of cocaine is approximately 1 h, with the onset of action between 8 s and 30 min depending on the route of administration. The duration of effect is reported to be between 5 and 90 min.[23] Conversely, the half-life of amphetamine is about 10 to 15 h, with its onset of action and duration of effect two to eight times as long as cocaine. This would lead to the expectation that amphetamine withdrawal would have a slower onset on action, last longer, and be less intense than cocaine withdrawal. Further controlled studies in humans need to be done to confirm this. Our current concepts of amphetamine withdrawal are based largely on clinical impressions and animal studies.

The main physical and psychological effects of cocaine and crack have been recently reviewed. Users feel stronger, more alert and energetic, confident and physically strong. Common physical effects include dry mouth, sweating, loss of appetite, and increased heart rate. When snorted, cocaine produces a slow wave of euphoria followed by a plateau and a "comedown." Smoked as crack, the drug has a much more intense and immediate effect. Excessive doses can cause severe medical problems including death from pulmonary edema, heart failure, and myocardial infarction.

Substantial numbers of people who are cocaine dependent will not report or have clinically evident withdrawal symptoms even after cessation of heavy and prolonged use.[24] This, combined with clinical observations, suggests that stimulant withdrawal is associated with considerable heterogeneity. It has been said to depend on dose of drug, pattern of use, duration of history, and pre-withdrawal psychopathology.[25] Patterns of use may vary from daily use to a common pattern of using for several days at a time followed by days of abstinence. This will have an effect on the appearance of withdrawal symptoms and their severity.

Stimulants do not produce dangerous physical withdrawal syndromes, and because of this there is no advantage to a gradual withdrawal of the drug. Patients should be advised to discontinue the drug abruptly. Advice and information should be given about the likely effects of cessation and consideration given to the setting for detoxification. Those patients who present with mild symptoms that last a matter of hours or days usually are not a management problem. Symptomatic treatment for agitation or anxiety with a drug of low abuse potential such as thioridazine may be necessary.

More severe withdrawal symptoms may require admission. Close observation will be necessary for those expressing suicidal ideas. Symptomatic relief for other symptoms such as anxiety and insomnia may be required. Having achieved abstinence, the next phase is to identify psychosocial problems and initiate interventions designed to maintain a drug-free state and deal with drug craving. A number of different pharmacological treatments have been used mainly in cocaine dependence to treat the dysphoric symptoms associated with withdrawal and to attempt to reduce craving. These are reviewed in Chapter 5.

The small numbers of studies, the absence of physical withdrawal symptoms, and the variation in patterns of drug use make stimulant withdrawal more difficult to characterize than with other groups of drugs. Cocaine has been studied because of the "crack" epidemic of the 1980s, and has led to an increase in our understanding of both the symptoms and the underlying neurochemistry of withdrawal. Numerous different agents have been used to attempt to treat the drug craving and mood disorders associated with withdrawal, all with limited success. Less is published about amphetamine withdrawal and details of ecstasy withdrawal are scarce. Any comparisons with cocaine should not ignore the differences in the drugs' properties and pharmacokinetics.

4.4 HYPNOTIC AND SEDATIVE WITHDRAWAL SYNDROME

In practice it is the benzodiazepines that dominate the market for both hypnotics and anxiolytics. Barbiturates such as secobarbital, pentobarbital, and amobarbital are under the same federal controls as morphine in the U.S. and in the U.K., and they are rarely prescribed.

DSM-IV-R[1] criteria for sedative, hypnotic, or anxiolytic withdrawal require two or more of the following to be present:

1. Autonomic hyperactivity (e.g., sweating or pulse rate greater than 100)
2. Increased hand tremor
3. Insomnia
4. Nausea or vomiting
5. Transient visual, tactile, or auditory hallucinations or illusions
6. Psychomotor agitation
7. Anxiety
8. Grand mal seizures

Physicians can then specify if perceptual disturbances are present. As in other classes of drug, the withdrawal symptoms are the opposite of the drug effects and are explained by the underlying changes in neurophysiology largely via the gamma aminobutyric acid (GABA) system. GABA is the most widely distributed inhibitory neurotransmitter in the central nervous system. Close to its receptors are specific receptors for the benzodiazepines and the barbiturates. When these are activated, the action of the GABA system is potentiated causing further inhibition. With continued drug use, the number of GABA receptors falls due to downregulation.

When GABA binds with its receptor it causes hyperpolarization of the neuron as the chloride channel is activated and hyperpolarization is reversed by increased entry of calcium to the cell. If drug use ceases, the increased intraneuronal calcium produces a state of hyperexcitability. The reduction in the number of GABA receptors has the effect of reducing the overall effect of the main inhibiting system resulting in the symptoms previously listed.

Benzodiazepines dependence is not a single entity and different classifications have been proposed. Perhaps the most useful division within the context of drug abuse is the division between high-dose and normal-dose dependence. Non-abusers who are dose dependent take their benzodiazepines within the recommended therapeutic range and remain on this regimen long term. These people may want to do without their medication but feel unable to because of the withdrawal symptoms experienced upon cessation of their medication. In high-dose misuse, up to ten times the normal recommended dosage may be consumed on a regular basis.

Benzodiazepine withdrawal can be classified in several ways. A division between minor and major withdrawal is sometimes used and this emphasizes the severity of the symptoms. Symptoms associated with low-dose withdrawal are nausea, vomiting, tremor, incoordination, restlessness, blurred vision, sweating, and anorexia. Depersonalization, heightened perceptions, and illusions are also described. In a review of recent studies, Alexander and Perry[15] concluded that symptoms occurred in 50% of those withdrawn from therapeutic doses of benzodiazepines with an average use of 3 years and most symptoms were mild to moderate.

Discontinuing high doses of benzodiazepines can produce all the minor symptoms discussed, but patients are also at risk of seizures, psychosis, and depression. Early studies indicate a high risk of severe withdrawal when high doses are discontinued. The incidence and the severity of withdrawal symptoms can be predicted to some extent by the dose and duration of use. The time course is influenced by the half-life of the drug. Those with a short action may begin to produce mild withdrawal symptoms within 1 to 5 days of ceasing use and usually disappear over 2 to 4 weeks. Drugs with a longer half-life may not produce withdrawal symptoms for 1 to 2 weeks after use ceases and they are likely to be less severe, but more prolonged.

4.4.1 Management of Withdrawal

Sudden withdrawal of benzodiazepines is not advised. For an uncomplicated low-dose withdrawal, a gradual tapering of the drug is recommended. If patients are on a short-acting drug, then they may be switched to a longer-acting drug with the rationale that less severe withdrawal symptoms occur with long-acting drugs. Diazepam has been the most widely studied, and conversion data from common benzodiazepines are available. Once stabilized this can then be reduced. A number of different schemes are available. The tapering dose can be calculated by dividing the total dose by 5 and reducing by this amount weekly. Most patients can be reduced to zero in 4 to 8 weeks. Slower withdrawal may be necessary toward the end of the reduction and consideration should be given to admission if withdrawal symptoms become very intense.

In high-dose withdrawal, the picture is often complicated by other illicit drug or alcohol use. A conversion to diazepam may be difficult because of problems in establishing dosage and frequency of use. Concomitant use of alcohol is particularly common. Most clinicians would withdraw the alcohol after establishing the patient on a stable dose of a long-acting benzodiazepine. Benzodiazepines are also commonly taken by opiate users to boost the opioid effect.[27] In North America it has been found that alprazolam was replacing diazepam as the drug of choice in this population. For those patients where an accurate and reliable history of drug intake is not available, then admission is indicated for tolerance testing performed to assess tolerance and severity of withdrawal before planning a detoxification regimen.

REFERENCES

1. American Psychiatric Association, *Diagnostic and Statistical Manual of Mental Disorders*, 4th ed. Washington, D.C.: American Psychiatric Association, 1994.
2. Smolka, M. and Schmidt, L.G., The influence of heroin dose and route of administration on the severity of opiate withdrawal syndrome, *Addiction*, 94, 1191, 1999.
3. Gossop, M., Bradley, M., and Philips, G., An investigation of withdrawal symptoms shown by opiate addicts during and subsequent to a 21 day in-patient methadone detoxification procedure, *Addict. Behav.*, 12, 1, 1987.
4. Gossop, M., Bradley, M., and Strang, J., Opiate withdrawal symptoms in response to 10 day and 21 day methadone withdrawal programs, *Br. J. Psychiatry*, 154, 560, 1989.
5. Prochaska, J.O. and DiClemente, C.C., *The Transtheoretical Approach: Crossing Traditional Boundaries of Therapy*, Homewood, IL: Dow Jones-Irwin, 1984.
6. Amato, L., Davoli, M., Minozzi, S., Ali, R., and Ferri, M., Methadone at tapered doses for the management of opioid withdrawal, *Cochrane Database Syst. Rev.*, July 20, 2005.
7. Hughes, J.R., Higgens, S.T., and Bickel, K.W., Common errors in pharmacologic treatment of drug dependence and withdrawal, *Comprehensive Ther.*, 20, 89, 1994.
8. Cook, C.C.H., Scannell, T.D., and Lepsedge, M.S., Another clinical trial that failed, *Lancet*, 524–525, 1988.
9. Bearn, J., Gossop, M., and Strang, J., Randomised double-blind comparison of lofexidine and methadone in the in-patient treatment of opiate withdrawal, *Drug Alcohol Depend.*, 43, 87, 1996.

10. Yang, G., Zhao, W., and Xu, K., The combined use of scopolamine, naltrexone, and naloxone as a rapid safe, effective detoxification treatment for heroin addicts, *Zhonghua Yi Xue Za ZHI*, 79, 679, 1999.

11. Golden, S.A. and Sakhrani, D.I., Unexpected delirium during Rapid Opioid Detoxification (ROD), *J. Addict. Dis.,* 23, 65, 2004.

12. Kosten, T.R., Morgan, C., and Kleber, H.D., Clinical trials of buprenorphine: detoxification and induction onto naltrexone, in Baline, J.D., Ed., *Buprenorphine: An Alternative Treatment for Opioid Dependence,* NIDA Research Monograph Series, 121, 101, 1994.

13. Gawin, F.H. and Kleber, H.D., Abstinence symptomology and psychiatric diagnosis in cocaine observers: clinical observations, *Arch. Gen. Psychiatry*, 43, 107, 1986.

14. Ellinwood, E.H., Jr. and Lee, T.H., Amphetamine abuse, in *Drugs of Abuse*, Balieres Clinical Psychiatry, 2, 3, 1996.

15. Alexander, B. and Perry, P., Detoxification from benzodiazepines, schedules and strategies, *J. Subst. Abuse Treat.,* 8, 9, 1991.

16. McDuff, D., Schwartz, R., Tommasello, M.S., Threpal, S., Donovan, T., and Johnson, J., Out-patient benzodiazepine detoxification procedure for methadone patients, *J. Subst. Abuse Treat.*, 10, 297, 1993.

17. Tyrer, P., Rutherford, D., and Huggett, T., Benzodiazepine withdrawal symptoms and propanolol, *Lancet*, 1, 520, 1981.

18. Seivewright, N.A. and Greenwood, J., What is important in drug misuse treatment. *Lancet*, 347, 373, 1996.

19. Kleber, H.D., Naltrexone, *J. Subst. Abuse Treat.*, 2, 117, 1985.

20. Pfohl, D.N., Allen, A.I., Atkinson, R.L., Knoppman, D.S., Malcolm, R.J., Mitchell, J.E., and Morley, J.E., Naltrexone hydrochloride: a review of serum transaminase elevations at high dosage, *NIDA Res. Monogr. Ser.,* 67, 66, 1986.

21. Weddington, W.W., Brown, B.S., Haertzen, C.A., Hess, J.M., Mahaffey, J.R., Kolar, A.F., and Jaffe, J.H., Comparison of amantadine and desipramine combined with psychotherapy for treatment of cocaine dependence, *Am. J. Drug Alcohol Abuse*, 17, 137, 1991.

22. Alterman, A.I., Droba, M., Antelo, R.E., Cornish, J.W., Sweeney, K.K., Parikh, G.A., and O'Brien, C.P., Amantadine may facilitate detoxification of cocaine addicts, *Drug Alcohol Depend.,* 31, 19, 1992.

23. Gawin, F.H., Allen, D., and Humblestone, B., Outpatient treatment of crack cocaine smoking with flupenthixol decanoate, *Arch. Gen. Psychiatry,* 46, 322, 1989.

24. Handelsman, L., Limpitlaw, L., Williams, D., Schmeidler, J., Paris, P., and Stimmel, B., Amantadine does not reduce cocaine use or craving in cocaine-dependent methadone maintenance patients, *Drug Alcohol Depend.,* 39, 173, 1995.

25. Lima, M.S., Pharmacological treatment of cocaine dependence: a systematic review, *Arch. Gen. Psychiatry*, 49, 900, 1992.

26. Kosten, T.R., Morgan, C.M., Falcione, J., and Schottenfeld, R.S., Pharmacotherapy for cocaine abusing methadone maintained patients using amantadine and despiramine, *Arch. Gen. Psychiatry,* 49, 894, 1992.

CHAPTER 5

Replacement Prescribing

Kim Wolff, Ph.D.
King's College London, Institute of Psychiatry, National Addiction Centre, London, U.K.

CONTENTS

5.1 OPIOID-SPECIFIC PRESCRIBING

Antagonists have zero efficacy and as such are very effective blockers of agonists. Their main limitations are that they can precipitate withdrawal in physically dependent drug users, and because they do not provide any reinforcement, there is little incentive for those dependent on illicit drugs to be compliant. Naltrexone is a long-acting, orally effective competitive antagonist at opioid receptors. It displaces any agonist present at the receptors and blocks the effects of any opioid subsequently administered. Naltrexone is predominantly metabolized by the liver and its major metabolite, 6-beta-naltrexol, is also an active opioid antagonist. The opiate-blocking effects of naltrexone last between 48 and 72 h. Naltrexone has not been shown to produce tolerance and therefore does not lead to physical dependence.[1]

Oral administration of naltrexone to an opioid-dependent individual results in the immediate appearance of a severe opioid withdrawal syndrome. It is therefore necessary to be completely detoxified from opioid prior to commencing naltrexone treatment. It is necessary to discontinue short-acting opioids such as heroin for approximately 5 to 7 days prior to commencing naltrexone. Longer-acting opioids such as methadone need to be discontinued for approximately 10 to 14 days before naltrexone can be successfully commenced. In the event of naltrexone being given prior to the end of detoxification, it is likely that withdrawal symptoms will appear. This, in turn, makes it much less likely that the individual will agree to taking naltrexone at any point subsequently despite reassurance from the prescribing doctor.

Successful naltrexone treatment depends on careful selection of individuals and understanding that naltrexone treatment is only a small part of the relapse prevention package. Psychological treatment looking at issues, such as craving, drug-refusal skills, and making appropriate lifestyle changes, should be administered at the same time as naltrexone. A positive outcome is more likely in those who are well supported by friends or family members and those who had good pre-morbid adjustment in terms of education, employment, and social class. Naltrexone treatment is contraindicated in people with acute hepatitis or liver failure. It is necessary to check liver function tests both prior to and during naltrexone treatment.

Individuals who are due to start on naltrexone should be informed of the possible side effects, which include gastrointestinal disturbances such as nausea, vomiting, abdominal pains, and diarrhea. They should also be warned of the potential dangers of trying to overcome the naltrexone blockade by taking large doses of opioids. This can lead to respiratory depression and death. It is also important for those prescribed naltrexone to understand that they will be unable to use opioid analgesics for mild pain. They should be advised about non-opiate alternatives. If opioid analgesia is required, this should be administered in a hospital setting under the supervision of trained staff. Naltrexone should be discontinued 72 h prior to elective surgery and reinstated once the surgical procedure has been performed.[2]

Prior to prescribing naltrexone for the first time, it is necessary to confirm that an individual is abstinent from opioids. This can be done by means of urine toxicology or by performing a "naloxone challenge." This involves the intravenous or intramuscular administration of the short-acting opiate antagonist naloxone. If opioid withdrawal symptoms are not precipitated, then it is appropriate to commence naltrexone approximately 1 h later. If opioid withdrawal symptoms are present, then naltrexone treatment should be deferred until the naloxone challenge has been repeated without the appearance of withdrawal symptoms.

Naltrexone (25 mg) should be given on the first day, followed by daily dosing of 50 mg thereafter. A dose of 50 mg naltrexone blocks the effects of 25 mg of heroin for up to 48 h; 150 mg of naltrexone blocks the effects for 72 h. To supervise the swallowing of naltrexone tablets and improve compliance, it is possible to prescribe naltrexone three times per week (i.e., 100 mg on Monday and Wednesday, 150 mg on Friday). Due to the variable nature of opioid dependence, the length of time that people are required to take naltrexone varies between individuals. Naltrexone prescribing should continue, in the absence of complications or contraindications, until the individual is confident that it is possible to resist the temptation to return to dependent use of opioid drugs. This time span may be only a few weeks but can be as long as a few years in some cases.

In summary, naltrexone is a competitive opioid antagonist that displaces opioid agonists from the opioid receptors and blocks the effects of opioid agonists subsequently administered. It is a useful adjunct to psychological relapse prevention methods in well-motivated individuals receiving treatment for opioid dependence.

5.2 STIMULANT-SPECIFIC PRESCRIBING

A useful pharmacotherapy for stimulant (cocaine and amphetamine) dependence remains elusive. As a rule, symptoms of stimulant withdrawal are not medically dangerous. Detoxification from these substances requires no treatment other than abstinence. However, many users find the symptoms of cocaine withdrawal intensely dysphoric and immediately relapse and reuse cocaine in order to fend off the symptoms. The addictive nature of stimulants, particularly crack, the freebase form of cocaine, is, in part, the result of their effects on the neurochemistry of the brain. Stimulant drugs act directly on the so-called brain reward pathways.

One of cocaine's primary effects in the brain is to block the presynaptic reuptake of dopamine, norepinephrine, and serotonin, whereas amphetamine and methamphetamine increase the release of these neurotransmitters. Chronic use of cocaine results in dopamine depletion through the increased activity of catechol-*o*-methyl transferase, and supersensitivity of the dopamine, norepinephrine, and serotonin receptors, while both catecholamine and indolamine transmitters are depleted. Chronic use of cocaine seems to compromise the body's ability to regenerate these neurotransmitters, causing withdrawal symptoms when the user stops. Withdrawal symptoms manifest as the inverse of the stimulant's effects. Acute tolerance, rebound depression (or the crash), and craving for stimulant drugs have been specifically attributed to dopamine depletion and receptor supersensitivity. Neurochemical changes also explain the withdrawal syndrome, which includes lethargy, depression, oversleeping, overeating, and craving for more cocaine. Extinguishing drug craving is one of the most difficult aspects of treating stimulant dependence.

5.2.1 Neurochemical Approach: Dopaminergic Agents and Selective Serotonin-Reuptake Inhibitors

The involvement of multiple neurotransmitter systems during stimulant use have complicated the search for pharmacological agents to address dependence. A variety of data suggest that dopamine is an important mediator for stimulant self-administration. As a result, drugs that modify dopaminergic neurotransmission are of interest as potential treatments for stimulant use. Both agonists and antagonists have been studied in this regard, agonists because they mimic the effects and act as a stimulant substitute, theoretically reducing or eliminating drug intake, and antagonists because they might reduce the reinforcing properties of stimulants and facilitate abstinence. However, a review of evidence shows little or no support for the clinical use of dopamine agonists, mazindol, phenytoin, nimodine, amantadine, bromocriptine, carbamazepine, buproprion (Zyban), and chlordiazepoxide in the treatment of cocaine dependence.[3]

5.2.1.1 Dopamine Agonists

Bromocriptine (Parlodel) is an agonist at the D_2 receptor. It acts by stimulating dopamine receptors in the brain and was thought to reduce some symptoms of cocaine withdrawal, have anticraving effects, and was effective as an antidepressant, alleviating the low mood that accompanies the cocaine crash. However, other more recent studies using a controlled approach have not supported the general usefulness of this drug.[4]

Amantadine (Symmetrel) is an indirect dopamine agonist. Open-label pilot studies in primary cocaine users and methadone-maintained cocaine users have indicated that amantadine might reduce cravings for cocaine.[5] The lack of efficacy of amantadine for the reduction of craving for cocaine recently reported by Hendelson[6] is consistent with other placebo-controlled clinical trials in methadone-maintained patients.[7] Amantadine, while well tolerated, is not particularly efficacious for the reduction of cocaine use or cocaine craving.[8]

Methylphenidate (Ritalin) may reduce cocaine cravings in patients with attention-deficit disorder, possibly because of its ability to stimulate the central nervous system. However, the abuse potential of this drug severely limits its, and other similar drugs', usefulness as a treatment for cocaine misuse.

5.2.1.2 Dopamine Antagonists

Flupenthixol, a dopamine antagonist, has also shown promise in treating cocaine withdrawal; however, Spiperone has not reduced the effects of cocaine in mice, rats, or dogs.[9]

5.2.1.3 Dopamine Partial Agonists

Aminoergolines (Terguride and SD208911), medications that act as partial agonists at the dopamine receptor, may be candidates for normalizing dopamine transmission. The efficacy of the partial agonist depends on the level of occupancy of a given receptor by full agonists, such as dopamine. Consequently, partial agonists function as antagonists during pharmacological stimulation due to stimulant use when transmitter activity is high. By occupying dopamine receptors and exerting low intrinsic activity, partial agonists might represent a novel antipsychotic agent. However, human self-administration studies have yet to be performed.

Buprenorphine: Recent evidence suggests that the dopamine reward system of the brain is also stimulated by μ-opiate agonists. Over the past 5 years there has been significant interest in buprenorphine, a partial agonist, as a potential treatment agent for cocaine abuse. Preclinical primate work suggests that buprenorphine might modulate dopaminergic systems to the degree of altering the reinforcing properties of cocaine. However, there may be inherent problems in prescribing a medication with opiate agonist properties to opiate-naive individuals in an effort to treat cocaine dependence, particularly in a population with a known vulnerability for addiction to substances with a demonstrated abuse liability.[10]

5.2.1.4 Selective Serotonin-Reuptake Inhibitors

In addition to the blockade of dopamine reuptake, cocaine is thought to produce an increase in serotonergic tone. Therefore, it was felt that drugs that modify serotonergic neurotransmission may also alter the behavioral effects of cocaine and be potentially useful as therapies for cocaine users. However, fluoxetine (Prozac) and lofepramine are important only if underlying depression is confirmed. Selective serotonin-reuptake inhibitors (SSRIs) should be used with caution if cocaine use persists because of the rare occurrence of the "serotonergic syndrome," which is characterized by changes in autonomic neuromotor and cognitive-behavioral function triggered by increased serotonergic stimulation.[11]

5.2.2 Clinical Approach, Tricyclic Antidepressants, and Antisensitizing Agents

The other main approach for the treatment of stimulant dependence is clinical because the clinical syndrome that evolves after the discontinuation of cocaine or amphetamine resembles a depressive disorder. And it is widely held that antidepressant medications may have clinical utility in alleviating drug craving and self-administration. Neurochemical and clinical rationales are not mutually exclusive, and an antidepressant agent that reduces the clinical phenomena observed after cessation of cocaine might also have significant dopaminergic activity that would be consistent with a neurochemical approach to treating cocaine use.

5.2.2.1 Tricyclic Antidepressants

Since chronic tricyclic antidepressant treatment has been shown to downregulate adrenergic and dopaminergic receptor sensitivities, it has been suggested that antidepressant agents could reverse the neuroreceptor adaptations to cocaine abuse.

Desipramine (Pertofran) has been studied as an adjunct to reducing cocaine use in patients because of its high degree of selective noradrenergic activity and inhibition of the norepinephrine transporter.

Imipramine (Tofranil): Tricyclics generally exert only modest anticraving and antieuphoriant effects, which may translate into reduced cocaine use and this is certainly the case with imipramine. Carroll[1] found that the antidepressant, anti-self-medication effect of imipramine was better in depressed users. Intravenous and freebase crack users showed poor outcome with imipramine. It seems likely that tricyclics such as imipramine are most effective in specific subgroups, e.g., nasal users who are exposed to less cocaine, or patients with comorbid depression, where depression plays a role in initiating or perpetuating cocaine use.

5.3 NEW APPROACHES

Immunopharmacotherapy is a new strategy to treat cocaine use. It has been developed in rodents by Carrera et al.,[12] who proposed generating an active immunization to cocaine to block the actions of the drug. Active immunization against cocaine is accomplished by linking stable cocaine-like conjugates with a foreign carrier protein to stimulate the immune system to produce antibodies that subsequently recognize and bind the drug, preventing it from entering the central nervous system and thereby exerting psychoactive effects. However, there are many problems to be addressed before immunization is to be effective in preventing or treating cocaine addiction in humans.

The National Institute on Drug Abuse (NIDA) is currently looking at ways to neutralize the drug in the bloodstream and reduce the amount available for brain uptake. Scientists are trying to develop catalytic antibodies, synthetic molecules that will target and break down cocaine molecules more quickly than the body's natural enzyme systems and, therefore, limit the amount of drug crossing the blood–brain barrier. The literature reveals no pharmacological agent that has been demonstrated in large double-blind studies to be significantly better than placebo for stimulant dependence in men and women. While several medications appear promising and will require more extensive investigation, many of the positive clinical reports are anecdotal and uncontrolled. At present, it remains difficult to justify routine clinical use of a single pharmacological agent.

REFERENCES

1. Carroll, K.M., Rounsaville, B.J., Nich, C., Gordon, L.T., Wirtz, P.W., and Gawin, F., One-year follow-up of psychotherapy and pharmacotherapy for cocaine dependence: delayed emergence of psychotherapy effects, *Arch. Gen. Psychiatry,* 51, 989, 1994.
2. Compton, P.A., Ling, W., Charuvastra, V.C., and Wesson, D.R., Buprenorphine as a pharmacotherapy for cocaine abuse: a review of the evidence, *J. Addict. Dis.,* 14, 97, 1995.
3. Sternbach, H., Serotonin syndrome: how to avoid it, identify and treat dangerous interactions, *Curr. Psych. Online,* 2, 5, 2002.
4. Extin, I.X. and Gold, M.S., The treatment of cocaine addicts: bromocriptine or desipramine, *Psychiatric Annals,* 18, 535, 1988.
5. Arndt, L., Desipramine treatment of cocaine dependence in MMT, *Arch. Gen. Psychiatry,* 49, 888, 1992.
6. Arndt, I.O., Dorozynsky, L., Woody, G., McLellan, A.T., and O'Brien, C.P., Desipramine treatment of cocaine dependence in methadone-maintained patients, *Arch. Gen. Psychiatry,* 49, 888, 1992.
7. Nunes, E.V., McGrath, P.J., Quitkin, F.M., Welikson, K.O., Stewart, J.E., Koenig, T., Wager, S., and Klein, D.F., Imipramine treatment of cocaine abuse: possible boundaries of efficacy, *Drug Alcohol Depend.,* 39, 185, 1995.
8. Carrera, M.R.A., Ashley, J.A., Parsons, L.H., Wirsching, P., Koob, G.F., and Janda, K.D., Suppression of psychoactive effects of cocaine by active immunisation, *Nature,* 378, 727, 1995.
9. Wittchen, H., Perkonigg, A., and Reed, V., Comorbidity of mental disorders and substance use disorders, *Eur. Addict. Res.,* 2, 36, 1996.
10. Kessler, R.C., McGonagle, K.A., Shanyang, Z., Nelson, C.B., Hughes, M., Eshleman, S., Wittchen, H., and Kendler, K.S., Lifetime and 12 month prevalence of DSM-III-R psychiatric disorders in the United States, *Arch. Gen. Psychiatry,* 51, 8, 1994.
11. Penick, E.C., Powell, B.J., Liskow, B.I., Jackson, J.O., and Nickel, E.J., The stability of coexisting psychiatric syndromes in alcoholic men after one year, *J. Stud. Alcohol,* 49, 395, 1988.

12. Carrera, M.R.A., Ashley, J.A., Parsons, L.H., Wirsching, P., Koob, G.F., and Janda, K.D., Suppression of psycho active effects of cocaine by active immunisation, *Nature,* 378, 727, 1995.

CHAPTER 6

Management of Comorbidity

Duncan Raistrick, M.B.B.S.
The Leeds Addiction Unit, Leeds, U.K.

CONTENTS

6.1 UNDERSTANDING COMORBIDITY

Comorbidity is defined as the coexistence of two or more psychiatric or psychological conditions; for the purposes of this chapter, one of these conditions will be substance misuse or substance dependence. It is usual to take ICD-10 or the *American Diagnostic and Statistical Manual*, now in version DSM-IV-R,[1] as the descriptive classification of these conditions. Practitioners are usually concerned with current comorbidity, but from the point of view of understanding etiology and deciding upon rational treatment approaches it may be more useful to think in the longer term. Estimates of comorbidity will be influenced by methodological factors including the diagnostic criteria, time frame, and the population sample: there will be marked differences, for example, between general population and treatment population samples, or even between groups assigned to different treatment programs. In spite of these difficulties, some general conclusions are evident.

Wittchen et al.[2] looked at key international studies of comorbidity in community population samples and concluded that there were strong similarities between different countries; summarizing two large studies from the U.S., they state: (1) over half of those individuals who have a substance misuse problem have also experienced other mental disorders within their lifetime, (2) dependence on, rather than misuse of, alcohol or other drugs is more likely to be associated with a mental disorder, (3) major depression, anxiety disorders, phobias, mania, schizophrenia, and conduct disorder in adolescence or adult antisocial behavior are all strongly associated with substance dependence, and (4) social phobia and adolescent conduct disorder are also associated with alcohol or drug misuse.

The National Comorbidity Survey of the general adult population in the U.S. studied lifetime and 12-month comorbidity in more than 8000 subjects: the lifetime prevalence for any substance misuse or dependence disorder was 26.6% and 12-month prevalence was 11.3%, with males having approximately twice the rates of women.[3] These data imply considerable variation and possibly substitution of mental disorders, one with another, over time. The stability of substance-related comorbidity is of importance in determining treatment regimens. Clinicians generally underestimate the presence of psychiatric and psychological disorders when assessing patients with substance misuse problems. Clinicians expect high levels of morbidity and often assume that symptoms are due to withdrawal, transient physical problems, or dependence itself. To determine the true prevalence of comorbidity in a treatment population, Driessen et al.[4] studied 100 inpatients' post-alcohol detoxification: they found 3% to have schizophrenia or schizoaffective disorders, 13% affective disorders, 22% phobic disorders, and 2% general anxiety. Alcohol dependence was judged to be secondary to the psychiatric condition in 60% of patients with schizophrenia, 48% with depression, and 72% with phobic disorder. This does not necessarily mean that a psychiatric condition that antedates substance misuse will persist beyond detoxification, or that there is any causal relationship.

It is important for the clinician to know what is driving an individual's substance use. Comorbidity does not imply cause and effect, but is one of several possibilities:

• Substance use and psychiatric disorder may coexist by chance.
• Substance use may cause psychiatric disorder.
• Psychiatric disorder may cause substance use.
• A third factor may mediate both substance use and psychiatric disorder.

Where a psychiatric disorder is seen to be of primary importance and driving the substance use, the psychiatric disorder should be the focus of treatment. However, a psychiatric disorder that initiated substance misuse or precipitated a relapse may be superseded by dependence driving the maintenance of substance use.

6.2 MAKING PRESCRIBING DECISIONS

As a matter of general principle there are several reasons doctors should be reserved when prescribing for people who misuse alcohol or other drugs: for those who also have a mental health problem there is a risk that prescribing sends out a message that taking drugs, prescribed or otherwise, is an appropriate way to deal with psychological distress. When undertaking a mental state examination, the doctor tries to balance benefits of pharmacotherapy against risk; risk is a function not only of the medication but also the treatment setting. In assessing risk, it is the ephemeral nature of psychological distress coexisting with substance misuse that is perhaps the most compelling reason to wait until a patient is drug free or stable before prescribing, and also a reason to consider hospital admission solely for the purpose of establishing a psychiatric diagnosis.

With a focus on alcohol, Allan[5] has recommended that patients presenting with anxiety and alcohol dependence should first be detoxified and reassessed after 6 weeks when only an expected 10% will be found to have persistent symptoms amounting to an anxiety state. The persistent anxiety can then be treated using conventional pharmacological or behavioral methods. She points out that patients may resist such an approach, preferring to deal with their psychological distress before tackling their substance use. People who are dependent on alcohol or other drugs usually succumb to a number of financial, family, health, and relationship problems, and it is not surprising that many will complain of depression; again it is not surprising that 80% or more will recover within a few weeks of abstinence without recourse to antidepressant treatment.

While abstinence may enforce an acceptance of problems accumulated while drinking or taking other drugs and this might be anticipated to increase depression, abstinence is also an opportunity to build self-efficacy and self-esteem, both powerful psychological antidepressants. Pharmacological antidepressants should be avoided unless there is unequivocal evidence of a biological depression of mood. The key point is that diagnoses of mental illness and substance use comorbidity made in haste will often evaporate. Nonetheless, it may be that the severity of symptoms is so great when a patient presents as to indicate immediate symptomatic prescribing without the benefit of a diagnosis. Equally, it may be that a provisional diagnosis, for example, alcoholic delirium or Wernicke encephalopathy, demands urgent treatment.

The general principle to observe and "wait and see" can be a difficult course to follow, and in addition to cases of obvious florid psychosis, there are times when urgent action (usually not pharmacotherapy) is required. For example, suicidal ideation is a common emergency for doctors specializing in addiction. Alcohol and other drugs are commonly found on toxicological screening of subjects who have committed suicide. Depressant drugs in particular are likely to impair judgment and, therefore, increase both the risk of any suicide attempt, but especially suicides involving violence or impulse, such as driving into a bridge or jumping in front of a train.

Murphy[6] has identified seven risk factors for suicide in "alcoholics":

- Depression
- Suicidal thoughts
- Poor social support
- Physical illness
- Unemployment
- Living alone
- Recent interpersonal loss

The risks accumulate over a number of years, suggesting that there is scope for preventive social and health care. In short, people who misuse alcohol or other drugs are at increased risk of committing suicide: pharmacological treatment risks providing a means of suicide and active, social therapy is more likely to be effective. Other psychiatric conditions may be less urgent than a suicide threat, but nonetheless complex in terms of reaching prescribing decisions.

Insomnia, which may result from psychological distress and may be a symptom of recreational drug use or may be part of a withdrawal syndrome, is ubiquitous and merits special mention. Alcohol and other sedatives increase slow wave sleep and reduce REM and are therefore effective hypnotics. Short-acting hypnotics and alcohol are, in normal amounts, metabolized through the night, causing rebound arousal and wakenings. For people who misuse depressant drugs, including alcohol, the rebound of REM may cause vivid nightmares and sleep disturbance, which persists for months after achieving abstinence. The use of stimulant drugs causes a similar overarousal.

Patients with addiction problems are often reluctant to accept nonpharmacological approaches to insomnia; however, advice to reduce smoking and coffee drinking in the evening and to exercise during the day should at least accompany any prescribing of hypnotics.

In summary, for many people who suffer from psychiatric or psychological disorders, substance use and misuse has utility. It is often the case that traditional medicine has less to offer than the patient's own self-medication regimen and that social rather than pharmacological interventions are really what is needed. It is particularly important for doctors to be clear about the purpose of their prescribing and to monitor its effectiveness. Where substance misuse and psychiatric disorder coexist, the case for not prescribing, even for psychiatric illness, should always be vigorously explored.

REFERENCES

1. American Psychiatric Association, *Diagnostic and Statistical Manual of Mental Disorders*, 4th ed. Washington, D.C.: American Psychiatric Association, 1994.
2. Wittchen, H., Perkonigg, A., and Reed, V., Comorbidity of mental disorders and substance use disorders, *Eur. Addict. Res.*, 2, 36, 1996.
3. Kessler, R.C., McGonagle, K.A., Shanyang, Z., Nelson, C.B., Hughes, M., Eshleman, S., Wittchen, H., and Kendler, K.S., Lifetime and 12 month prevalence of DSM-III-R psychiatric disorders in the United States, *Arch. Gen. Psychiatry*, 51, 8, 1994.

4. Driessen, M., Arolt, V., John, U., Veltrup, C., and Dilling, H., Psychiatric comorbidity in hospitalized alcoholics after detoxification treatment, *Eur. Addict. Res.*, 2, 17, 1996.
5. Allan, C.A., Alcohol problems and anxiety disorders — a critical review, *Alcohol Alcohol.*, 30, 145, 1995.
6. Murphy, G.E., *Suicide in Alcoholism*, New York: Oxford University Press, 1992.

CHAPTER 7

Toxicologic Issues

Kim Wolff, Ph.D.
King's College London, Institute of Psychiatry, National Addiction Centre, London, U.K.

CONTENTS

7.1 HEAT AND DRUG STABILITY

The variety of different body matrices that can be analyzed to determine the presence or absence of different psychoactive substances is extensive, ranging from semen to cerumen. There are, however, practical limitations to the extent to which different biological samples can be used, and the mechanism of collection and supervision of samples are critical to the procedure. This chapter focuses on those biological samples that are commonly used for testing within various drug treatment settings, namely, urine, saliva, blood, and hair. Urinalysis is routinely used in hospital-based services, blood in forensic environments, hair analysis for medicolegal cases, and saliva tests have been used in the prison services and outreach units.

Many would advocate that the assessment of psychoactive drug use could reliably be achieved using self-report from the drug user (client). However, there are issues around the method of inquiry — the context, purpose, interviewer characteristics, etc.[1] — that may bias self-report. Circumstances where the drug user sees the self-report to the inquirer about drug use as influential on his own continued treatment or possible loss of privileges are particular examples.

The drug being tested for and the period of time that the clinician wishes to consider influence the choice of body fluid. Blood and, to a lesser degree, saliva are likely to give the most accurate measurement of drugs currently active in the system, whereas urine provides a somewhat broader time period, but with less quantitative accuracy. Hair provides a substantially longer time frame.[2,3]

The routine drug testing strategy most widely adopted is to send urine samples to a laboratory for an initial screen to detect psychoactive drugs of interest. Analysis is performed using a semi-automated commercially available immunoassay or thin layer chromatography (TOXILAB) test. Several types of the former test exist and include radioimmunoassay, RIA:Europ/DPC, enzyme-mediated immunoassay test, Syva:EMIT, and fluorescence polarization immunoassay, FPIA. Recently, several rapid detection devices (near patient test, NPT) for drugs of abuse screening have been marketed in the U.K. Such tests offer a more rapid turnaround of results to aid clinical decision making.[4] However, all initial drug screen tests are nonspecific and identify only in a nonquantitative fashion the class of drug present, e.g., opiates, amphetamines, or benzodiazepines, etc.

Ideally, any positive test result should then be confirmed by a second test working on different physicochemical principles to the screening test. Gas and liquid chromatography with mass spectrometric detection are regarded as the "gold standard" and are favored where legally defensible results are required. It cannot be overemphasized that the confirmation of drug screening test results is essential. For amphetamine-specific immunoassays, the confirmation test provides the opportunity to differentiate legitimate medicines. For instance, pseudoephedrine and phentermine give a positive test result (cross-react) with tests for illicit drugs like amphetamine and 3,4-methylenedioxymethamphetamine, MDMA. For opiate drugs, initial immunoassay tests for morphine cross-react with codeine, dihydrocodeine, pholcodeine, 6-monoactetylmorphine (6-MAM), morphine-3-glucuronide, and morphine-6-glucuronide. Consequently, if more than one of these substances is present in a urine sample, the test result will relate to the concentration of the sum of all these opiates and their metabolites. In this way an inaccurate picture of the window-of-detection of opiate drugs in urine may be concluded. The clinical benefit of the confirmation test is that it is able to verify the specific substance(s) present. For example, a confirmation test can detect the presence of 6-MAM, the only specific indicator (metabolite) of heroin use.

7.2 ANALYSIS USING OTHER BODY FLUIDS

The advantages of urine sampling for detecting drugs of abuse are the higher drug concentrations; the large volume of urine; the opportunity to concentrate urine samples, which in turn, increases drug concentrations, and thus the possibility of detection; and the fact that urine collection is a non-invasive procedure. Urine testing is the most reliable and interpretable process available to the clinician and is the technique universally supported by laboratories across the country. Urine testing is recommended as essential to help confirm opiate dependence before commencing substitute prescribing with methadone or buprenorphine. Random urine tests are also used to monitor illicit drug use during treatment. Hair testing is more common in occupational health settings and for medicolegal cases where a longer history of drug use is required. Providing the client's hair is of sufficient length (hair grows at a rate of 1 cm/month) and thickness (50 to 100 strands are needed), a drug history covering a 3-month period may be obtained. Cannabis use, however, is very difficult to detect in hair and different rates of drug deposition in the hair strand have been identified for different races, treated (bleached hair), and in blond compared to black-haired people. Blood (and possibly saliva) provides an accurate picture of the immediate situation and is best suited for therapeutic drug monitoring, which has been reported for methadone treatment.

Sample integrity has frequently been an issue with urinalysis and every effort should be made to avoid substitution or adulteration of specimens. Simple observational checks of foaming, color, and temperature are valuable. Collection cups with temperature indicator strips are available for immediate monitoring of specimen temperature. For workplace or pre-employment testing, medicolegal work and sport testing, chain-of-custody procedures, tamper-free collection vesicles, and documentation to accompany each sample are required.

Dilution is a commonly reported problem. The U.K. National External Quality Assessment Scheme (UKNEQAS) for drugs of abuse screening in urine reported that 86% of samples found adulterated had been diluted.[4] As it is possible to drink large volumes of water and lower urine drug concentrations below the positive cutoff, thresholds for tests of urine creatinine and specific gravity have been proposed (Table 7.1).

There has been a huge growth in the development of NPT kits. Most are predominantly for urine sample collection and have the advantage of offering rapid results. Such tests include FRONT-LINE (Boehringer Mannheim) and Rapi Tests (Morwell Diagnostics), EZ-Screen (for cannabis and

Table 7.1   Checks for Urine Sample Adulteration

Problem	Check to Confirm
Dilution	Creatinine <20 mg/dl (1.77 mmol/L)
	Specific gravity <1.003
Substitution	Creatinine 5 mg/dl (0.44 mmol/L)
	Specific gravity 1.001 or 1.020
Concentration	pH values of <4 and >8 are abnormal
Temperature	Values <32°C and >38°C are abnormal
Adulteration (bleach, nitrate)	Sample will not smell like urine
	Nitrite level >500 g/ml

cocaine), Triage (for benzodiazepines, methadone, and cocaine; Biosite Diagnostic), Abuscreen ONTRAK (for cannabis and morphine; Roche Diagnostics), ONTRAK TESTCUP (for opiates; Roche Diagnostics). There have been many reported limitations for these immunoassay test devices. For cannabinoids, the accuracy varies from 52 to 90%; for opiates 37 to 90%; for amphetamines 44 to 83%; and for cocaine 72 to 92%.[5] Another reported failing of the NPT kits has been the lack of available information about cross-reactivity,[3] which is important in drug treatment services where poly substance use is commonplace. Urine samples for use with NPT kits also have the same issues with authenticity as those collected for laboratory-based testing and in addition concern has been raised that without onsite staff training the number of false-positive and false-negative test results could be unacceptably high. Confirmation of the test result with all initial tests is recommended as good practice.

Most recently, oral fluid immunoassay test kits have also become available (Cozart RapiScan, www.cozart.co.uk) offering a less invasive testing procedure. Oral fluid screening is, however, subject to contamination of the buccal cavity from drugs taken intranasally or sublingually, i.e., cannabis and buprenorphine, respectively. Additionally, the pH of saliva (the main component of oral fluid) can be changed during the sample collection procedure by chewing, which may alter (reduce) the diffusion of the drugs of interest into the oral fluid sample. This could result in false-negative test results. Cost is also prohibitive and currently there is little evidence-based information about these products.[6]

Accurate interpretation of the drug-screening test within a clinical setting, alongside other relevant information, remains the key to the usefulness of any test.

REFERENCES

1. Magura, S., Casriel, C., Goldsmith, D.S., Strug, D.L., and Lipton, D.S., Contingency contracting with poly drug-abusing methadone patients, *Addict. Behav.,* 13, 113, 1988.
2. Strang, J., Marsh, A., and Desouza. N., Hair analysis for drugs of abuse, *Lancet*, 1, 740, 1990.
3. American Association for Clinical Chemistry, Protocol issues in urinalysis of abused substances: report of the Substance-abuse Testing Committee, *Clin. Chem.,* 34, 605, 1989.
4. Braithwaite, R.A., Jarvie, D.R., Minty, P.S.B., Simpson, D., and Widdop, B., Screening for drugs of abuse. I: Opiates, amphetamines and cocaine, *Ann. Clin. Biochem.,* 32, 123, 1995.
5. Decrease, R., Magura, A., Lifshitz, M., and Tilson, J., *Drug Testing in the Workplace,* American Society of Clinical Pathologists, Chicago, 1989, 1–11.
6. Fraser, A.D., Clinical toxicology of drugs used in the treatment of opiate dependency, *Clin. Toxicol. I Clin. Lab. Med.,* 10(2), 375, 1990.

CHAPTER 8

Medical Aspects of Drug Abuse

Shoshana Zevin, M.D.[1] **and Neal L. Benowitz, M.D.**[2]

[1] Department of Internal Medicine, Shaare Zedek Medical Center, Jerusalem, Israel
[2] Division of Clinical Pharmacology and Experimental Therapeutics, University of California, San Francisco, California

CONTENTS

Drug abuse is associated with many medical problems and complications stemming both from regular use and from overdoses. Another serious medical complication arising from drug abuse is the withdrawal syndrome, which manifests during abstinence from the drug.

Drug abuse affects a number of organ systems. Central nervous system (CNS) symptoms can range from headaches and altered mental status to life-threatening situations like coma and seizures (Tables 8.1 and Table 8.2). Cardiovascular manifestations of drug abuse include alterations in blood pressure, heart rate, as well as arrhythmias and organ ischemia. Respiratory arrest, pulmonary edema, and pneumothorax may occur. Metabolic effects such as alterations in body temperature, electrolytes, and acid–base disturbances are commonly seen (Table 8.3). Reproductive consequences, ranging from impaired fertility to intrauterine growth retardation, premature births, and neonatal syndromes, may also occur.

Infectious complications from intravenous drug use include viral infections such as HIV and hepatitis B, as well as bacterial infections including bacterial endocarditis, osteomyelitis, and abscesses.

In this chapter we describe the specific clinical syndromes associated with drugs of abuse.

Table 8.1   Drugs of Abuse Commonly Causing Altered Mental Status

Agitation	Amphetamines
	Cocaine
	Phencyclidine
	Phenylpropanolamine
Hallucinations	Khat
	LSD
	Marijuana
	Mescaline
	Phencyclidine
	Solvents
Psychosis	Amphetamines
	Khat
	LSD
	Phencyclidine
	Phenylpropanolamine
Stupor/Coma	Barbiturates
	Benzodiazepines
	Ethanol
	Opiates
	Phencyclidine
	"Crash" after binging on cocaine or amphetamines

Table 8.2   Drugs of Abuse Commonly Causing
            Seizures

Amphetamines
Cocaine
Meperidine
Phencyclidine
Phenylpropanolamine
Propoxyphene
Ethanol and sedative–hypnotic drug withdrawal

Table 8.3   Drugs of Abuse Commonly Causing Temperature
            Disturbances

Hyperthermia	Amphetamines
	Cocaine
	LSD
	Phencyclidine
	Ethanol and/or sedative–hypnotic drug withdrawal
Hypothermia	Barbiturates
	Benzodiazepines
	Opiates

Table 8.4   Effects of Stimulant Intoxication

CNS Effects	Cardiovascular Effects	Metabolic Effects	Respiratory Effects
Irritability	Tachycardia[a]	Hyperthermia	Respiratory arrest
Euphoria	Hypertension	Rhabdomyolysis	
Insomnia	Cardiovascular collapse		
Anxiety			
Aggressiveness			
Delirium (agitated)			
Psychosis			
Stupor			
Coma			
Seizures			

[a] Except alpha-adrenergic agonists, which cause reflex bradycardia.

8.1 STIMULANTS

Stimulant drugs act primarily through activation of the sympathetic nervous system. In moderate doses they result in an elevated mood, increased energy and alertness, and decreased appetite. During intoxication they have profound central nervous system, cardiovascular system, and metabolic effects (Table 8.4).

8.1.1 Cocaine

Cocaine is one of the most frequent causes of medical complications of drug abuse.[1–3] Its actions include blockade of reuptake of catecholamines and dopamine by the neurons, release and/or blockade of the reuptake of serotonin, and centrally mediated neural sympathetic activation.[4,5] In addition to stimulating the sympathetic nervous system, cocaine also has a local anesthetic effect due to blockade of fast sodium channels in neural tissue and the myocardium.

Cocaine may be injected intravenously, smoked, snorted, or orally ingested. Its half-life is approximately 60 min. After intravenous injection or smoking there is a rapid onset of CNS manifestations; the effects may be delayed 30 to 60 min after snorting, mucosal application, or oral ingestion. The duration of cocaine effect is dependent on the route of administration, and is usually about 90 min after oral ingestion. Acute cocaine intoxication

Table 8.5   Medical Complications of Cocaine Intoxication and Abuse

CNS	Headache
	Stroke (ischemic and hemorrhagic)
	Transient neurological deficit
	Subarachnoid hemorrhage
	Seizures
	Toxic encephalopathy
	Coma
Cardiovascular	Hypertension
	Aortic dissection
	Arrhythmia (sinus tachycardia, supraventricular tachycardia, ventricular tachycardia/fibrillation)
	Shock
	Sudden death
	Myocarditis
	Myocardial ischemia and infarction
	Other organ ischemia: renal infarction, intestinal infarction, limb ischemia
Respiratory	Pulmonary edema
	Respiratory arrest
	"Crack lung"
	Pneumothorax
	Pneumomediastinum
Metabolic	Hyperthermia
	Rhabdomyolysis
	Renal failure (myoglobinuria)
	Coagulopathy
	Lactic acidosis
Reproductive/Neonatal	Spontaneous abortion
	Placental abruption
	Placenta previa
	Intrauterine growth retardation
	"Crack baby syndrome"
	Cerebral infarction
Infectious	HIV/AIDS[a]
	Hepatitis B[a]
	Infectious endocarditis[a]
	Frontal sinusitis with brain abscess[b]
	Fungal cerebritis[a]
	Wound botulism
	Tetanus

[a] Associated with contaminated needles.
[b] Associated with intranasal insufflation.
Source: Modified from Benowitz.[24]

usually resolves after about 6 h, but some manifestations, such as myocardial infarction and stroke, may occur many hours after use, and a cocaine "crash" syndrome may last for several days after cocaine binging.

Most of the toxic manifestations of cocaine are due to excessive central and sympathetic nervous system stimulation. CNS stimulation causes behavioral changes, mood alterations, and psychiatric abnormalities. Autonomic stimulation causes cardiovascular system abnormalities, such as alterations in blood pressure, heart rate, arrhythmias, and hyperthermia (Table 8.5). Some of these manifestations, especially in the CNS and cardiovascular systems, can be life-threatening.

8.1.1.1 *Central Nervous System*

In moderate doses cocaine produces arousal and euphoria, but also anxiety and restlessness. Acute intoxication may result in severe psychiatric disturbances, such as acute anxiety, panic attacks, delirium, or acute psychosis.[6] Chronic cocaine intoxication can produce paranoid psychosis, similar to schizophrenia.[7] There is evidence suggesting that chronic cocaine use may lead to permanent neurological abnormalities. Brain atrophy, particularly in the frontal cortex and basal ganglia, has been found in chronic cocaine abusers, as well as cerebral blood perfusion deficits in frontal, periventricular, and temporal areas.[7,8] Abnormalities in cerebral glucose metabolism, as well as reduction in β-ATP/Pi ratios in cerebral cortex, were found in chronic cocaine addicts. These changes are similar to those observed after cerebral hypoxia.[9]

Headache: Headache is quite common in cocaine users, and has been reported in 13 to 50% of the users surveyed. In some patients the headaches were triggered by cocaine, whereas others reported them in association with cocaine withdrawal.[8,10] Some patients experienced migraine headaches. In some instances, headaches may be induced by hypertension. Persistent headaches, despite normalization of blood pressure, should raise concern about a possible stroke.

Stroke and transient neurologic defects: A variety of neurologic signs have been reported in patients with cocaine intoxication, among them dizziness, vertigo, tremor, and blurred vision. Transient hemiparesis has also been observed, and may be the result of cerebral vasospasm.[11,12] Strokes are being increasingly recognized in cocaine abuse, particularly in young patients. In one case-control study, the odds ratio for women aged 15 to 44 years who used cocaine or amphetamines was 7.[13] Among the patients with strokes, about 50% have cerebral hemorrhage, 30% subarachnoid hemorrhage, and 20% ischemic stroke.[8,10,14] This distribution differs from the one found in the general population, where ischemia and not hemorrhage accounts for the majority of strokes. There was also a report of acute subdural hematoma associated with cocaine use.[15] The mechanism of stroke is thought be an acute elevation of blood pressure induced by increased sympathetic activity, which may cause rupture of cerebral aneurysm; or vasospasm or cerebral vasoconstriction.[16] Interestingly, anticardiolipin antibodies, which are associated with an increased risk of stroke, were found in 27% of asymptomatic cocaine users, and in 5 of 7 cocaine users with thromboembolism.[17] Chronic cocaine abuse has been associated with acute dystonic reactions, which in some cases have been precipitated by neuroleptics, and in others without neuroleptics. Acute dystonia was reported after cocaine use as well as during cocaine withdrawal.[18,19] Choreoathetoid movements lasting up to 6 days have also been described.[20]

Seizures: Seizures are seen in about 1.4 to 2.8% of cocaine abusers admitted to a hospital.[8,10,18,21,22] They are usually generalized, tonic-clonic in character, and may occur soon after taking cocaine, or after a delay of several hours. Seizures may be associated with recreational cocaine use, but are more common in intoxication or "body packer" syndrome.[8,21] Children can have seizures as a first manifestation of cocaine exposure.[10] The mechanism of cocaine-related seizures is not clear, and may be related to its local anesthetic properties.

Toxic encephalopathy and coma: Often patients present after several days of cocaine binge; at first they may experience severe anxiety, hyperactivity, and paranoia, which last for about 6 to 8 h, and then may become hypersomnolent and depressed. This latter phase can last 2 to 3 days.

Other complications associated with cocaine abuse are frontal sinusitis and brain abscess after chronic cocaine snorting.[23] Cocaine snorting is also associated with atrophy of nasal mucosa, necrosis, and perforation of the nasal septum.[18]

8.1.1.2 Cardiovascular System

Blood pressure: Intense sympathetic stimulation induced by cocaine results in hypertension and tachycardia. Hypertension is a combined result of increased cardiac output and increased systemic vascular resistance. Hypertension may cause stroke, aortic dissection, and acute pulmonary edema.

Myocardial ischemia: Myocardial infarction has been well documented in cocaine abuse. It is the end result of a combination of several factors including coronary vasospasm, increased myocardial oxygen demand due to increased myocardial work load, and thrombosis.[24–27] Most patients with cocaine-related ischemia present within 1 h of cocaine use, when the plasma concentrations of cocaine are the highest; however, some patients present hours after cocaine use. The late presentation may be caused by delayed coronary vasoconstriction induced by major cocaine metabolites.[26,28] However, only between 4 and 6% of patients presenting to emergency rooms with cocaine-associated chest pain have acute coronary syndrome.[26,29] Ambulatory electrocardiographic (ECG) monitoring of chronic cocaine users during the first week of cocaine withdrawal demonstrated recurrent episodes of ST segment elevation, probably due to vasospasm.[30] Myocarditis presenting as patchy myocardial necrosis has been observed after acute cocaine intoxication, and is believed to result from intense catecholamine stimulation.[24,30] Clinically, this results in ST segment elevations and/or T wave inversions, with an elevated CPK-MB fraction. In chronic cocaine use, the result may be myocardial fibrosis and cardiomyopathy. Other organs may be affected by ischemia resulting from vasoconstriction, including renal infarction and ischemic colitis and mesenteric ischemia,[31–33] which can be life-threatening. These patients usually present with intense flank or diffuse abdominal pain.

Arrhythmia: Arrhythmia is common in cocaine intoxication; in acute intoxication it results from sympathetic stimulation; and later it may be the result of myocardial ischemia or myocarditis. The most common arrhythmia is sinus tachycardia; other arrhythmias include atrial tachycardia and fibrillation, ventricular tachycardia, including *torsade de pointes* and conduction disturbances due to local anesthetic effects of cocaine, with wide complex tachycardia.[30] Ventricular fibrillation can be a cause of sudden death, and asystole has also been reported. QT prolongation was observed in patients after cocaine exposure.[34]

Shock: Shock may develop in patients with cocaine intoxication as a result of reduced cardiac output due to myocardial ischemia, direct myocardial depression, myocarditis, or arrhythmia, and as a result of vasodilatation due to either local anesthetic effects of cocaine on blood vessels, or its effects on the brain stem. Hypovolemia may also be present in agitated and/or hyperthermic patients.

Sudden death: Most deaths occur within minutes to hours of acute cocaine intoxication, and most are the result of arrhythmia due to either massive catecholamine release or ischemia. Many convulse prior to death. Another syndrome associated with sudden death during cocaine intoxication is "excited delirium," in which the victim manifests aggressive and bizarre behavior accompanied by hyperthermia, and then suddenly dies.[35–38] Death due to medical reasons related to cocaine intoxication accounts for about 11% of all cocaine-related deaths; the majority of cocaine-related deaths are due to trauma and homicide.[14,39]

Pulmonary: Pulmonary edema is a common finding at autopsies of victims of cocaine intoxication. It can occur in acute intoxication either because of myocardial dysfunction or as a result of a massive increase in the afterload due to vasoconstriction. Noncardiogenic pulmonary edema has also been reported.[24] A syndrome called "crack lung" has been described, and consists of fever, pulmonary infiltrates, bronchospasm, and eosinophilia.[40–42] Alveolar macrophages from crack cocaine smokers were deficient in cytokine production and in their ability to kill bacteria and tumor cells.[43] Respiratory arrest can occur as a result of CNS depression. Pneumomediastinum and pneumothorax have been described in patients who snort or smoke cocaine, presumably due to increased airway pressure during a Valsalva maneuver.

Metabolic complications: Severe hyperthermia has been described in patients with acute cocaine intoxication; the mechanism probably is muscular hyperactivity due to agitation or seizures and increased metabolic rate. However, cocaine, even in small doses, was shown to impair sweating and cutaneous vasodilatation, as well as heat perception.[44] Consistent with these findings, it was found that on hot days (with ambient temperature above 31°C), the number of deaths from accidental cocaine overdose was 33% higher compared to that on days with lower temperatures.[45] Hyperthermia is also part of the "agitated delirium" syndrome, where it accompanies extremely violent and agitated behavior, in sometimes fatal cocaine intoxications.[36,37] Victims of the "agitated delirium" syndrome were more likely to be young, male, and black, compared to the victims of accidental cocaine overdose.[37,38] Hyperthermia, if untreated, can result in brain damage, rhabdomyolysis with renal failure, coagulation abnormalities, and death. Rhabdomyolysis in acute cocaine intoxication is most often the result of muscular hyperactivity and hyperthermia, but can also be due to muscular ischemia due to vasoconstriction. It presents as muscular pains, which can also occur in the chest wall, and must be distinguished from the pain of myocardial ischemia. Lactic acidosis may be a complication of prolonged muscular hyperactivity.

Reproductive/neonatal: Cocaine use during pregnancy can result in an increased incidence of spontaneous abortion, placenta previa, and abruption of the placenta. Placental ischemia results in intrauterine growth retardation.[46,47] Neonates born to cocaine-addicted mothers have various neurologic abnormalities, including irritability, tremulousness, poor feeding, hypotonia or hypertonia, and hyperreflexia. This syndrome may last for 8 to 10 weeks.[24,47] There is a dose–response relationship between adverse neonatal effects and maternal cocaine exposure.[47]

Withdrawal: Abstinence after prolonged use of cocaine can result in a "cocaine crash," manifesting as anxiety, depression, exhaustion, and craving for cocaine. Suicidal ideation is common. The symptoms can last for several weeks to several months after the cessation of use.[48]

8.1.2 Natural Stimulants

Ephedrine and khat belong to a group of natural stimulants. Ephedrine is found in a variety of plants, as well as in many Chinese medicines and is part of many nonprescription decongestants. The khat shrub grows in Ethiopia, and khat leaves are chewed in East African countries, particularly in Yemen and Somalia.[18,49] The active ingredient in khat leaves is (–)cathinone. Both ephedrine and cathinone resemble amphetamine in structure.

8.1.2.1 Ephedrine

Ephedrine acts directly on alpha and beta-adrenergic receptors, and also stimulates the release of norepinephrine. It exhibits fewer CNS effects compared to amphetamine. Pseudoephedrine is a dextro isomer of ephedrine, and has similar alpha-, but less beta-adrenergic activity. Both drugs are marketed as nonprescription medications for nasal decongestion, and are ingredients in many cold medications and bronchodilators. Ephedrine-containing dietary supplements (also known as ma-huang) are widely used for weight loss and energy enhancement. The main manifestations of ephedrine intoxication are cardiovascular, with elevation of blood pressure and heart rate.[50] Hypertension due to ephedrine intoxication, even if moderate, can result in neurologic complications including headache, confusion, seizures, and stroke, both ischemic and hemorrhagic.[51] There have also been reports of intracerebral vasculitis and hemorrhage associated with ephedrine abuse.[52] Severe headache, focal neurologic deficit, or changes in mental status in ephedrine intoxication should raise the possibility of stroke. Fatalities may result from myocardial infarction, arrhythmia, seizures, or stroke.[53]

Use of dietary supplements containing ephedrine (ma-huang), even in doses recommended by the manufacturer, has been associated with severe cardiovascular events, including myocardial infarction, sudden death, and stroke.[54,55] Many of the adverse effects occurred in young people without risk factors for cardiovascular disease.

Another, little recognized complication of chronic use of ephedra-containing products is kidney stones, which have been found to contain ephedrine and pseudoephedrine.[56]

8.1.2.2 Khat

Khat has CNS effects quite similar to amphetamine; but due to the bulkiness of the plant the actual amounts of the active ingredient, cathinone, which is actually ingested, are usually not large. Social use of khat causes increase in energy level and alertness, but also mood lability, anxiety, and insomnia.[57] Khat abuse may result in mania-like symptoms, paranoia, and acute schizophrenia-like psychosis. In most cases of khat-induced psychosis, heavy khat consumption preceded the episodes.[49,57,58] Most of the cases are resolved within weeks with cessation of khat use. There is one case report of leukoencephalopathy associated with heavy khat use.[59] No specific physical withdrawal syndrome is recognized, but there is a psychological withdrawal characterized by depression, hypersomnia, and loss of energy.[49,57]

Khat intoxication may result in cardiovascular toxicity with hypertension and tachycardia, but severe hypertension has not been observed.[57,60] Khat chewing may be a precipitating factor for myocardial infarction, probably due to its catecholamine-releasing properties. As compared to non-chewers, khat chewers presenting with acute myocardial infarction were more likely to be young and without cardiovascular risk factors, and were more likely to present during or immediately after khat-chewing sessions.[61]

There is an association between khat use and gastric ulcers, and also between its use and constipation, although causation is not clear.[57]

Babies born to khat-chewing mothers are likely to suffer from intrauterine growth retardation. Long-term chewing of khat (for more than 25 years) was found to be strongly associated with oral cancer.[49]

8.1.3　Synthetic Stimulants

Amphetamine, along with its analogues methamphetamine and methylphenidate, are sympathomimetics; they act by releasing biogenic amines from storage sites both in the CNS and the peripheral nervous system as well as by directly stimulating alpha- and beta-adrenergic receptors. Thus, they produce CNS stimulation and arousal, and serious mental changes and cardiovascular effects during intoxication.

8.1.3.1　Amphetamine

Amphetamine is one of the most potent CNS stimulators. It exists as a racemic solution, but dextroamphetamine (D-isomer) is three to four times more potent than levoamphetamine with regard to CNS stimulation. It is mainly administered orally or intravenously. Clinically amphetamine effects are very similar to those of cocaine, but amphetamine has a longer half-life compared to cocaine (10 to 15 h), and the duration of amphetamine-induced euphoria is four to eight times longer than for cocaine.

CNS effects: During acute intoxication with amphetamines, patients commonly present with euphoria, restlessness, agitation, and anxiety.[18,62] Suicidal ideation, hallucinations, and confusion are seen in 5 to 12% of the patients with acute intoxication. In one sample of drug users, 55% of amphetamine users reported having at least one adverse effect (anxiety, depression, paranoia, sleep and appetite disturbances).[3] Seizures may occur in about 3% of the patients presenting in the hospital with amphetamine intoxication.[22,62] Stroke has been reported in patients with amphetamine intoxication; it is usually hemorrhagic and results from hypertension.[13,63,64] There have also been reports of cerebral vasculitis and hemorrhage with chronic abuse of amphetamine.[65-67] Chronic amphetamine abuse may precipitate psychiatric disturbances, such as paranoia and psychosis, that can persist for weeks.[68,69]

Movement disorders: Chronic high-dose amphetamine use is associated with stereotypic behavior, dyskinesias, and also with chorea, especially in patients with preexisting basal ganglia disorders. Amphetamines exacerbate tics in patients who already have them, and may induce tics, although the causation is unclear.[18]

Cardiovascular effects: The major effects seen during acute intoxication are hypertension and tachycardia. Arrhythmia can occur, including ventricular fibrillation. Myocardial ischemia and infarction have been reported; the underlying mechanisms are increased myocardial oxygen demand and/or coronary vasospasm.[25,62,70,71] Chronic abuse has been reported to result in cardiomyopathy.[72] Systemic necrotizing vasculitis, resembling periarteritis nodosa, has been associated with chronic amphetamine abuse.[73]

Metabolic and other effects: Acute amphetamine intoxication can manifest with sweating, tremor, muscle fasciculations, and rigidity. Hyperthermia can develop and may be life-threatening if not treated promptly.[74] The mechanisms underlying hyperthermia are muscle hyperactivity and seizures. The same mechanisms may also cause rhabdomyolysis with attendant renal failure. Chronic amphetamine abuse can result in weight loss of up to 20 to 30 lb and malnutrition.[18]

Withdrawal: Amphetamine withdrawal peaks in 2 to 4 days of abstinence, and can last several weeks. The main symptom is depression, occasionally with suicidal ideation.[48]

8.1.3.2 Methamphetamine

Methamphetamine is an amphetamine analogue; it has an increased CNS penetration and a longer half-life; its effects may persist for 6 to 24 h longer than amphetamine. It can be ingested orally, smoked, or snorted.[75] Methamphetamine produces more CNS stimulation with fewer peripheral effects compared to amphetamine,[76] but large doses may result in hypertension. Stroke, both ischemic and hemorrhagic, has been reported with methamphetamine abuse, and in some cases the stroke was delayed by 10 to 12 h after last use.[77,78] The mechanisms may be hypertension, thrombosis, vasospasm, and vasculitis. Rhabdomyolysis has also been described in association with methamphetamine abuse.[79]

8.1.3.3 Methylphenidate

Methylphenidate is structurally related to amphetamine; in therapeutic doses it is a mild CNS stimulant, with more mental than motor effects, and it has minimal peripheral effects in therapeutic doses. It is used clinically for the treatment of attention-deficit disorder and narcolepsy. However, when abused and used in high doses it may cause generalized CNS stimulation with symptoms similar to amphetamine, including seizures. A case of cerebral vasculitis associated with therapeutic doses of methylphenidate was reported.[80]

8.1.3.4 Phenylpropanolamine

Phenylpropanolamine (PPA) is primarily an alpha-adrenergic agonist, both direct and indirect through release of norepinephrine. It is structurally related to amphetamine. Phenylpropanolamine is an ingredient in many cold and anorectic agents. Phenylpropanolamine combined with caffeine has been sold as a look-alike "amphetamine." PPA has a low therapeutic index, and doses two to three times in excess of recommended may result in toxicity. Susceptible individuals, particularly those suffering from hypertension or autonomic insufficiency with attendant denervation hypersensitivity of adrenergic receptors, may experience adverse effects even with therapeutic doses. The main manifestations of phenylpropanolamine toxicity are cardiovascular; however, CNS stimulant effects usually appear at higher doses.

Cardiovascular effects: The main effect of phenylpropanolamine is hypertension due to its alpha-adrenergic properties. Because it has only slight beta-adrenergic activity, there is no tachycardia; rather, a reflex bradycardia is usually present.[81] Patients with phenylpropanolamine-induced hypertension are at risk for stroke, both ischemic and hemorrhagic.[81–83] A strong association was found between the risk of hemorrhagic stroke in women aged 18 to 49 years and use of phenylpropanolamine-containing appetite suppressants and cold medications. No increase in risk was found in men.[84] These findings prompted the FDA to remove phenylpropanolamine from over-the-counter medications.[85,86] Headache is a common feature, and may reflect an acutely elevated blood pressure, or may be the first manifestation of stroke. Patients with a severe headache, altered mental status, or neurologic deficit should be evaluated for stroke even if their blood pressure is not elevated. There are also case reports of chest pain, myocardial infarction, and ECG repolarization abnormalities.[81] The duration of intoxication is about 6 h.

CNS effects: When taken in large doses and/or chronically abused, phenylpropanolamine causes symptoms similar to amphetamine, including anxiety, agitation, and psychosis.[81,87] There are individuals at risk for psychiatric side effects from phenylpropanolamine even at therapeutic doses: these are individuals with past psychiatric history, children younger than 6 years, and post-partum women.[88,89] Seizures have also been reported, though often when phenylpropanolamine was combined with other drugs, such as caffeine. Case reports of cerebral vasculitis and hemorrhage with phenylpropanolamine use have been described.[90]

8.2 HALLUCINOGENS

The primary effects of hallucinogenic drugs are altered perception and mood. The specific effects differ in different drug classes. They are also accompanied by autonomic changes (Table 8.6). Most hallucinogens do not induce physical dependence. The specific mechanisms of action are not known for many of the drugs, but there are indications that they act as adrenergic and serotoninergic agonists. The changes in mood and perception are probably related to their serotoninergic actions.[91,92] After prolonged or high-dose use of the drugs, there is evidence of depletion of serotonin and dopamine in the neurons in the brain. The psychiatric effects may be quite severe, and require medication. Sometimes the psychosis may be prolonged long beyond the presence of the drug in the body, and there may be chronic psychiatric impairment and memory disturbances, possibly related to damage to serotoninergic neurons in the brain.

**Table 8.6   Manifestations of Hallucinogen Intoxication
and Abuse**

Neuropsychiatric:

Acute	Euphoria
	Altered time perception
	Heightened visual and color perception
	Anxiety
	Disorientation
	Delirium
	Panic attacks
	Suicidal ideation
	Hallucinations
Chronic	Depression
	Drowsiness
	Anxiety
	Panic disorder
	Psychosis
	Impaired memory
	Flashbacks (LSD)
Medical	Hypertension
	Tachycardia
	Nausea
	Vomiting
	Muscle pains
	Trismus (MDMA)
	Flushing
	Arrhythmia (MDMA)
	Cardiovascular collapse
	Respiratory arrest
	Stroke (MDMA)
	Hyperthermia
	Seizures
	Hepatotoxicity (MDMA)
	SIADH (MDMA)

8.2.1 Phenylethylamine Derivatives

8.2.1.1 Mescaline

Mescaline is a phenylethylamine derivative. Its use probably dates from as long as 5700 years ago.[93] It is found in peyote cactus, and can be ingested orally or intravenously. It is structurally related to epinephrine. The precise mechanism of action is unknown, but it is thought to alter the activity of serotonin, norepinephrine, and dopamine receptors.[76] The signs of intoxication appear within 30 min of ingestion, peak at 4 h, and last 8 to 14 h. The psychic phase lasts about 6 h.[94] There are both physiological and psychological manifestations of mescaline.

Physiological effects: These are mainly manifestations of autonomic adrenergic activation: dilated pupils, increased sweating, elevated systolic blood pressure and temperature. Large doses of mescaline may induce hypotension, bradycardia, and respiratory depression.[95] Some users may experience nausea, vomiting, or dizziness, which usually resolve within an hour.[96] A fatal case of Mallory–Weiss lacerations has been described after mescaline ingestion.[97] Peyote ceremonial tea, which had been stored for a prolonged time, was contaminated with botulism.[98]

Psychological effects: These begin several hours after the ingestion. Typically there is a feeling of euphoria, a sense of physical power, and distortion of sensation. There is an increased color perception.[95,99] Sometimes there are visual hallucinations, especially of vivid colors. Users may also experience feelings of depersonalization, disorientation, anxiety, emotional lability, and/or emotional outbursts.[96] There is no physical dependence for mescaline.[95,99]

8.2.1.2 TMA-2 (2,4,5-Trimethoxyamphetamine)

TMA is a synthetic analogue of mescaline and amphetamine. It is more potent than mescaline, but resembles mescaline in the effects.[100]

8.2.1.3 DOM/STP (4-Methyl-2,5-Dimethoxyamphetamine)

This is another amphetamine analogue. It has a narrow therapeutic index. Low doses of 2 to 3 mg cause perceptual distortion and mild sympathetic stimulation, but doses two to three times that produce hallucinations and more severe sympathetic stimulation.[76,101]

8.2.1.4 PMA (para-Methoxyamphetamine)

This is a very potent hallucinogen and CNS stimulant. Overdose may present with severe sympathetic stimulation including seizures, hyperthermia, coagulopathy, and rhabdomyolysis (like in amphetamine intoxication) and can result in fatalities.[102–104] PMA is a more potent CNS stimulant compared to other amphetamines, and there were reports of fatalities where PMA was substituted for MDMA.[104]

8.2.1.5 DOB (4-Bromo-2,5-Dimethoxyamphetamine)

DOB, otherwise called bromo-DOM, is one of the most potent phenylethylamine derivatives; it has about 100 times the potency of mescaline. It is long-acting, with effects starting within an hour, reaching their full strength after 3 to 4 h, and lasting up to 10 h.[105] The manifestations of intoxication are mood enhancement with visual distortion. There are case reports of severely intoxicated patients with hallucinations, agitation, and sympathetic stimulation.[106] DOB, when ingested in large doses, can have an ergot-like effect, and cause severe generalized peripheral vasospasm with tissue ischemia.[76]

8.2.1.6   MDA (3,4-Methylenedioxyamphetamine)

MDA is an amphetamine derivative included in the category of "designer drugs." While in small doses it produces mild intoxication with a feeling of euphoria, large doses can cause hallucinations, agitation, and delirium.[76] It also can produce intense sympathetic stimulation, with hypertension, tachycardia, seizures, and hyperthermia. Death has been reported after MDA use, usually as a result of seizures or hyperthermia.[107]

8.2.1.7   MDMA (3,4-Methylenedioxymethamphetamine)

MDMA is one of the most popular "designer drugs" today, and is used recreationally by a large number of young people.[108] It is also known as "Ecstasy," "Adam," and "M&M." It was "rediscovered" in the 1970s as an adjunct to psychotherapy, but its use for this purpose has since diminished.

Psychological effects: After ingestion of 75 to 150 mg, users experience a sense of euphoria, heightened awareness, improved sense of communication, but also some impairment in the performance of psychomotor tasks.[95,109] Women tend to have more intense psychoactive effects of MDMA compared to men.[110] Acute neuropsychiatric complications have been reported, and include anxiety, insomnia, depression, paranoia, confusion, panic attacks, and psychosis.[109,111–113] Adverse effects during the 24 h following use include lack of energy, restlessness, insomnia, lack of appetite, and difficulty concentrating.[114] Chronic effects of MDMA abuse include depression, drowsiness, anxiety, panic disorder, aggressive outbursts, psychosis, and memory disturbance.[115–117] The memory disturbance and impaired cognitive performance were found in chronic users who were abstinent, as well as in former users as long as a year after stopping.[118–123] Although the exact mechanism of action is not known, there is some evidence from animal studies, as well as from human subjects, that MDMA can cause damage to serotoninergic neurons in the brain.[109,124,125] Chronic users of MDMA were found to have a lower density of 5-HT transporters in cortex compared to nonusers; there was a dose–response with the extent of use.[120,126,127] These effects were more pronounced in women compared to men.[127]

Medical effects: Stimulatory effects of MDMA are apparent even in mild intoxication, and include increased blood pressure and heart rate, decreased appetite, and dry mouth. The recreational doses of MDMA significantly increased heart rate and blood pressure.[128,129] Also common are nausea, vomiting, trismus (jaw clenching), teeth grinding, hyperreflexia, muscle aches, hot and cold flushes, and nystagmus. Additional side effects reported include paresthesias, blurred vision, and motor tics. There are several reports of MDMA-induced arrhythmias, asystole, and cardiovascular collapse. Other potentially fatal complications include seizures, hyperthermia, and rhabdomyolysis with acute renal failure.[118,130] There are several case reports of hepatotoxicity, including hepatic failure requiring transplantation, following MDMA ingestion,[130–134] and several cases of inappropriate antidiuretic hormone secretion (SIADH) with severe hyponatremia and seizures.[135–139] CNS complications including stroke (ischemic and hemorrhagic), subarachnoid hemorrhage, and cerebral venous sinus thrombosis have been reported following MDMA ingestion. One syndrome of MDMA intoxication has been reported specifically in the setting of crowding and vigorous dancing, such as in "raves" or clubs. It includes several manifestations: hyperthermia, dehydration, seizures, rhabdomyolysis, disseminated intravascular coagulation, and acute renal failure.[118,140] This is thought to be the consequence of the combination of sympathomimetic effects including cutaneous vasoconstriction and extreme physical exertion in hot and poorly ventilated conditions, although some features are those of serotonin syndrome.[141] There are two case reports of MDMA intoxication, one of them fatal, after regular recreational doses in HIV patients on ritonavir therapy.[142,143] The mechanism is probably inhibition of CYP2D6, which metabolizes amphetamines, by ritonavir.

Reproductive/neonatal effects: A prospective study following 136 women exposed to MDMA during pregnancy found a significantly increased risk (15.4%) of congenital defects, particularly cardiovascular and musculoskeletal anomalies.[144]

8.2.1.8 MDEA (3,4-Methylenedioxy-N-ethylamphetamine)

This is an analogue of MDMA, with effects similar to those of MDMA.

8.2.2 Lysergic Acid Diethylamide

Lysergic acid diethylamide (LSD) is a synthetic ergoline, and it is the third most-frequently used drug among adolescents, after alcohol and marijuana.[145,146] The main site of action of LSD is serotoninergic receptor 5-HT_2.[147] The effects of LSD, psychological and physical, are dose-related. With oral doses of 20 to 50 μg the onset of effects is after 5 to 10 min, with peak effects occurring 30 to 90 min post-ingestion. Duration of the effects may be 8 to 12 h, and recovery lasts between 10 and 12 h, when normal cognition alternates with altered mood and perception. Cognitive effects include distortion of time and altered visual perception with very vivid color perception. Euphoria and anxiety may be experienced. There are also signs of sympathetic stimulation, with dilated pupils, tachycardia, elevated blood pressure and temperature, and facial flushing. Tremors and hyperreflexia are also common.[95,148] A "bad trip" may be experienced during LSD intoxication: terrifying hallucinations, which precipitate panic attacks, disorientation, delirium, or depression with suicidal ideation. A "bad trip" may occur with first-time use, as well as after recurrent use. Five major categories of psychiatric adverse effects have been described: anxiety and panic attacks, self-destructive behavior, such as attempting to jump out of the window, hallucinations, acute psychosis, and major depressive reactions.[148] Patients who have taken very high doses of LSD have presented with manifestations of intense sympathetic stimulation including hyperthermia, coagulopathy, circulatory collapse, and respiratory arrest.[149] Another danger of LSD abuse is accidents and trauma while trying to drive during intoxication, or during the recovery phase.

There may be chronic toxic effects associated with LSD abuse. Effects that have been described include:

1. Prolonged psychosis, especially among users with preexisting psychiatric morbidity
2. Prolonged or intermittent major depression
3. Disruption of personality
4. Post-hallucinogen perceptual disorder (PHPD)

The last syndrome is characterized by flashbacks, when imagery experienced during LSD intoxication returns without taking the drug. Flashbacks may occur months, and even years, after LSD use. It has been reported that 50% of users experienced flashbacks during the 5 years after their last use of LSD.[148-150] In most cases flashbacks occur after LSD has been used more than ten times.[149] Rarely, the flashbacks may be frightening hallucinations; in extreme cases these have been associated with homicide or suicide. Flashbacks may be triggered by stress, illness, and marijuana and alcohol use.[95,148]

8.2.3 Disassociative Anesthetics

8.2.3.1 Phencyclidine

Phencyclidine (PCP) was developed as an anesthetic, but its psychiatric side effects precluded its use in humans. In the1960s PCP became a popular street drug. It is most commonly smoked, but can also be ingested orally, snorted, or injected intravenously. PCP is also commonly used as an additive to other drugs, such as marijuana, mescaline, and LSD. The mechanisms of action of PCP include anesthesia without depression of ventilation, and its main site of action is probably blockade of the cationic channel of the NMDA receptor, as well as sigma opioid receptors.[151,152] It also inhibits the reuptake of dopamine and norepinephrine, and has direct alpha-adrenergic effects.

Table 8.7   Manifestations of Phencyclidine Intoxication

Mild (≤5 mg)	Confusional state
	Uncommunicative
	Agitated, combative
	Bizarre behavior
	Nystagmus
	Ataxia
	Myoclonus
	Muscle rigidity or catalepsy
	Hypertension
Severe (≤20 mg)	Coma
	Eyes may be open
	Myosis
	Nystagmus
	Muscle rigidity
	Extensor posturing, opisthotonus
	Increased deep tendon reflexes
	Hypertension
	Hyperthermia
	Seizures
Massive (500 mg)	Prolonged coma
	Hypoventilation
	Respiratory arrest
	Hypertension
	Prolonged and fluctuating confusional state upon
	recovery from coma

Source: Modified from Benowitz.[186]

The effects of PCP are dose-dependent (Table 8.7). Smoking causes a rapid onset of effects; the half-life of PCP may range from 11 to 51 h.[153]

Psychiatric effects: At low doses of 1 to 5 mg, PCP produces euphoria, relaxation, and a feeling of numbness. There may also be a feeling of altered body image and sensory distortion. At higher doses there may be agitation, bizarre behavior, and psychosis resembling paranoid schizophrenia. The patients may alternate between agitation and a catatonic-like state. There is also analgesia, which may lead to self-injury.[153,154]

Physical effects: In mild intoxication the most prominent sign is nystagmus, both vertical and horizontal, and numbness in extremities. In severe intoxication there are signs of adrenergic stimulation, with hypertension, tachycardia, flushing, and hyperthermia sometimes complicated by rhabdomyolysis and acute renal failure, and also of cholinomimetic stimulation with sweating, hypersalivation, and miosis, and dystonic reactions, ataxia, and myoclonus may also occur. With high doses PCP causes seizures, coma with extensor posturing, respiratory arrest, and circulatory collapse.[154,155] The eyes may remain open during coma. Coma may be prolonged, even up to several weeks. Death may result directly from intoxication (seizures, hyperthermia) or from violent behavior. Chronic effects of PCP abuse include memory impairment, personality changes, and depression, which may last up to a year after stopping. There is probably no physical dependence on PCP, but after stopping there is craving.

8.3 MARIJUANA

Marijuana is obtained from the *Cannabis sativa* plant; it is a mixture of crushed leaves, seeds, and twigs from the plant. There are many active ingredients in the plant, but the ingredient accounting for the majority of the effects is delta-9-tetrahydrocannabinol (THC). There is a great variability in the amount of THC in different plants and in different batches of marijuana. Hashish is a resinous sap of the *Cannabis* plant, and typically contains 20 to 30 times the amount of THC compared to the equal weight of marijuana. THC exerts its effects through binding to G protein type CB_1

cannabinoid receptors in the brain (CB_2 cannabinoid receptors have been identified in spleen macrophages and other immune cells). Endogenous cannabinoids, including anandamide and 2-arachidonylglycerol, have been identified.[156–158] The endogenous cannabinoids produce effects similar to those of THC when administered to animals. Their physiological functions are not yet fully understood, and probably involve neuromodulation of pain and stress and immunomodulation.

Today marijuana is the most commonly used illicit drug in the U.S.[159–161] Marijuana is usually smoked; one "joint" typically contains 10 to 30 mg of THC; the onset of action is within 10 to 20 min, and the effects last up to 2 to 3 h.[153] However, during the past 20 years improved cultivation techniques resulted in a greatly increased potency of cannabis products. Today a joint may contain up to 150 mg of THC.[158,162] Acute effects of marijuana include relaxation and sometimes euphoria, and also perceptual changes, such as enhanced vividness of colors, music, and emotions.[158,162] There may be a feeling of depersonalization. These effects may last for 2 h or more, depending on the dose. There is impairment of concentration, psychomotor performance, and problem solving. Driving skills may be affected. High doses of THC may cause hallucinations, anxiety, panic, and psychosis.[153,163,164] These effects can last for several days. Physical effects include impairment of balance, conjunctival infection, increased heart rate, orthostatic hypotension, peripheral vasoconstriction with cold extremities, dry mouth, and increased appetite.[158,162] There are reports of intravenously injected marijuana extract, which results in rapid onset of nausea, vomiting, fever, and diarrhea, and is followed by hypotension, acute renal failure, thrombocytopenia, and rhabdomyolysis.[165]

Chronic users of marijuana have been reported to experience an amotivation syndrome, in which apathy, lack of energy, and loss of motivation persist for days or longer.[163] Chronic and heavy users of marijuana exhibit impaired performance on tests of memory and attention even after 19-h abstinence.[166–169] The impaired performance was significantly correlated with the duration of cannabis use.[166] However, it is not clear whether there is any permanent neurological damage, or whether the impairment is due to prolonged release of cannabis from tissues.[168,169] Chronic use of marijuana may result in inhibition of secretion of reproductive hormones, and cause impotence in men and menstrual irregularities in women.[170] No clear association was found between maternal cannabis use during pregnancy and adverse perinatal outcomes or birth defects, when cigarette smoking and other drug use were taken into account.[162,171] However, there is a suggestion that in utero exposure to marijuana led to deficits in sustained attention and memory between ages 4 and 9.[172]

Chronic smokers of marijuana are at risk for chronic obstructive lung disease, and marijuana tar is carcinogenic and appears to be associated with development of respiratory tract carcinoma and head and neck cancer in young adults.[41,43,173–177] There are also reports of spontaneous pneumothorax in daily marijuana smokers, although the patients smoked tobacco as well. The mechanism is sustained Valsalva maneuver during forced inhalation.[178]

Chronic cannabis use has been shown to lead to the development of tolerance and dependence, and withdrawal syndrome has been demonstrated. About 8 to 10% of cannabis users will develop dependence.[158,179–182] Cannabis withdrawal syndrome is characterized by restlessness, anxiety, insomnia, anorexia, muscle tremors, and craving for marijuana.[158,183,184]

8.4 OPIOIDS

Opioids have been used and abused since ancient times. They are indispensable in clinical use for pain management, and are also used as cough suppressants and antidiarrheal agents. They are abused for their mood-altering effects, and tolerance and physical and psychological dependence account for continued abuse. Patients who use narcotic analgesics for pain relief may develop physical dependence, but rarely develop psychological dependence on the drug. Opioids are a diverse group of drugs, among them derivatives of the naturally occurring opium (morphine, heroin, codeine), synthetic (methadone, fentanyl), and endogenous compounds (enkephalins, endorphins, and dynorphins). Morphine-like analgesic drugs are also known as narcotics. There

Table 8.8   Opiate Receptor Subtypes

Receptor Subtype	Prototype Drug	Major Action
μ_1	All opiates and most opioid peptides	Supraspinal analgesia Prolactin release Catalepsy
μ_2	Morphine	Respiratory depression Gastrointestinal transit Growth hormone release Cardiovascular effects
δ	Enkephalins	Spinal analgesia Growth hormone release
κ	Dynorphin Ketocyclazocine	Spinal analgesia Sedation Inhibition of vasopressin release
ϵ	β-Endorphin	?
σ	N-allylnormetazocine	Psychotomimetic effects

Source: Modified from Olson et al.[257]

are several subtypes of opiate receptors (mu, delta, and kappa), which differ in their affinity to different agonists and antagonists, and in their effects (Table 8.8). Opiate receptors are present in different concentrations in different regions of the nervous system. Some of the receptors involved in analgesia are located in the periaqueductal gray matter; the receptors believed to be responsible for reinforcing effects are in the ventral tegmental area and the nucleus accumbens. There are opiate receptors in the locus ceruleus, which plays an important role in control of autonomic activity; their activation results in inhibition of locus ceruleus firing. After opiate withdrawal there is an increase in locus ceruleus neuronal firing, resulting in autonomic hyper-activity characteristic of opiate withdrawal. Tolerance develops to many of the opiate effects, but differentially to different effects.[185,186]

In general, opioids cause analgesia and sedation, respiratory depression, and slowed gastrointes-tinal transit. Severe intoxication results in coma and respiratory depression, which may progress to apnea and death (Table 8.9).[187] Adverse side effects from opiates are seen in drug abusers who

Table 8.9   Medical Complications of Opiate Intoxication and Withdrawal

Intoxication		
	CNS	Stupor or coma Myosis Seizures (propoxyphene, meperidine)
	Respiratory	Hypoventilation Cough suppression Respiratory arrest Pulmonary edema
	Cardiovascular	Hypotension Bradycardia Conduction abnormalities (propoxyphene)
	Metabolic	Hypothermia Cool, moist skin
Withdrawal		Anxiety Insomnia Chills Myalgias, arthralgias Nausea, vomiting Anorexia Diarrhea Yawning Midriasis Tachycardia Diaphoresis, lacrimation

take an overdose (intentional or unintentional), but also in medical patients who are treated with opiates. Morphine, heroin, methadone, propoxyphene, and fentanyl derivatives account for about 98% of all opiate deaths and hospital admissions.[188] In the 1990s there was a significant increase in the medical use of opioid analgesics in the U.S. (particularly morphine, fentanyl, hydromorphone, and oxycodone); however, no increase was seen in emergency department admissions due to abuse of these drugs.[189]

Even though different opioid drugs have similar effects, the cross-tolerance is not complete. This is explained by the discovery of different subtypes of mu and delta receptors with differential binding of opioid agonists.[190–192]

8.4.1 Opiate Effects

8.4.1.1 Analgesic Effects

Opioid receptors mu_1 play a major role in analgesia; analgesic effects are mediated through central, spinal, and peripheral mechanisms. Analgesia is dose-dependent, and in high doses opioids produce anesthesia. Tolerance to analgesic effects develops less rapidly compared to tolerance to mood or respiratory effects.[185]

8.4.1.2 Mental Effects

Mood: Opiate drugs have reinforcing properties, possibly mediated through dopaminergic neuron activation in the ventral tegmental area and nucleus accumbens. Usually, the effect on the mood is relaxation and euphoria, although patients who take opiates for pain relief more often report dysphoria after taking the drug. Tolerance to euphoria-inducing effects develops rapidly.

Sedation: Sedation is dose-dependent, and is often accompanied by stereotypic dreaming.[185] Tolerance develops rapidly. Sedation is a first sign of opiate intoxication; respiratory depression does not occur unless the patient is sedated.

8.4.1.3 Gastrointestinal Effects

Nausea and vomiting: Nausea and vomiting are prominent side effects of opiates, resulting from their actions on the chemoreceptor trigger zone in the medulla. However, tolerance usually develops to these effects. Different opiates have different likelihoods for causing nausea.

Constipation: Opioid drugs decrease gastrointestinal motility and peristalsis, acting in the spinal cord and gastrointestinal tract, thus causing constipation. Tolerance does not develop to this effect, and so constipation persists even in chronic users.[193] The constipating effect of opiates is used for symptomatic treatment of diarrhea.

8.4.1.4 Respiratory Effects

Respiratory depression: Respiratory depression is the most serious adverse effect of opiates; it is dose-dependent, and respiratory arrest is almost always the cause of death from opiate overdose. Respiratory arrest occurs within minutes of the intravenous overdose. After overdose from an oral, intramuscular, or subcutaneous route, sedation almost always precedes respiratory arrest. Tolerance to respiratory depression develops, but is lost rapidly after abstinence. All opioid agonists produce the same degree of respiratory depression given the same degree of analgesia. The mechanism is through mu_2 receptor stimulation in respiratory centers in the brain stem.[194] Opioids are medically used for the relief of dyspnea in terminally ill patients with cancer; this effect may also be mediated by opioid receptors in the bronchioles and alveolar walls.[187]

Pulmonary edema: Pulmonary edema occurs with several opioid drugs, and is noncardiogenic. The precise mechanisms are unknown but probably involve hypoperfusion with tissue injury and cytokine-induced pulmonary capillary endothelial injury. Pulmonary edema is particularly common with heroin intoxication, and may be precipitated by the administration of naloxone (which reverses venodilation and redistributes blood to the central circulation).

Cough suppression: Opiates cause cough suppression by acting in the medulla; the doses needed are usually lower than for analgesia.

8.4.1.5 Other Effects

Pupillary constriction: Miosis is invariably present in opiate intoxication, unless anoxic brain damage is present.

Pruritus: Pruritis is very common in patients receiving opiates, as well as in addicts. It is caused by histamine release mediated by the mu receptors.[195]

Urinary retention: This effect is mediated through spinal cord opiate receptors.[196]

Individual narcotic agents have specific effects, which are discussed below.

8.4.2 Specific Narcotic Agents

Morphine: Morphine has an elimination half-life of 1.7 h, but its 6-glucuronide metabolite is also pharmacologically active. Morphine can be administered by intravenous, subcutaneous, oral, and rectal routes. While well absorbed, morphine undergoes significant first-pass metabolism when given orally, and thus requires high doses to achieve the desired effects. Although the oral route is the accepted route of administration for pain control in patients with chronic pain, it is not often utilized by drug addicts. Neuroexcitatory side effects, not mediated by opioid receptors, including delirium, myoclonus, seizures, hyperalgesia, and allodynia, have occurred with morphine, and are probably related to the accumulation of metabolites such as morphine-3-glucuronide.[197,198]

Heroin: Heroin (diacetyl-morphine) is a synthetic derivative of morphine. In the body, it is rapidly converted to 6-acetylmorphine, and then to morphine. The conversion to morphine occurs within minutes. In addition to the effects common to all opiates, there have been reports of acute rhabdomyolysis with myoglobinuria during heroin intoxication.[199,200] In some case the patients have been comatose, lying with pressure on their muscles, but in other cases rhabdomyolysis occurred with alert patients, accompanied by muscle pains, weakness, and swelling.[201,202] Chronic abuse of heroin has been associated with progressive nephrotic syndrome resulting in renal failure.[203] The histopathology is focal segmental glomerulosclerosis. There is a broad spectrum of neuropathological changes in the brains of heroin abusers. Some are related to prolonged anoxia or vasculitis. Spongiform leukoencephalopathy has been described following inhalation of pre-heated heroin. Two cases of delayed-onset spongiform leukoencephalopathy following intravenous heroin overdose were also reported.[201,202,204,205] There was also a report of extrapyramidal toxicity after recovery from intranasal heroin overdose.[206]

Codeine: Codeine, one of the substances found in opium, is about 20% as potent as morphine as an analgesic. It is mostly used as a cough suppressant, and as an ingredient in pain medications. To be effective as an analgesic, codeine must be converted to morphine; this reaction is performed by the isozyme CYP2D6 of the P450 enzymes. The majority of the dose is glucuronidated, and the glucuronide is inactive as an analgesic. The enzyme converting codeine to morphine is subject to genetic polymorphism. About 10% of Caucasians are poor metabolizers, meaning that they do not convert codeine to morphine, and thus do not derive therapeutic benefit from codeine. Inhibition of CYP2D6 resulted in diminished effects of codeine, and caused codeine-dependent patients to use less codeine.[207,208]

Methadone: Methadone is a synthetic long-acting opiate agonist. It is well absorbed orally, and does not undergo significant first-pass metabolism. It has a half-life of approximately 35 h.

Methadone is mainly used as a maintenance therapy for heroin addicts, but occasionally is also used to treat chronic pain. There have been reports of deaths associated with methadone treatment, mostly as a result of too rapid dose increases in subjects who may have lost their tolerance.[209]

Propoxyphene: Propoxyphene is a derivative of methadone, but unlike methadone, it is only a mild analgesic. It has a half-life of about 15 h, but is metabolized to norpropoxyphene, a potentially toxic metabolite with a longer half-life (about 30 h). Propoxyphene has been associated with a high incidence of toxicity, because in addition to being a respiratory depressant, it also acts as a local anesthetic, and has potent membrane-stabilizing effects. Propoxyphene is an ingredient in many compound analgesics, but it is also abused.[210] The main cause of death in propoxyphene intoxication is cardiac abnormalities[211] resulting from its membrane-stabilizing effects. Conduction abnormalities with wide QRS that respond to sodium bicarbonate, and cardiovascular collapse have been described.[212] Seizures have also been associated with propoxyphene intoxication.[211] Unlike respiratory depression, cardiac abnormalities and seizures do not respond to naloxone, since these effects are not mediated through opiate receptors.

Fentanyl: Fentanyl and related drugs are synthetic opioid agonists structurally related to meperidine. Fentanyl is 50 to 100 times more potent than morphine, and has a half-life of about 4 h. Fentanyl is administered intravenously and transdermally, and is used for surgical anesthesia, especially for cardiac surgery; transdermal fentanyl is used for post-operative analgesia and for chronic pain management.[213] Fentanyl derivatives that are "street-synthesized" belong to a group of "designer drugs," and include alpha-methyl-fentanyl ("China White") and 3-methyl-fentanyl (3MF). Due to the very high potency of fentanyl and related drugs, respiratory depression may occur very rapidly. There are some reports of seizures associated with fentanyl anesthesia,[214] and a syndrome of delayed respiratory depression with truncal muscular rigidity occurring after recovering from fentanyl anesthesia has been reported.[215]

Hydromorphone: This is a synthetic derivative of morphine that is seven to ten times more potent compared to morphine. Its half-life is 2.5 h. Hydromorphone intoxication presents with all the signs of typical opiate intoxication.

Hydrocodone: Hydrocodone is almost identical to codeine. It is converted in the body to hydromorphone. Like other opiates, it can cause respiratory depression and death.

Oxycodone: This compound is a codeine derivative. Its potency and half-life are comparable to those of morphine. Deaths due to respiratory depression following oxycodone ingestion have been reported.[216]

Oxymorphone: This compound is seven to ten times more potent than morphine. It produces all the signs of classic opiate intoxication.

Meperidine: Meperidine is a synthetic opiate. Its half-life is about 3 h, but its metabolite, normeperidine, has a half-life of 15 to 34 h, and thus accumulates in plasma with repeated dosing. In patients with renal failure the half-life of normeperidine may be as long as 3 to 4 days. Normeperidine is pharmacologically active, and has both mu-mediated effects as well as other effects not mediated by opioid receptors. Acute intoxication with meperidine presents like morphine intoxication, with respiratory depression, and can be reversed with naloxone. Patients treated with high doses of meperidine, or patients with renal failure, may accumulate high levels of normeperidine resulting in a syndrome characterized by irritability, myoclonus, and seizures.[217–220] Because of the side effects on the one hand, and lack of any specific benefits on the other, meperidine use has been declining since the 1990s.[189]

Pentazocine: Pentazocine is both an opiate agonist and an antagonist. It is an agonist for kappa, delta, and sigma receptors,[221] but antagonizes mu receptors. This renders pentazocine less likely to be abused. Pentazocine produces analgesia in nontolerant patients, but may produce withdrawal in tolerant individuals. The action on sigma and kappa receptors probably mediates a psychotomimetic reaction.[222] Pentazocine also potentiates the release of catecholamines from adrenal glands, and in high doses can cause elevated blood pressure and tachycardia.[188] There are two case reports of fibrous myopathy following intramuscular pentazocine abuse.[223,224]

8.4.3   Opiate Withdrawal

Abstinence after prolonged use of opiates results in the opiate withdrawal syndrome (Table 8.9). The severity of the symptoms depends on the duration of use and the daily dose of the opiates taken before the cessation of use; it is usually more severe in drug abusers than in patients taking opiates for pain relief. Opiate withdrawal can be precipitated by naloxone, and can occur even after a single dose of an opiate. Acute withdrawal after naloxone usually results in nausea and vomiting, profuse sweating, diarrhea, fatigue, and aches and pains, which may last up to 12 h.[225] During unassisted opiate withdrawal the patient will experience craving for the drug, usually 4 to 6 h after the last administered dose of short-acting opiates such as morphine or heroin (the interval may be 12 to 24 h for methadone). If no drug is administered at this point, there will be a feeling of intense discomfort, with anxiety, agitation, myalgias, sweating, and increased bowel movement. The symptoms will increase over the next 36 to 48 h, reach their peak at 36 to 72 h, and resolve over the next 7 to 10 days. The withdrawal symptoms are not life-threatening. They can be treated specifically with opiate replacement (usually methadone) in doses that will make the patient comfortable, and/or with supportive treatment including clonidine (a central alpha-agonist with some opiate-like effects), or benzodiazepines for anxiety.

8.5 SEDATIVE–HYPNOTICS

8.5.1   Benzodiazepines

Benzodiazepines belong to the category of CNS depressant drugs, and are used in clinical practice as sedative–hypnotic and anxiolytic agents. Some benzodiazepines are also used as anti-epileptics and anesthetics. Their principal mechanism of action is potentiation of gamma-aminobu-tyric acid (GABA) — an inhibitory neurotransmitter — activity in the brain. GABA binds to the receptor opening chloride channels. The influx of chloride ions hyperpolarizes the cell membrane and prevents its firing. Benzodiazepines bind to a different site on the GABA receptor, potentiating the effects of GABA on chloride flux and enhancing the inhibitory effects of GABA.[226] Prolonged use of benzodiazepines results in tolerance. The possible mechanisms are downregulation of the GABA receptors, and configurational changes of the receptor-agonist complex resulting in dimin-ished agonist sensitivity.[227–229]

There are many drugs in the benzodiazepine class, which share the same pharmacodynamic properties. They differ in their pharmacokinetics, and the differences in elimination half-life and in duration of action indicate their different uses (Table 8.10A). Benzodiazepines are classified as very short acting (midazolam), short acting (triazolam), intermediate acting (alprazolam), long acting (diazepam), and very long acting (flurazepam). Most of the benzodiazepines, except oxazepam and lorazepam, which are glucuronidated, are metabolized by liver cytochrome P450 and have active metabolites. Tolerance usually develops to benzodiazepines' effects after continuous use, slowly for long-acting drugs (after about 1 month or more) and more rapidly for short-acting ones. Most users of benzodiazepines obtain the drugs by prescription. Benzodiazepines are abused usually by people who abuse other drugs as well.[230,231] However, inappropriate chronic use by patients is also com-mon.[231,232] Because benzodiazepines cause physical and psychological dependence, they are gener-ally recommended for limited periods of time (several weeks) and the doses carefully titrated.[230,233,234] Side effects of use include daytime drowsiness, aggravation of depression, and memory impairment, especially anterograde amnesia.[233,235–238] Benzodiazepine use in elderly individuals has been asso-ciated with falls and hip fractures, due to drowsiness and ataxia.[239] Chronic benzodiazepine exposure in elderly individuals was associated with functional impairment similar to that caused by medical conditions.[234] However, discontinuation of benzodiazepines results in normalization of memory and psychomotor performance.[240,241] Short-acting benzodiazepines, in particular triazolam, have been associated with withdrawal symptoms during treatment. The symptoms include rebound insomnia

Table 8.10A Commonly Used Benzodiazepines

Drug	Elimination Half-Life (h)
Very short-acting	
Triazolam	1.5–3
Midazolam	2–5
Short-acting	
Alprazolam	10–20
Lorazepam	10–20
Oxazepam	5–10
Temazepam	10–17
Intermediate-acting	
Chlordiazepoxide	10–29
Clonazepam	20–30
Diazepam	30–60
Nitrazepam	15–24
Long-acting	
Clorazepate	50–80
Flurazepam	50–100

Table 8.10B Commonly Used Barbiturates

Drug	Elimination Half-Life (h)	Duration of Effect (h)
Ultrashort-acting		
Thiopental	8–10	<0.5
Methohexital	3–5	<0.5
Short-acting		
Pentobarbital	15–50	>3–4
Secobarbital	15–50	>3–4
Intermediate-acting		
Amobarbital	10–40	>4–6
Aprobarbital	14–34	>4–6
Butabarbital	35–50	>4–6
Long-acting		
Phenobarbital	80–120	>6–12
Mephobarbital	10–70	>6–12

Source: Adapted from Olson.[257]

and anxiety when the drug is stopped. The use of triazolam as a hypnotic has also been associated with global amnesia[242] and affective and psychiatric disturbances.[236]

Intoxication with benzodiazepines results in CNS depression. In general, they have a very high toxic-therapeutic ratio, and doses 15 to 20 times the therapeutic dose may not cause serious side effects. With high doses the patients present with lethargy, ataxia, or slurred speech (Table 8.11). With very high doses, and especially when there is co-ingestion of alcohol or barbiturates, coma and respiratory depression may occur. Rapid intravenous injection of diazepam and midazolam may cause respiratory arrest. Respiratory depression has also been reported with short-acting benzodiazepines, particularly triazolam.

Withdrawal: Withdrawal usually occurs after sudden cessation of benzodiazepines; it is usually associated with a prolonged use of high doses, but also after therapeutic doses when the drug was used for several months. The symptoms include anxiety, panic attacks, insomnia, irritability, agitation, tremor, and anorexia (Table 8.11). Withdrawal from high doses of benzodiazepines and from short-acting benzodiazepines is usually more severe, and may result in seizures and psychotic reactions.[243] The time course of the withdrawal syndrome depends on the half-life of the specific compound.

8.5.2 Barbiturates

Barbiturates are clinically used as sedative–hypnotic drugs, and also for the treatment of epilepsy and induction of anesthesia. They modulate GABA receptor binding sites and potentiate the effects

Table 8.11   Manifestations of Sedative–Hypnotic Drug Intoxication and Withdrawal

Intoxication	
Mild	Sedation
	Disorientation
	Slurred speech
	Ataxia
	Nystagmus
Moderate	Coma, arousable by painful stimuli
	Hypoventilation
	Depressed deep tendon reflexes
Severe	Coma, unarousable
	Absent corneal, gag, and deep tendon reflexes
	Hypoventilation, apnea
	Hypotension, shock
	Hypothermia
Withdrawal	Anxiety
	Insomnia
	Irritability
	Agitation
	Anorexia
	Tremor
	Seizures (short-acting benzodiazepines and barbiturates)

Source: Modified from Benowitz.[186]

of the inhibitory neurotransmitter GABA. In high concentrations the barbiturates may enhance chloride ion flux independently.[244] There are several classes of barbiturates based on their elimination half-life (Table 8.10B). The commonly used antiepileptic agent phenobarbital has a half-life of 80 to 120 h. Serious toxicity may occur when the ingested dose is five to ten times the therapeutic. Intoxication with barbiturates results in progressive encephalopathy and coma. Mild intoxication may present as oversedation, slurred speech, ataxia, and nystagmus. Severe intoxication may present with coma, absent reflexes, hypothermia, hypotension, and respiratory depression. Apnea and shock may occur. The time course of intoxication depends on the pharmacokinetics of the specific drug; for phenobarbital coma may last for 5 to 7 days. Barbiturates are usually abused as a "treatment" for unpleasant symptoms of stimulant intoxication; in this context, short-acting drugs, such as pentobarbital and secobarbital, are often used.[245]

Withdrawal: Withdrawal symptoms upon cessation of barbiturates occur after prolonged use even of therapeutic doses, although severe withdrawal is seen most commonly in polydrug abusers. The presentation is similar to that of benzodiazepine withdrawal, but there may be a greater risk of seizures with barbiturate withdrawal (Table 8.11).

8.5.3 Solvents

Solvent abuse has been a problem for many years, particularly among adolescents. The most frequently abused agents are glues, paint thinners, nail lacquer removers, lighter fluids, cleaning solutions, aerosols, and gasoline.[246,247] The most frequently encountered chemical is toluene, which is an ingredient in glues, paint thinners, and some petroleum products. Other chemicals are acetone in nail lacquer remover, naphtha, fluorinated hydrocarbons, trichloroethylene, and others. The methods of inhalation are breathing the substance from a plastic bag placed directly over the nose or the mouth, inhaling directly from the container or from impregnated rags, and spraying aerosols directly into the mouth. All the solvents are lipid-soluble, and thus easily cross the blood–brain barrier and cell membranes. They typically produce similar effects.

The acute effects of solvent inhalation begin within minutes, and last 15 to 45 min after inhalation. Habitual abusers of solvents may have a rash around the nose and mouth from inhaling, and may have the odor of solvent on their breath.[248] The typical effects are feelings of euphoria,

Table 8.12   Manifestations of Solvent Intoxication and Abuse

Mild	Euphoria
	Disinhibition
	Dizziness
	Slurred speech
	Lack of coordination
	Sneezing and coughing
Moderate	Lethargy, stupor
	Hallucinations
	Nausea, vomiting
	Diarrhea
	Ataxia
	Tremors
	Myalgias
	Paresthesias
Severe	Coma
	Seizures
Chronic	Cerebellar syndrome: ataxia, nystagmus, tremor (toluene)
	Parkinsonism (toluene)
	Peripheral neuropathy: symmetrical, motor, mainly involving
	hands and feet (*n*-hexene, naphtha)

disinhibition, and dizziness (Table 8.12). There may also be slurred speech, lack of coordination, and impaired judgment.[248,249] More severe intoxication may result in nausea and vomiting, diarrhea, tremor, ataxia, paresthesia, diffuse pains, and hallucinations. Seizures and coma may ensue.[247–250] The acute intoxication usually resolves quickly. Toluene abuse has been associated with renal tubular acidosis and severe hypokalemia, as well as interstitial nephritis, and acute tubular necrosis.[251] There are deaths associated with acute solvent abuse, about half of them the result of accidents such as asphyxiation from the plastic bag. Almost all the rest are thought to be from cardiac causes, including ventricular fibrillation and pulmonary edema.[249] Persistent toxic effects have been reported in chronic frequent abusers of volatile substances (Table 8.12). These include cerebellar syndrome, parkinsonism, and peripheral neuropathy and cognitive impairments. On magnetic resonance imaging (MRI), cerebral atrophy is seen, particularly in the areas of corpus callosum and cerebellar vermis; SPECT studies have demonstrated areas of hypoperfusion in the brain.[252–254] Cerebellar syndrome is associated mainly with toluene abuse and presents with nystagmus, ataxia, and tremor. It may be reversible with continued abstinence.[248] However, MRI changes demonstrating cerebral and cerebellar atrophy were found.[254] There was a report of parkinsonism in a young patient who chronically abused lacquer thinner; the symptoms persisted for more than 3 months after cessation of use.[255] Peripheral neuropathy, predominantly motor and symmetrical, is associated with *n*-hexene and naphtha. Symptoms usually start weeks after the first exposure, and the deterioration may continue for several months after the cessation of solvents. There are reports of hepatitis and liver failure, renal failure, and aplastic anemia associated with chronic solvent abuse.[256]

ACKNOWLEDGMENT

The authors acknowledge the support of NIH Grant DD01696.

REFERENCES

1. Gawin FH, Ellinwood EH, Jr. Cocaine and other stimulants. Actions, abuse, and treatment. *N Engl J Med* 1988;318(18):1173–82.
2. Boghdadi MS, Henning RJ. Cocaine: pathophysiology and clinical toxicology. *Heart Lung* 1997;26(6):466–83.

3. Williamson S, Gossop M, Powis B, Griffiths P, Fountain J, Strang J. Adverse effects of stimulant drugs in a community sample of drug users. *Drug Alcohol Depend* 1997;44(2–3):87–94.

4. Fleckenstein AE, Gibb JW, Hanson GR. Differential effects of stimulants on monoaminergic transporters: pharmacological consequences and implications for neurotoxicity. *Eur J Pharmacol* 2000;406(1):1–13.

5. Ramamoorthy S, Blakely RD. Phosphorylation and sequestration of serotonin transporters differentially modulated by psychostimulants. *Science* 1999;285(5428):763–6.

6. Lowenstein DH, Massa SM, Rowbotham MC, Collins SD, McKinney HE, Simon RP. Acute neurologic and psychiatric complications associated with cocaine abuse. *Am J Med* 1987;83(5):841–6.

7. Majewska MD. Cocaine addiction as a neurological disorder: Implications for treatment. *NIDA Res Monogr* 1996;163:1–26.

8. Daras M. Neurologic complications of cocaine. *NIDA Res Monogr* 1996;163:43–65.

9. Christensen JD, Kaufman MJ, Levin JM, Mendelson JH, Holman BL, Cohen BM, et al. Abnormal cerebral metabolism in polydrug abusers during early withdrawal: a 31P MR spectroscopy study. *Magn Reson Med* 1996;35(5):658–63.

10. Mueller PD, Benowitz NL, Olson KR. Cocaine. *Emerg Med Clin North Am* 1990;8(3):481–93.

11. Rowbotham MC. Neurologic aspects of cocaine abuse [clinical conference]. *West J Med* 1988;149(4):442–8.

12. Effiong C, Ahuja TS, Wagner JD, Singhal PC, Mattana J. Reversible hemiplegia as a consequence of severe hyperkalemia and cocaine abuse in a hemodialysis patient. *Am J Med Sci* 1997;314(6):408–10.

13. Petitti DB, Sidney S, Quesenberry C, Bernstein A. Stroke and cocaine or amphetamine use. *Epidemiology* 1998;9(6):596–600.

14. Tardiff K, Gross E, Wu J, Stajic M, Millman R. Analysis of cocaine-positive fatalities. *J Forensic Sci* 1989;34(1):53–63.

15. Keller TM, Chappell ET. Spontaneous acute subdural hematoma precipitated by cocaine abuse: case report. *Surg Neurol* 1997;47(1):12–4.

16. Kaufman MJ, Levin JM, Ross MH, Lange N, Rose SL, Kukes TJ, et al. Cocaine-induced cerebral vasoconstriction detected in humans with magnetic resonance angiography. *JAMA* 1998;279(5):376–80.

17. Fritsma GA, Leikin JB, Maturen AJ, Froelich CJ, Hryhorczuk DO. Detection of anticardiolipin antibody in patients with cocaine abuse. *J Emerg Med* 1991;9 Suppl 1:37–43.

18. Sanchez-Ramos JR. Psychostimulants. *Neurol Clin* 1993;11(3):535–53.

19. Catalano G, Catalano MC, Rodriguez R. Dystonia associated with crack cocaine use. *South Med J* 1997;90(10):1050–2.

20. Daras M, Koppel BS, Atos Radzion E. Cocaine-induced choreoathetoid movements ("crack dancing"). *Neurology* 1994;44(4):751–2.

21. Winbery S, Blaho K, Logan B, Geraci S. Multiple cocaine-induced seizures and corresponding cocaine and metabolite concentrations. *Am J Emerg Med* 1998;16(5):529–33.

22. Zagnoni PG, Albano C. Psychostimulants and epilepsy. *Epilepsia* 2002;43 Suppl 2:28–31.

23. Naveen RA. Brain abscess: A complication of cocaine inhalation. *NY State J Med* 1988;88:548–50.

24. Benowitz NL. Clinical pharmacology and toxicology of cocaine [published erratum appears in *Pharmacol Toxicol* 1993 Jun;72(6):343]. *Pharmacol Toxicol* 1993;72(1):3–12.

25. Ghuran A, Nolan J. Recreational drug misuse: Issues for the cardiologist. *Heart* 2000;83(6):627–33.

26. Lange RA, Hillis LD. Cardiovascular complications of cocaine use. *N Engl J Med* 2001;345(5):351–8.

27. Benzaquen BS, Cohen V, Eisenberg MJ. Effects of cocaine on the coronary arteries. *Am Heart J* 2001;142(3):402–10.

28. Mittleman MA, Mintzer D, Maclure M, Tofler GH, Sherwood JB, Muller JE. Triggering of myocardial infarction by cocaine. *Circulation* 1999;99(21):2737–41.

29. Feldman JA, Fish SS, Beshansky JR, Griffith JL, Woolard RH, Selker HP. Acute cardiac ischemia in patients with cocaine-associated complaints: results of a multicenter trial. *Ann Emerg Med* 2000;36(5):469–76.

30. Nademanee K. Cardiovascular effects and toxicities of cocaine. *J Addict Dis* 1992;11(4):71–82.

31. Boutros HH, Pautler S, Chakrabarti S. Cocaine-induced ischemic colitis with small-vessel thrombosis of colon and gallbladder. *J Clin Gastroenterol* 1997;24(1):49–53.

32. Linder JD, Monkemuller KE, Raijman I, Johnson L, Lazenby AJ, Wilcox CM. Cocaine-associated ischemic colitis. *South Med J* 2000;93(9):909–13.

33. Niazi M, Kondru A, Levy J, Bloom AA. Spectrum of ischemic colitis in cocaine users. *Dig Dis Sci* 1997;42(7):1537–41.

34. Gamouras GA, Monir G, Plunkitt K, Gursoy S, Dreifus LS. Cocaine abuse: Repolarization abnormalities and ventricular arrhythmias. *Am J Med Sci* 2000;320(1):9–12.

35. Mirchandani HG, Rorke LB, Sekula-Perlman A, Hood IC. Cocaine-induced agitated delirium, forceful struggle, and minor head injury. A further definition of sudden death during restraint. *Am J Forensic Med Pathol* 1994;15(2):95–9.

36. Wetli CV, Mash D, Karch SB. Cocaine-associated agitated delirium and the neuroleptic malignant syndrome. *Am J Emerg Med* 1996;14(4):425–8.

37. Ruttenber AJ, McAnally HB, Wetli CV. Cocaine-associated rhabdomyolysis and excited delirium: Different stages of the same syndrome. *Am J Forensic Med Pathol* 1999;20(2):120–7.

38. Ruttenber AJ, Lawler Heavner J, Yin M, Wetli CV, Hearn WL, Mash DC. Fatal excited delirium following cocaine use: epidemiologic findings provide new evidence for mechanisms of cocaine toxicity. *J Forensic Sci* 1997;42(1):25–31.

39. Marzuk PM, Tardiff K, Leon AC, Hirsch CS, Stajic M, Portera L, et al. Fatal injuries after cocaine use as a leading cause of death among young adults in New York City. *N Engl J Med* 1995;332(26):1753–7.

40. Kissner DG, Lawrence WD, Selis JE, Flint A. Crack lung: pulmonary disease caused by cocaine abuse. *Am Rev Respir Dis* 1987;136(5):1250–2.

41. Tashkin DP. Airway effects of marijuana, cocaine, and other inhaled illicit agents. *Curr Opin Pulm Med* 2001;7(2):43–61.

42. Albertson TE, Walby WF. Respiratory toxicities from stimulant use. *Clin Rev Allergy Immunol* 1997;15(3):221–41.

43. Baldwin GC, Tashkin DP, Buckley DM, Park AN, Dubinett SM, Roth MD. Marijuana and cocaine impair alveolar macrophage function and cytokine production. *Am J Respir Crit Care Med* 1997;156(5):1606–13.

44. Crandall CG, Vongpatanasin W, Victor RG. Mechanism of cocaine-induced hyperthermia in humans. *Ann Intern Med* 2002;136(11):785–91.

45. Marzuk PM, Tardiff K, Leon AC, Hirsch CS, Portera L, Iqbal MI, et al. Ambient temperature and mortality from unintentional cocaine overdose. *JAMA* 1998;279(22):1795–800.

46. Bateman DA, Chiriboga CA. Dose–response effect of cocaine on newborn head circumference. *Pediatrics* 2000;106(3):E33.

47. Chiriboga CA, Brust JC, Bateman D, Hauser WA. Dose–response effect of fetal cocaine exposure on newborn neurologic function. *Pediatrics* 1999;103(1):79–85.

48. Lago JA, Kosten TR. Stimulant withdrawal. *Addiction* 1994;89(11):1477–81.

49. Yousef G, Huq Z, Lambert T. Khat chewing as a cause of psychosis. *Br J Hosp Med* 1995;54(7):322–6.

50. Battig K. Acute and chronic cardiovascular and behavioural effects of caffeine, aspirin and ephedrine. *Int J Obes Relat Metab Disord* 1993;17 Suppl 1:S61–4.

51. Bruno A, Nolte KB, Chapin J. Stroke associated with ephedrine use. *Neurology* 1993;43(7):1313–6.

52. Wooten MR, Khangure MS, Murphy MJ. Intracerebral hemorrhage and vasculitis related to ephedrine abuse. *Ann Neurol* 1983;13(3):337–40.

53. MMWR. Adverse events associated with ephedrine-containing products — Texas, December 1993–September 1995. *MMWR Morb Mortal Wkly Rep* 1996;45(32):689–93.

54. Haller CA, Benowitz NL. Adverse cardiovascular and central nervous system events associated with dietary supplements containing ephedra alkaloids. *N Engl J Med* 2000;343(25):1833–8.

55. Samenuk D, Link MS, Homoud MK, Contreras R, Theohardes TC, Wang PJ, et al. Adverse cardiovascular events temporally associated with ma huang, an herbal source of ephedrine. *Mayo Clin Proc* 2002;77(1):12–6.

56. Powell T, Hsu FF, Turk J, Hruska K. Ma-huang strikes again: Ephedrine nephrolithiasis. *Am J Kidney Dis* 1998;32(1):153–9.

57. Luqman W, Danowski TS. The use of khat (*Catha edulis*) in Yemen. Social and medical observations. *Ann Intern Med* 1976;85(2):246–249.

58. Pantelis C, Hindler CG, Taylor JC. Use and abuse of khat (*Catha edulis*): A review of the distribution, pharmacology, side effects and a description of psychosis attributed to khat chewing. *Psychol Med* 1989;19(3):657–68.

59. Morrish PK, Nicolaou N, Brakkenberg P, Smith PE. Leukoencephalopathy associated with khat misuse. *J Neurol Neurosurg Psychiatry* 1999;67(4):556.

60. Hassan NA, Gunaid AA, Abdo Rabbo AA, Abdel Kader ZY, al Mansoob MA, Awad AY, et al. The effect of Qat chewing on blood pressure and heart rate in healthy volunteers. *Trop Doct* 2000;30(2):107–8.

61. Al Motarreb A, Al Kebsi M, Al Adhi B, Broadley KJ. Khat chewing and acute myocardial infarction. *Heart* 2002;87(3):279–80.

62. Derlet RW, Rice P, Horowitz BZ, Lord RV. Amphetamine toxicity: Experience with 127 cases. *J Emerg Med* 1989;7(2):157–61.

63. Agaba EA, Lynch RM, Baskaran A, Jackson T. Massive intracerebral hematoma and extradural hematoma in amphetamine abuse. *Am J Emerg Med* 2002;20(1):55–7.

64. El Omar MM, Ray K, Geary R. Intracerebral haemorrhage in a young adult: consider amphetamine abuse. *Br J Clin Pract* 1996;50(2):115–6.

65. Matick H, Anderson D, Brumlik J. Cerebral vasculitis associated with oral amphetamine overdose. *Arch Neurol* 1983;40(4):253–4.

66. Shaw HE, Jr., Lawson JG, Stulting RD. *Amaurosis fugax* and retinal vasculitis associated with methamphetamine inhalation. *J Clin Neuroophthalmol* 1985;5(3):169–76.

67. Buxton N, McConachie NS. Amphetamine abuse and intracranial haemorrhage. *J R Soc Med* 2000;93(9):472–7.

68. Harris D, Batki SL. Stimulant psychosis: symptom profile and acute clinical course. *Am J Addict* 2000;9(1):28–37.

69. Flaum M, Schultz SK. When does amphetamine-induced psychosis become schizophrenia? *Am J Psychiatry* 1996;153(6):812–5.

70. Costa GM, Pizzi C, Bresciani B, Tumscitz C, Gentile M, Bugiardini R. Acute myocardial infarction caused by amphetamines: A case report and review of the literature. *Ital Heart J* 2001;2(6):478–80.

71. Waksman J, Taylor RN, Jr., Bodor GS, Daly FF, Jolliff HA, Dart RC. Acute myocardial infarction associated with amphetamine use. *Mayo Clin Proc* 2001;76(3):323–6.

72. Smith HJ, Roche AH, Jausch MF, Herdson PB. Cardiomyopathy associated with amphetamine administration. *Am Heart J* 1976;91(6):792–7.

73. Welling TH, Williams DM, Stanley JC. Excessive oral amphetamine use as a possible cause of renal and splanchnic arterial aneurysms: a report of two cases. *J Vasc Surg* 1998;28(4):727–31.

74. Callaway CW, Clark RF. Hyperthermia in psychostimulant overdose. *Ann Emerg Med* 1994; 24(1):68–76.

75. Albertson TE, Derlet RW, Van Hoozen BE. Methamphetamine and the expanding complications of amphetamines. *West J Med* 1999;170(4):214–9.

76. Buchanan JF, Brown CR. 'Designer drugs.' A problem in clinical toxicology. *Med Toxicol Adverse Drug Exp* 1988;3(1):1–17.

77. Rothrock JF, Rubenstein R, Lyden PD. Ischemic stroke associated with methamphetamine inhalation. *Neurology* 1988;38(4):589–92.

78. Perez JA, Jr., Arsura EL, Strategos S. Methamphetamine-related stroke: four cases. *J Emerg Med* 1999;17(3):469–71.

79. Richards JR, Johnson EB, Stark RW, Derlet RW. Methamphetamine abuse and rhabdomyolysis in the ED: A 5-year study. *Am J Emerg Med* 1999;17(7):681–5.

80. Schteinschnaider A, Plaghos LL, Garbugino S, Riveros D, Lazarowski A, Intruvini S, et al. Cerebral arteritis following methylphenidate use. *J Child Neurol* 2000;15(4):265–7.

81. Pentel P. Toxicity of over-the-counter stimulants. *JAMA* 1984;252(14):1898–903.

82. Kikta DG, Devereaux MW, Chandar K. Intracranial hemorrhages due to phenylpropanolamine. *Stroke* 1985;16(3):510–2.

83. Edwards M, Russo L, Harwood-Nuss A. Cerebral infarction with a single oral dose of phenylpropanolamine. *Am J Emerg Med* 1987;5(2):163–4.

84. Kernan WN, Viscoli CM, Brass LM, Broderick JP, Brott T, Feldmann E, et al. Phenylpropanolamine and the risk of hemorrhagic stroke. *N Engl J Med* 2000;343(25):1826–32.

85. Mersfelder TL. Phenylpropanolamine and stroke: the study, the FDA ruling, the implications. *Cleve Clin J Med* 2001;68(3):208–9, 213–9, 223.

86. SoRelle R. FDA warns of stroke risk associated with phenylpropanolamine; cold remedies and drugs removed from store shelves. *Circulation* 2000;102(21):E9041–3.

87. Mueller SM. Neurologic complications of phenylpropanolamine use. *Neurology* 1983;33(5): 650–2.

88. Goodhue A, Bartel RL, Smith NB. Exacerbation of psychosis by phenylpropanolamine. *Am J Psychiatry* 2000;157(6):1021–2.

89. Lake CR, Masson EB, Quirk RS. Psychiatric side effects attributed to phenylpropanolamine. *Pharmacopsychiatry* 1988;21(4):171–81.

90. Glick R, Hoying J, Cerullo L, Perlman S. Phenylpropanolamine: An over-the-counter drug causing central nervous system vasculitis and intracerebral hemorrhage. Case report and review. *Neurosurgery* 1987;20(6):969–74.

91. Aghajanian GK, Marek GJ. Serotonin model of schizophrenia: emerging role of glutamate mechanisms. *Brain Res Brain Res Rev* 2000;31(2–3):302–12.

92. Aghajanian GK, Marek GJ. Serotonin and hallucinogens. *Neuropsychopharmacology* 1999;21(2 Suppl):16s–23s.

93. Bruhn JG, De Smet PAGM, El Seedi HR, Beck O. Mescaline use for 5700 years. *Lancet* 2002;359(9320):1866.

94. Hollister LE, Hartman AM. Mescaline, lysergic acid diethylamide and psilocybin: comparison of clinical syndromes, effects on color perception and biochemical measures. *Comprehensive Psychiatry* 1962;3:235–241.

95. Leikin JB, Krantz AJ, Zell-Kanter M, Barkin RL, Hryhorczuk DO. Clinical features and management of intoxication due to hallucinogenic drugs. *Med Toxicol Adverse Drug Exp* 1989;4(5):324–50.

96. Kapadia GJ, Fayez MB. Peyote constituents: chemistry, biogenesis, and biological effects. *J Pharm Sci* 1970;59(12):1699–727.

97. Nolte KB, Zumwalt RE. Fatal peyote ingestion associated with Mallory-Weiss lacerations. *West J Med* 1999;170(6):328.

98. Hashimoto H, Clyde VJ, Parko KL. Botulism from peyote. *N Engl J Med* 1998;339(3):203–4.

99. Mack RB. Marching to a different cactus: peyote (mescaline) intoxication. *N C Med J* 1986;47(3):137–8.

100. Shulgin AT. Profiles of psychedelic drugs: TMA-2. *J Psychedelic Drugs* 1976;8:169.

101. Shulgin AT. Profiles of psychedelic drugs: STP. *J Psychedelic Drugs* 1977;9:171–172.

102. James RA, Dinan A. Hyperpyrexia associated with fatal paramethoxyamphetamine (PMA) abuse. *Med Sci Law* 1998;38(1):83–5.

103. Kraner JC, McCoy DJ, Evans MA, Evans LE, Sweeney BJ. Fatalities caused by the MDMA-related drug paramethoxyamphetamine (PMA). *J Anal Toxicol* 2001;25(7):645–8.

104. Byard RW, Gilbert J, James R, Lokan RJ. Amphetamine derivative fatalities in South Australia — is "Ecstasy" the culprit? *Am J Forensic Med Pathol* 1998;19(3):261–5.

105. Shulgin A. Profiles of psychedelic drugs: DOB. *J Psychoactive Drugs* 1981;13(1):99.

106. Buhrich N, Morris G, Cook G. Bromo-DMA: the Australasian hallucinogen? *Aust NZ J Psychiatry* 1983;17(3):275–9.

107. Simpson DL, Rumack BH. Methylenedioxyamphetamine. Clinical description of overdose, death, and review of pharmacology. *Arch Intern Med* 1981;141(11):1507–9.

108. Strote J, Lee JE, Wechsler H. Increasing MDMA use among college students: results of a national survey. *J Adolesc Health* 2002;30(1):64–72.

109. Steele TD, McCann UD, Ricaurte GA. 3,4-Methylenedioxymethamphetamine (MDMA, "Ecstasy"): pharmacology and toxicology in animals and humans. *Addiction* 1994;89(5):539–51.

110. Liechti ME, Gamma A, Vollenweider FX. Gender differences in the subjective effects of MDMA. *Psychopharmacology* (Berlin) 2001;154(2):161–8.

111. McCann UD, Ricaurte GA. MDMA ("ecstasy") and panic disorder: induction by a single dose. *Biol Psychiatry* 1992;32(10):950–3.

112. Alciati A, Scaramelli B, Fusi A, Butteri E, Cattaneo ML, Mellado C. Three cases of delirium after "ecstasy" ingestion. *J Psychoactive Drugs* 1999;31(2):167–70.

113. Vaiva G, Boss V, Bailly D, Thomas P, Lestavel P, Goudemand M. An "accidental" acute psychosis with ecstasy use. *J Psychoactive Drugs* 2001;33(1):95–8.

114. Vollenweider FX, Gamma A, Liechti M, Huber T. Psychological and cardiovascular effects and short-term sequelae of MDMA ("ecstasy") in MDMA-naive healthy volunteers. *Neuropsychopharmacology* 1998;19(4):241–51.

115. Morgan MJ, McFie L, Fleetwood H, Robinson JA. Ecstasy (MDMA): Are the psychological problems associated with its use reversed by prolonged abstinence? *Psychopharmacology* (Berlin) 2002;159(3):294–303.

116. MacInnes N, Handley SL, Harding GF. Former chronic methylenedioxymethamphetamine (MDMA or ecstasy) users report mild depressive symptoms. *J Psychopharmacol* 2001;15(3):181–6.

117. Gerra G, Zaimovic A, Ampollini R, Giusti F, Delsignore R, Raggi MA, et al. Experimentally induced aggressive behavior in subjects with 3,4-methylenedioxy-methamphetamine ("Ecstasy") use history: psychobiological correlates. *J Subst Abuse* 2001;13(4):471–91.

118. McCann UD, Slate SO, Ricaurte GA. Adverse reactions with 3,4-methylenedioxymethamphetamine (MDMA; "Ecstasy"). *Drug Saf* 1996;15(2):107–115.

119. Ricaurte GA, McCann UD. Assessing long-term effects of MDMA (Ecstasy). *Lancet* 2001;358(9296):1831–2.

120. Reneman L, Lavalaye J, Schmand B, de Wolff FA, van den Brink W, den Heeten GJ, et al. Cortical serotonin transporter density and verbal memory in individuals who stopped using 3,4-methylenedioxymethamphetamine (MDMA or "ecstasy"): preliminary findings. *Arch Gen Psychiatry* 2001;58(10):901–6.

121. Gouzoulis Mayfrank E, Daumann J, Tuchtenhagen F, Pelz S, Becker S, Kunert HJ, et al. Impaired cognitive performance in drug free users of recreational ecstasy (MDMA). *J Neurol Neurosurg Psychiatry* 2000;68(6):719–25.

122. Parrott AC, Sisk E, Turner JJ. Psychobiological problems in heavy "ecstasy" (MDMA) polydrug users. *Drug Alcohol Depend* 2000;60(1):105–10.

123. Verkes RJ, Gijsman HJ, Pieters MS, Schoemaker RC, de Visser S, Kuijpers M, et al. Cognitive performance and serotonergic function in users of ecstasy. *Psychopharmacology* (Berlin) 2001;153(2):196–202.

124. McCann UD, Ridenour A, Shaham Y, Ricaurte GA. Serotonin neurotoxicity after (+/–)3,4-methylenedioxymethamphetamine (MDMA; "Ecstasy"): a controlled study in humans. *Neuropsychopharmacology* 1994;10(2):129–38.

125. Kish SJ, Furukawa Y, Ang L, Vorce SP, Kalasinsky KS. Striatal serotonin is depleted in brain of a human MDMA (Ecstasy) user. *Neurology* 2000;55(2):294–6.

126. McCann UD, Szabo Z, Scheffel U, Dannals RF, Ricaurte GA. Positron emission tomographic evidence of toxic effect of MDMA ("Ecstasy") on brain serotonin neurons in human beings. *Lancet* 1998;352(9138):1433–7.

127. Reneman L, Booij J, de Bruin K, Reitsma JB, de Wolff FA, Gunning WB, et al. Effects of dose, sex, and long-term abstention from use on toxic effects of MDMA (ecstasy) on brain serotonin neurons. *Lancet* 2001;358(9296):1864–9.

128. Lester SJ, Baggott M, Welm S, Schiller NB, Jones RT, Foster E, et al. Cardiovascular effects of 3,4-methylenedioxymethamphetamine. A double-blind, placebo-controlled trial. *Ann Intern Med* 2000;133(12):969–73.

129. Mas M, Farre M, de la Torre R, Roset PN, Ortuno J, Segura J, et al. Cardiovascular and neuroendocrine effects and pharmacokinetics of 3, 4-methylenedioxymethamphetamine in humans. *J Pharmacol Exp Ther* 1999;290(1):136–45.

130. Henry JA. Ecstasy and the dance of death. *Br Med J* 1992;305(6844):5–6.

131. Milroy CM, Clark JC, Forrest AR. Pathology of deaths associated with "ecstasy" and "eve" misuse. *J Clin Pathol* 1996;49(2):149–53.

132. Jones AL, Simpson KJ. Review article: mechanisms and management of hepatotoxicity in ecstasy (MDMA) and amphetamine intoxications. *Aliment Pharmacol Ther* 1999;13(2):129–33.

133. Brauer RB, Heidecke CD, Nathrath W, Beckurts KT, Vorwald P, Zilker TR, et al. Liver transplantation for the treatment of fulminant hepatic failure induced by the ingestion of ecstasy. *Transpl Int* 1997;10(3):229–33.

134. Garbino J, Henry JA, Mentha G, Romand JA. Ecstasy ingestion and fulminant hepatic failure: liver transplantation to be considered as a last therapeutic option. *Vet Hum Toxicol* 2001;43(2):99–102.

135. Maxwell DL, Polkey MI, Henry JA. Hyponatraemia and catatonic stupor after taking "ecstasy" [see comments]. *Br Med J* 1993;307(6916):1399.

136. Satchell SC, Connaughton M. Inappropriate antidiuretic hormone secretion and extreme rises in serum creatinine kinase following MDMA ingestion. *Br J Hosp Med* 1994;51(9):495.

137. Forsling M, Fallon JK, Kicman AT, Hutt AJ, Cowan DA, Henry JA. Arginine vasopressin release in response to the administration of 3,4-methylenedioxymethamphetamine ("ecstasy"): Is metabolism a contributory factor? *J Pharm Pharmacol* 2001;53(10):1357–63.

138. Henry JA, Fallon JK, Kicman AT, Hutt AJ, Cowan DA, Forsling M. Low-dose MDMA ("ecstasy") induces vasopressin secretion. *Lancet* 1998;351(9118):1784.

139. Wilkins B. Cerebral oedema after MDMA ("ecstasy") and unrestricted water intake. Hyponatraemia must be treated with low water input. *Br Med J* 1996;313(7058):689–90.

140. Williams H, Dratcu L, Taylor R, Roberts M, Oyefeso A. "Saturday night fever": Ecstasy related problems in a London accident and emergency department. *J Accid Emerg Med* 1998;15(5): 322–6.

141. Mueller PD, Korey WS. Death by "ecstasy": The serotonin syndrome? *Ann Emerg Med* 1998;32(3 Pt 1):377–80.

142. Henry JA, Hill IR. Fatal interaction between ritonavir and MDMA. *Lancet* 1998;352(9142):1751–2.

143. Harrington RD, Woodward JA, Hooton TM, Horn JR. Life-threatening interactions between HIV-1 protease inhibitors and the illicit drugs MDMA and gamma-hydroxybutyrate. *Arch Intern Med* 1999;159(18):2221–4.

144. McElhatton PR, Bateman DN, Evans C, Pughe KR, Thomas SH. Congenital anomalies after prenatal ecstasy exposure. *Lancet* 1999;354(9188):1441–2.

145. Webb E, Ashton CH, Kelly P, Kamali F. Alcohol and drug use in UK university students. *Lancet* 1996;348(9032):922–5.

146. Golub A, Johnson BD, Sifaneck SJ, Chesluk B, Parker H. Is the U.S. experiencing an incipient epidemic of hallucinogen use? *Subst Use Misuse* 2001;36(12):1699–729.

147. Jacobs BL. How hallucinogenic drugs work. *Am Sci* 1987;75:386–392.

148. Schwartz RH. LSD. Its rise, fall, and renewed popularity among high school students. *Pediatr Clin North Am* 1995;42(2):403–13.

149. Abraham HD, Aldridge AM. Adverse consequences of lysergic acid diethylamide. *Addiction* 1993;88(10):1327–34.

150. Kawasaki A, Purvin V. Persistent palinopsia following ingestion of lysergic acid diethylamide (LSD). *Arch Ophthalmol* 1996;114(1):47–50.

151. Contreras PC, Monahan JB, Lanthorn TH, Pullan LM, DiMaggio DA, Handelmann GE, et al. Phencyclidine. Physiological actions, interactions with excitatory amino acids and endogenous ligands. *Mol Neurobiol* 1987;1(3):191–211.

152. Sonders MS, Keana JF, Weber E. Phencyclidine and psychotomimetic sigma opiates: recent insights into their biochemical and physiological sites of action. *Trends Neurosci* 1988;11(1):37–40.

153. Brust JC. Other agents. Phencyclidine, marijuana, hallucinogens, inhalants, and anticholinergics. *Neurol Clin* 1993;11(3):555–61.

154. McCarron MM, Schulze BW, Thompson GA, Conder MC, Goetz WA. Acute phencyclidine intoxication: Clinical patterns, complications, and treatment. *Ann Emerg Med* 1981;10(6):290–7.

155. Aniline O, Pitts FN, Jr. Phencyclidine (PCP): a review and perspectives. *Crit Rev Toxicol* 1982;10(2):145–77.

156. Martin BR, Mechoulam R, Razdan RK. Discovery and characterization of endogenous cannabinoids. *Life Sci* 1999;65(6–7):573–95.

157. Ameri A. The effects of cannabinoids on the brain. *Prog Neurobiol* 1999;58(4):315–48.

158. Ashton CH. Pharmacology and effects of cannabis: a brief review. *Br J Psychiatry* 2001;178:101–6.

159. Gruber AJ, Pope HG, Jr. Marijuana use among adolescents. *Pediatr Clin North Am* 2002;49(2):389–413.

160. Gledhill Hoyt J, Lee H, Strote J, Wechsler H. Increased use of marijuana and other illicit drugs at US colleges in the 1990s: results of three national surveys. *Addiction* 2000;95(11):1655–67.

161. Harris D, Jones RT, Shank R, Nath R, Fernandez E, Goldstein K, et al. Self-reported marijuana effects and characteristics of 100 San Francisco medical marijuana club members. *J Addict Dis* 2000;19(3):89–103.

162. Hall W, Solowij N. Adverse effects of cannabis. *Lancet* 1998;352(9140):1611–6.

163. Johns A. Psychiatric effects of cannabis. *Br J Psychiatry* 2001;178:116–22.

164. Nunez LA, Gurpegui M. Cannabis-induced psychosis: a cross-sectional comparison with acute schizophrenia. *Acta Psychiatr Scand* 2002;105(3):173–8.

165. Farber SJ, Huertas VE. Intravenously injected marijuana syndrome. *Arch Int Med* 1976;136:337–339.

166. Solowij N, Stephens RS, Roffman RA, Babor T, Kadden R, Miller M, et al. Cognitive functioning of long-term heavy cannabis users seeking treatment. *JAMA* 2002;287(9):1123–31.

167. Pope HG, Jr., Yurgelun Todd D. The residual cognitive effects of heavy marijuana use in college students. *JAMA* 1996;275(7):521–7.

168. Pope HG, Jr., Gruber AJ, Hudson JI, Huestis MA, Yurgelun Todd D. Neuropsychological performance in long-term cannabis users. *Arch Gen Psychiatry* 2001;58(10):909–15.

169. Pope HG, Jr. Cannabis, cognition, and residual confounding. *JAMA* 2002;287(9):1172–4.

170. Hollister LE. Health aspects of cannabis. *Pharmacol Rev* 1986;38(1):1–20.

171. Fergusson DM, Horwood LJ, Northstone K. Maternal use of cannabis and pregnancy outcome. *BJOG* 2002;109(1):21–7.

172. Fried PA, Smith AM. A literature review of the consequences of prenatal marihuana exposure. An emerging theme of a deficiency in aspects of executive function. *Neurotoxicol Teratol* 2001;23(1): 1–11.

173. Taylor FMd. Marijuana as a potential respiratory tract carcinogen: a retrospective analysis of a community hospital population. *South Med J* 1988;81(10):1213–6.

174. Wu TC, Tashkin DP, Djahed B, Rose JE. Pulmonary hazards of smoking marijuana as compared with tobacco. *N Engl J Med* 1988;318(6):347–51.

175. Taylor DR, Poulton R, Moffitt TE, Ramankutty P, Sears MR. The respiratory effects of cannabis dependence in young adults. *Addiction* 2000;95(11):1669–77.

176. Van Hoozen BE, Cross CE. Marijuana. Respiratory tract effects. *Clin Rev Allergy Immunol* 1997;15(3):243–69.

177. Zhang ZF, Morgenstern H, Spitz MR, Tashkin DP, Yu GP, Marshall JR, et al. Marijuana use and increased risk of squamous cell carcinoma of the head and neck. *Cancer Epidemiol Biomarkers Prev* 1999;8(12):1071–8.

178. Feldman AL, Sullivan JT, Passero MA, Lewis DC. Pneumothorax in polysubstance-abusing marijuana and tobacco smokers: three cases. *J Subst Abuse* 1993;5(2):183–6.

179. von Sydow K, Lieb R, Pfister H, Hofler M, Sonntag H, Wittchen HU. The natural course of cannabis use, abuse and dependence over four years: a longitudinal community study of adolescents and young adults. *Drug Alcohol Depend* 2001;64(3):347–61.

180. Swift W, Hall W, Teesson M. Characteristics of DSM-IV and ICD-10 cannabis dependence among Australian adults: results from the National Survey of Mental Health and Wellbeing. *Drug Alcohol Depend* 2001;63(2):147–53.

181. Rosenberg MF, Anthony JC. Early clinical manifestations of cannabis dependence in a community sample. *Drug Alcohol Depend* 2001;64(2):123–31.

182. Coffey C, Carlin JB, Degenhardt L, Lynskey M, Sanci L, Patton GC. Cannabis dependence in young adults: an Australian population study. *Addiction* 2002;97(2):187–94.

183. Budney AJ, Hughes JR, Moore BA, Novy PL. Marijuana abstinence effects in marijuana smokers maintained in their home environment. *Arch Gen Psychiatry* 2001;58(10):917–24.

184. Kouri EM, Pope HG, Jr. Abstinence symptoms during withdrawal from chronic marijuana use. *Exp Clin Psychopharmacol* 2000;8(4):483–92.

185. Foley KM. Opioids. *Neurol Clin* 1993;11(3):503–22.

186. Benowitz NL. Substance abuse: dependence and treatment. In: Melmon KL, Morrelli HF, Hoffman BB, Nierenberg DW, Eds. *Clinical Pharmacology*. 3 ed: New York: McGraw-Hill; 1992. p. 763–786.

187. Zebraski SE, Kochenash SM, Raffa RB. Lung opioid receptors: pharmacology and possible target for nebulized morphine in dyspnea. *Life Sci* 2000;66(23):2221–31.

188. Karch SB. *The Pathology of Drug Abuse.* Boca Raton, FL: CRC Press; 1993.

189. Joranson DE, Ryan KM, Gilson AM, Dahl JL. Trends in medical use and abuse of opioid analgesics. *JAMA* 2000;283(13):1710–4.

190. Pasternak GW. Insights into mu opioid pharmacology: the role of mu opioid receptor subtypes. *Life Sci* 2001;68(19–20):2213–9.

191. Pasternak GW. The pharmacology of mu analgesics: from patients to genes. *Neuroscientist* 2001;7(3):220–31.

192. Zaki PA, Bilsky EJ, Vanderah TW, Lai J, Evans CJ, Porreca F. Opioid receptor types and subtypes: the delta receptor as a model. *Annu Rev Pharmacol Toxicol* 1996;36:379–401.

193. Pappagallo M. Incidence, prevalence, and management of opioid bowel dysfunction. *Am J Surg* 2001;182(5A Suppl):11s–18s.

194. Ling GS, Spiegel K, Lockhart SH, Pasternak GW. Separation of opioid analgesia from respiratory depression: evidence for different receptor mechanisms. *J Pharmacol Exp Ther* 1985;232(1):149–55.

195. Ballantyne JC, Loach AB, Carr DB. Itching after epidural and spinal opiates. *Pain* 1988;33(2):149–60.

196. Dray A. Epidural opiates and urinary retention: new models provide new insights [editorial]. *Anesthesiology* 1988;68(3):323–4.

197. Smith MT. Neuroexcitatory effects of morphine and hydromorphone: evidence implicating the 3-glucuronide metabolites. *Clin Exp Pharmacol Physiol* 2000;27(7):524–8.

198. Mercadante S. Opioid rotation for cancer pain: rationale and clinical aspects. *Cancer* 1999;86(9):1856–66.

199. Chan P, Lin TH, Luo JP, Deng JF. Acute heroin intoxication with complications of acute pulmonary edema, acute renal failure, rhabdomyolysis and lumbosacral plexitis: a case report. *Chung Hua I Hsueh Tsa Chih* (Taipei) 1995;55(5):397–400.

200. Richter RW. Muscle damage in heroin addicts. *N Engl J Med* 1971;284(15):920.

201. Klockgether T, Weller M, Haarmeier T, Kaskas B, Maier G, Dichgans J. Gluteal compartment syndrome due to rhabdomyolysis after heroin abuse. *Neurology* 1997;48(1):275–6.

202. Rice EK, Isbel NM, Becker GJ, Atkins RC, McMahon LP. Heroin overdose and myoglobinuric acute renal failure. *Clin Nephrol* 2000;54(6):449–54.

203. Dubrow A, Mittman N, Ghali V, Flamenbaum W. The changing spectrum of heroin-associated nephropathy. *Am J Kidney Dis* 1985;5(1):36–41.

204. Niehaus L, Meyer BU. Bilateral borderzone brain infarctions in association with heroin abuse. *J Neurol Sci* 1998;160(2):180–2.

205. Buttner A, Mall G, Penning R, Weis S. The neuropathology of heroin abuse. *Forensic Sci Int* 2000;113(1–3):435–42.

206. Schoser BG, Groden C. Subacute onset of oculogyric crises and generalized dystonia following intranasal administration of heroin. *Addiction* 1999;94(3):431–4.

207. Kathiramalainathan K, Kaplan HL, Romach MK, Busto UE, Li NY, Sawe J, et al. Inhibition of cytochrome P450 2D6 modifies codeine abuse liability. *J Clin Psychopharmacol* 2000;20(4):435–44.

208. Romach MK, Otton SV, Somer G, Tyndale RF, Sellers EM. Cytochrome P450 2D6 and treatment of codeine dependence. *J Clin Psychopharmacol* 2000;20(1):43–5.

209. Drummer OH, Opeskin K, Syrjanen M, Cordner SM. Methadone toxicity causing death in ten subjects starting on a methadone maintenance program. *Am J Forensic Med Pathol* 1992;13(4):346–50.

210. Ng B, Alvear M. Dextropropoxyphene addiction — a drug of primary abuse. *Am J Drug Alcohol Abuse* 1993;19(2):153–8.

211. Lawson AA, Northridge DB. Dextropropoxyphene overdose. Epidemiology, clinical presentation and management. *Med Toxicol Adverse Drug Exp* 1987;2(6):430–44.

212. Stork CM, Redd JT, Fine K, Hoffman RS. Propoxyphene-induced wide QRS complex dysrhythmia responsive to sodium bicarbonate — A case report. *J Toxicol Clin Toxicol* 1995;33(2):179–83.

213. Yee LY, Lopez JR. Transdermal fentanyl. *Ann Pharmacother* 1992;26(11):1393–9.

214. Sprung J, Schedewie HK. Apparent focal motor seizure with a jacksonian march induced by fentanyl: a case report and review of the literature. *J Clin Anesth* 1992;4(2):139–43.

215. Caspi J, Klausner JM, Safadi T, Amar R, Rozin RR, Merin G. Delayed respiratory depression following fentanyl anesthesia for cardiac surgery. *Crit Care Med* 1988;16(3):238–40.

216. Drummer OH, Syrjanen ML, Phelan M, Cordner SM. A study of deaths involving oxycodone. *J Forensic Sci* 1994;39(4):1069–75.

217. Stock SL, Catalano G, Catalano MC. Meperidine associated mental status changes in a patient with chronic renal failure. *J Fla Med Assoc* 1996;83(5):315–9.

218. Hassan H, Bastani B, Gellens M. Successful treatment of normeperidine neurotoxicity by hemodialysis. *Am J Kidney Dis* 2000;35(1):146–9.

219. Kussman BD, Sethna NF. Pethidine-associated seizure in a healthy adolescent receiving pethidine for postoperative pain control. *Paediatr Anaesth* 1998;8(4):349–52.

220. Latta KS, Ginsberg B, Barkin RL. Meperidine: a critical review. *Am J Ther* 2002;9(1):53–68.

221. Zabetian CP, Staley JK, Flynn DD, Mash DC. [3H]-(+)-Pentazocine binding to sigma recognition sites in human cerebellum. *Life Sci* 1994;55(20):L389–95.

222. Pfeiffer A, Brantl V, Herz A, Emrich HM. Psychotomimesis mediated by kappa opiate receptors. *Science* 1986;233(4765):774–6.

223. Das CP, Thussu A, Prabhakar S, Banerjee AK. Pentazocine-induced fibromyositis and contracture. *Postgrad Med J* 1999;75(884):361–2.

224. Sinsawaiwong S, Phanthumchinda K. Pentazocine-induced fibrous myopathy and localized neuropathy. *J Med Assoc Thai* 1998;81(9):717–21.

225. Farrell M. Opiate withdrawal. *Addiction* 1994;89(11):1471–5.

226. Tallman JF, Gallager DW, Mallorga P, Thomas JW, Strittmatter W, Hirata F, et al. Studies on benzodiazepine receptors. *Adv Biochem Psychopharmacol* 1980;21:277–83.

227. Miller LG, Greenblatt DJ, Roy RB, Summer WR, Shader RI. Chronic benzodiazepine administration. II. Discontinuation syndrome is associated with upregulation of gamma-aminobutyric acid A receptor complex binding and function. *J Pharmacol Exp Ther* 1988;246(1):177–82.

228. Lader M. Biological processes in benzodiazepine dependence. *Addiction* 1994;89(11):1413–8.

229. Bateson AN. Basic pharmacologic mechanisms involved in benzodiazepine tolerance and withdrawal. *Curr Pharm Des* 2002;8(1):5–21.

230. Woods JH, Winger G. Current benzodiazepine issues. *Psychopharmacology* (Berlin) 1995;118(2):107–15; discussion 118, 120–1.

231. Griffiths RR, Weerts EM. Benzodiazepine self-administration in humans and laboratory animals — implications for problems of long-term use and abuse. *Psychopharmacology* (Berlin) 1997;134(1):1–37.

232. Michelini S, Cassano GB, Frare F, Perugi G. Long-term use of benzodiazepines: tolerance, dependence and clinical problems in anxiety and mood disorders. *Pharmacopsychiatry* 1996;29(4):127–34.

233. Ashton H. Guidelines for the rational use of benzodiazepines. When and what to use. *Drugs* 1994;48(1):25–40.

234. Nelson J, Chouinard G. Guidelines for the clinical use of benzodiazepines: pharmacokinetics, dependency, rebound and withdrawal. Canadian Society for Clinical Pharmacology. *Can J Clin Pharmacol* 1999;6(2):69–83.

235. Vgontzas AN, Kales A, Bixler EO. Benzodiazepine side effects: role of pharmacokinetics and pharmacodynamics. *Pharmacology* 1995;51(4):205–23.

236. Fraser AD. Use and abuse of the benzodiazepines. *Ther Drug Monit* 1998;20(5):481–9.

237. Buffett Jerrott SE, Stewart SH. Cognitive and sedative effects of benzodiazepine use. *Curr Pharm Des* 2002;8(1):45–58.

238. Buffett Jerrott SE, Stewart SH, Teehan MD. A further examination of the time-dependent effects of oxazepam and lorazepam on implicit and explicit memory. *Psychopharmacology* (Berlin) 1998;138(3–4):344–53.

239. Wysowski DK, Baum C, Ferguson WJ, Lundin F, Ng MJ, Hammerstrom T. Sedative–hypnotic drugs and the risk of hip fracture. *J Clin Epidemiol* 1996;49(1):111-3.

240. Rickels K, Lucki I, Schweizer E, Garcia Espana F, Case WG. Psychomotor performance of long-term benzodiazepine users before, during, and after benzodiazepine discontinuation. *J Clin Psychopharmacol* 1999;19(2):107–13.

241. Kilic C, Curran HV, Noshirvani H, Marks IM, Basoglu M. Long-term effects of alprazolam on memory: a 3.5 year follow-up of agoraphobia/panic patients. *Psychol Med* 1999;29(1):225–31.

242. Morris HHd, Estes ML. Traveler's amnesia. Transient global amnesia secondary to triazolam. *JAMA* 1987;258(7):945–6.

243. Petursson H. The benzodiazepine withdrawal syndrome. *Addiction* 1994;89(11):1455–9.

244. Ito T, Suzuki T, Wellman SE, Ho IK. Pharmacology of barbiturate tolerance/dependence: GABAA receptors and molecular aspects. *Life Sci* 1996;59(3):169–95.

245. Coupey SM. Barbiturates. *Pediatr Rev* 1997;18(8):260–4.

246. Kurtzman TL, Otsuka KN, Wahl RA. Inhalant abuse by adolescents. *J Adolesc Health* 2001;28(3):170–80.

247. Brouette T, Anton R. Clinical review of inhalants. *Am J Addict* 2001;10(1):79–94.

248. Ron MA. Volatile substance abuse: a review of possible long-term neurological, intellectual and psychiatric sequelae. *Br J Psychiatry* 1986;148:235–46.

249. al-Alousi LM. Pathology of volatile substance abuse: a case report and a literature review. *Med Sci Law* 1989;29(3):189–208.

250. Meadows R, Verghese A. Medical complications of glue sniffing. *South Med J* 1996;89(5):455–62.

251. Crowe AV, Howse M, Bell GM, Henry JA. Substance abuse and the kidney. *QJM* 2000;93(3):147–52.

252. Rosenberg NL, Grigsby J, Dreisbach J, Busenbark D, Grigsby P. Neuropsychologic impairment and MRI abnormalities associated with chronic solvent abuse. *J Toxicol Clin Toxicol* 2002;40(1):21–34.

253. Kucuk NO, Kilic EO, Ibis E, Aysev A, Gencoglu EA, Aras G, et al. Brain SPECT findings in long-term inhalant abuse. *Nucl Med Commun* 2000;21(8):769–73.

254. Kamran S, Bakshi R. MRI in chronic toluene abuse: low signal in the cerebral cortex on T2-weighted images. *Neuroradiology* 1998;40(8):519–21.

255. Uitti RJ, Snow BJ, Shinotoh H, Vingerhoets FJ, Hayward M, Hashimoto S, et al. Parkinsonism induced by solvent abuse. *Ann Neurol* 1994;35(5):616–9.

256. Schuckit MA. *Drug and Alcohol Abuse*. 3 ed. New York: Plenum Press; 1989.

257. Olson KR, Pentel PR, Kelly MT. Physical agreement and differential diagnosis of the poisoned patient. *Med Toxicol* 1987;2:52–81.

258. Albertson TE. Barbiturates. In: Olson KR, Ed. *Poisoning and Drug Overdose*. 3 ed. Stamford, CT: Appleton & Lange; 1999.

CHAPTER 9

Emergency Management of Drug Abuse

Brett A. Roth, M.D.,[1] **Neal L. Benowitz, M.D.,**[2] **and Kent R. Olson, M.D.**[2]

[1] University of Texas Southwestern Medical Center, Dallas, Texas
[2] Division of Clinical Pharmacology and Experimental Therapeutics, University of California, San Francisco, California

CONTENTS

The management of complications from drug abuse demands a variety of skills from airway management to control of seizures and shock. Several reviews have addressed the issues of general resuscitation[1–3] and toxidromes.[4–8] The purpose of this chapter is to present a series of management strategies for the emergency physician or other clinical personnel caring for patients with acute complications from drug abuse. Immediate interventions (e.g., resuscitation and stabilization), secondary interventions (e.g., emergency care after the patient is stable), as well as diagnostic workup (e.g., laboratory data, imaging), and disposition of the patient are discussed. This chapter proposes a variety of treatment approaches based on a review of the pertinent literature and clinical experience. A general treatment approach based on symptom complex (i.e., seizures, coma, hyperthermia) is presented since initial management decisions frequently have to be made without the benefit of a reliable history. This is followed by a brief review of the each particular drug of abuse (i.e., psychostimulants, opiates, hallucinogens). The reader is referred to Chapter 8 for a detailed description of the clinical toxicology associated with each drug of abuse.

It should be emphasized that the adverse reaction to a drug may depend on the unique characteristics of an individual (i.e., presence of cardiovascular disease) as well as the type of drug abused. These protocols serve as guidelines only and an individualized approach to management should be made whenever possible.

9.1 DECREASED MENTAL STATUS: COMA, STUPOR, AND LETHARGY

9.1.1 General Comments

In the setting of drug overdose, coma usually reflects global depression of the brain's cerebral cortex. This can be a direct effect of the drug on specific neurotransmitters or receptors or an indirect process such as trauma or asphyxia. Treatment deals largely with maintaining a functional airway, the administration of potential antidotes, and evaluation for underlying medical conditions. The following section describes the appropriate use of antidotes and the approach to the patient with a decreased level of consciousness from drug abuse.

Level vs. content of consciousness: It is often useful to distinguish between the *level* and the *content* of consciousness. Alertness and wakefulness refer to the level of consciousness; awareness is a reflection of the content of consciousness.[9] In referring to coma, stupor, and lethargy here we address the level of consciousness as it applies to the drug-abusing patient along a clinical spectrum with deep coma on one end, stupor in the middle, and lethargy representing a mildly decreased level of consciousness. Agitation, delirium, and psychosis are addressed in a subsequent section with a greater focus on *content* of consciousness, i.e., presence or absence of hallucinations, paranoia, severe depression, etc.

Attributes of a good antidote: The ideal antidote should be safe, effective, rapidly acting, and easy to administer. It should also have low abuse potential, and act as long as the intoxicating drug. The following standard antidotes are of potentially great benefit and little harm in all patients.

Thiamine: Thiamine is an important cofactor for several metabolic enzymes that are vital for the metabolism of carbohydrates and for the proper function of the pentose–phosphate pathway.[10] When thiamine is absent or deficient, Wernicke's encephalopathy, classically described as a triad of oculomotor abnormalities, ataxia, and global confusion, may result. Although Wernicke's is rare, empiric treatment for this disease is safe,[11] inexpensive (wholesale price of 100 mg of thiamine is approximately $1), and cost-effective.[12]

Dextrose: Hypoglycemia is a common cause of coma or stupor and should be assessed or treated empirically in all patients with deceased level of consciousness. Concerns about 50% dextrose causing an increase in infarct size and mortality in stroke,[13-15] as well as increasing serum hypertonicity in hyperosmolar patients, have been raised when arguing the benefits of routine administration of 50% dextrose. Animal models of stroke[16] that showed worse outcomes associated with hyperglycemic subjects used large doses of dextrose (approximately 2 mg/kg) as opposed to the 0.3 g/kg (25 g in a 70-kg adult) routinely given as part of the coma cocktail. Also, one ampoule of 50% dextrose in water should only raise the serum glucose level of a 70-kg patient by about 60 mg/dl (0.3 mOsm) if it distributes into total body water prior to any elimination or metabolism.[17]

Naloxone: A 19th-century method for treating opiate overdose:

> The surface of the body may be stimulated by whipping,… the patient should be made to walk around for 6–8 hours.[18]

Shoemaker, 1896

Fortunately, the use of modern antidotes such as naloxone can provide a more effective and less abusive reversal of opiate-induced narcosis. In addition to reversing respiratory depression and eliminating the need for airway interventions, naloxone may assist in the diagnosis of opiate overdose and eliminate the need for diagnostic studies such as lumbar puncture and computed tomography (CT) scanning. Despite its advances over 19th-century treatments for narcotic overdose, naloxone may not always be the best approach to management. The risk of "unmasking," or exposing the effects of dangerous co-ingestions such as cocaine or PCP[19] and of precipitating opiate withdrawal must be considered. The main effects of naloxone include the reversal of coma and respiratory depression induced by *exogenous* opiates, but it also reverses miosis, analgesia, bradycardia, and gastrointestinal stasis.[20] Presumably related to the reversal of the effects of *endogenous* opioid peptides, such as endorphins and enkephalins, naloxone has also been reported to have nonspecific benefit (e.g., reversing properties) for the treatment of ethanol, clonidine, captopril, and valproic acid.[21-24] These "nonspecific" responses are usually not as complete as a true reversal of opiate-induced coma by naloxone. The current literature raises many serious concerns about the safety of naloxone. Pulmonary edema,[25–30] hypertension,[31–33] seizures,[34] arrhythmias,[33,35] and cardiac arrest[36] have been reported following naloxone administration. In addition, reversing the sedating effects of a drug like heroin may produce acute withdrawal symptoms,[37] which, although they are not life-threatening, can cause the patient to become agitated, demanding, or even violent.[38] Considering the great number of patients who have received large doses of naloxone as part of controlled trials for shock,[39–42] stroke,[43–46] and spinal cord injuries,[47–49] as part of healthy volunteer studies,[50,51] and for overdose management,[52,53] all without significant complications, the use of naloxone appears relatively safe.[17] Opioid withdrawal symptoms commonly occur in addicted patients given naloxone.[37] While withdrawal symptoms are treatable, the best approach is avoidance. Withdrawal symptoms may be avoided either by (1) withholding opioid antagonists from known drug addicts and supporting the airway with traditional methods (e.g., endotracheal intubation) or (2) by titrating the dose of naloxone slowly such that enough antidote is given to arouse the patient but not to precipitate withdrawal. The latter can be done by administering small doses (0.2 to 0.4 mg) intravenously in a repetitive manner. While conjunctival[54] and nasal[55,56] testing for opioid addiction have been described, these tests are impractical in the patient with altered mental status in whom immediate action is necessary.

Nalmefene: Nalmefene ($t_{1/2}$ = 8 to 9 hours) is a methylene analogue of naltrexone that, like naloxone, is a pure opioid antagonist. It was developed to address concerns about the short duration of action of naloxone (~60 min). Studies have proved it to be as safe and effective with a duration of action at least twice as long as naloxone.[57] Other reports suggest a duration of action of up to 4 h.[57–59] However, 4 h is still not long enough to safely manage patients who have overdosed on long-lasting opiates such as methadone ($t_{1/2}$ up to 48 h) or propoxyphene ($t_{1/2}$ of active metabolite up to 36 h), or in those patients with delayed absorption. The use of nalmefene may potentially be advantageous due to (1) less risk of recurrent respiratory depression in the patient who leaves the emergency department against medical advise, (2) fewer doses of antagonist needed, cutting down on nursing time, and (3) fewer complications resulting from fluctuations in levels of consciousness (e.g., sedation, aspiration, occult respiratory insufficiency).[60] The dose is 0.25 to 1.0 mg IVP, with the lower dose recommended to avoid opiate withdrawal. The disadvantage of nalmefene is its cost (average wholesale price of nalmefene is $31.21/1 mg versus $5.52/0.4 mg of naloxone). Current use of nalmefene has been limited to the reversal of procedural sedation,[61] alcohol dependence,[62] and avoidance of opiate side effects in patients receiving epidural analgesia.[63]

Flumazenil: Flumazenil is a highly selective competitive inhibitor of benzodiazepines at the GABA/benzodiazepine-receptor complex.[64] Like naloxone it is a pure antagonist lacking agonist properties or abuse potential. It has been shown to be safe and effective for the reversal of benzodiazepine-induced sedation in volunteer studies[65] and in patients undergoing short procedures such as endoscopy.[66–70] There has been some debate about the role of flumazenil in the treatment of patients presenting with an acute drug overdose. Although initially recommended with caution for this population,[71,72] recent advice would be to administer it only when there is a reliable history of benzodiazepine ingestion and the likelihood of a significant proconvulsant or proarrhythmic coingestion or benzodiazepine dependency is limited. Adverse effects including precipitation of benzodiazepine withdrawal,[73,74] seizures,[75–78] ballism,[79] arrhythmias,[80,81] and even death[82,83] have occurred. In a review of 43 cases of seizure activity associated with flumazenil administration, 42% of the patients had ingested overdoses of cyclic antidepressants.[75] In addition to patients with concurrent cyclic antidepressant poisoning, *high-risk populations* include patients who have been receiving benzodiazepines for a seizure disorder or an acute convulsive episode, patients with concurrent major sedative–hypnotic drug withdrawal, patients who have recently been treated with repeated doses of parenteral benzodiazepines, and overdose patients with myoclonic jerking or seizure activity before flumazenil administration.[75] To minimize the likelihood of a seizure, it is recommended that flumazenil not be administered to patients who have used benzodiazepines for the treatment of seizure disorders or to patients who have ingested drugs that place them at risk for the development of seizures[75] (e.g., cyclic antidepressants, cocaine, amphetamines, diphenhydramine, lithium, methylxanthines, isoniazid, propoxyphene, buproprion HCl, etc.). As with nalox-one, flumazenil may also uncover the effects of a more serious intoxication such as cocaine, making the patient unmanageable. Because benzodiazepine overdoses are associated with only rare mortality[84] and only mild morbidity (the major complication being aspiration pneumonia),[85] a conservative approach with supportive airway maneuvers (e.g., endotracheal intubation) seems safest. Despite concerns over side effects, the use of flumazenil in patients with acute overdose is justified under certain circumstances. When there is a reliable history of a single drug ingestion supported by clinical manifestations consistent with benzodiazepine intoxication, and the likelihood of a significant proconvulsant or proarrhythmic co-ingestion or benzodiazepine dependency is limited, reversal of sedation may be warranted.[17] One case report described continuous flumazenil infusion for 16 days without adverse effects for clonazepam-induced sedation.[86] Errors can be avoided by obtaining a thorough history and by performing a thorough physical examination as well as a screening electrocardiogram to exclude the possibility of significant cyclic antidepressant intoxication; correction of hypoxia, hypotension, acidosis, and arrhythmias; and then by adminis-tering the agent slowly. Greenblatt[85] showed that of 99 cases in which patients overdosed on benzodiazepines only 12 were known to ingest benzodiazepines alone. Given the high incidence of co-ingestions in the drug-abusing population the risk for unmasking proconvulsants such as cocaine or amphetamine must be considered high. It is interesting that flumazenil has been credited with the reversal of paradoxical benzodiazepine-induced agitation[87] and hepatic encephalopathy[88] and that it is being investigated as a treatment aid for benzodiazepine withdrawal.[89]

9.1.2 Stepwise Approach to Management

9.1.2.1 Immediate Interventions

1. **Airway, Breathing, Circulation:** Maintain the airway and assist ventilation if necessary. Administer supplemental oxygen. Treat hypotension, and resuscitate as per previous reviews.[2,90]
2. **Thiamine:** Administer thiamine,100 mg IVP over 2 min to all the following patients:

   a. Patients with altered mental status if the patient has signs or symptoms of Wernicke's encephal-opathy
   b. Patients who are malnourished[91]
   c. Patients with a history of alcoholism[10]
   d. Patients with prolonged history of vomiting[92]
   e. Patients who are chronically ill[93]

Comment: There is no need to withhold hypertonic dextrose (D_{50}, D_{25}) until thiamine admin-istration since thiamine uptake into cells is slower than the entry of dextrose into cells.[94] Previous reports describing adverse reactions to IV thiamine[95] have recently been disputed. In a review by Wrenn et al.[11] the incidence of adverse reactions to IV thiamine ($n = 989$) was 1.1% and consisted of transient local irritation in all patients except one who developed generalized pruritus. Thiamine may also be administered intramuscularly (IM) or by mouth (po).

3. **Dextrose**

   Bedside fingerstick glucose level: Perform rapid bedside testing in all patients. If hypoglycemia is detected then the patient should receive hypertonic dextrose (25 g of 50% hypertonic dextrose solution IVP).
   Comment: This approach avoids giving dextrose solution to patients who do not need it (eliminating concerns that hyperglycemia impairs cerebral resuscitation) and detects the vast majority of hypoglycemic patients. Relying on physical signs and symptoms such as tachycardia and diaphoresis in combination with a history of diabetes mellitus is an unreliable way to predict hypoglycemia, missing up to 25% of hypoglycemic patients.[17]

Borderline rapid assay results: In any patient with borderline rapid assay results (60 to 100 mg/dl) a decision on whether or not to treat should be based on the clinical suspicion of hypoglycemia and a repeat rapid assay. Alternatively, simply treat all patients with borderline blood sugar results.

Comment: Rapid reagent assays for blood glucose may, at times, be inaccurate. Failure to detect hypoglycemia has been described in 6 to 8% of patients tested in the prehospital setting,[96,97] but results are generally more accurate inside of the hospital. False-negative results have also been reported in neonatal populations[98] and in patients with severe anemia.[99] False-positive tests (false hypoglycemia) has occurred in patients with severe peripheral vascular disease,[100] shock,[101] and hyperthermia.[102] Because most errors occur in patients with borderline glucose readings (60 to 100 mg/dl),[17] the recommendation to treat borderline glucose values is made. This also makes sense in light of recent reports that describe individual variability in response to borderline hypoglycemia;[103] e.g., patients with poorly controlled diabetes mellitus may experience clinical symptoms of hypoglycemia at greater glucose concentrations than nondiabetics.

Empiric treatment: In patients where rapid bedside testing for serum glucose is not available, administer 25 g of 50% hypertonic dextrose solution IVP after collecting a specimen of blood for glucose analysis at a later time.

4. Naloxone/Nalmefene:

a. **Restraint:** Consider restraining and disrobing the patient prior to administration.

b. **Antidote:** All patients with classic signs (RR < 12, pupils miotic, needle marks) and symptoms of opioid intoxication should receive naloxone.

　　Comment: Because of nalmefene's expense, naloxone is generally recommended. Nalmefene may be advantageous in the patient who leaves the emergency department against medical advice or if close monitoring of the patient is not possible. The usual initial dose is 0.25 mg IV followed by repeated doses until adequate response is achieved.

　　Comment: Hoffman et al.,[104] using a clinical criteria of respiratory rate less than 12 breaths/min, circumstantial evidence of opioid abuse, or miosis, decreased the use of naloxone by 75 to 90% while still administering it to virtually all naloxone responders who had a final diagnosis of opiate overdose.

c. **Initial doses:** Small doses (0.2 to 0.4 mg IV of naloxone) should be given to patients who are breathing, and at possible risk for withdrawal. If no response, repeat or titrate the same dose IV every minute until 2.0 mg of naloxone or 1.0 mg of nalmefene have been given or the patient wakes up.

　　Comment: If the patient is not suspected to be at risk for opiate withdrawal (i.e., most children) and there is no risk of unmasking a dangerous co-intoxicant such as cocaine or phencyclidine (PCP), 2.0 mg of naloxone may be given initially.

d. **High-dose antidote:** If there is still no response to a total of 2.0 mg of naloxone and opiate overdose is highly suspected by history or clinical presentation, one can give 10 to 20 mg of naloxone in one bolus dose. Certain opiates (i.e., propoxyphene, pentazocine, diphenoxylate, butorphanol, nalbuphine, codeine) may require larger doses of naloxone due to higher affinity for the kappa receptors.[105]

　　Comment: Reversal of opioid toxicity, once achieved, will be sustained for approximately 20 to 60 min ($t_{1/2}$ = 1 h). Because the duration of action of most opioids exceeds the duration of action of naloxone, the patient may require repeated bolus doses or to be started on a continuous infusion at a dose sufficient to prevent the reappearance of respiratory depression (see Section 9.10.2 on opiates).

　　Comment: A true response to naloxone or nalmefene is a dramatic improvement. Anything less should be considered a sign of a coexisting intoxication or illness, a nonspecific improvement from the reversal of endogenous opiates, or the presence of anoxic encephalopathy from prolonged respiratory depression. If dramatic improvement is noted, further management depends on the type of narcotic involved and the amount taken (Table 9.1).

e. **Dose in respiratory arrest:** Patients with respiratory arrest should either be given larger does (0.4 to 2.0 mg of naloxone) or endotracheally intubated and artificially ventilated.

Table 9.1   Half-Lives and Observation Times Required after Acute Narcotic Overdose

Opioid	Duration of Action via IV Route	$t_{1/2}$	Observation Time (h)
Propoxyphene (Darvon, Doloxene)	May be >24 h	6-12[a]	24
Methadone (Dolophine, Amidone)	May be days	15[b]–72[c]	24–36 or longer
Morphine	Usually 2–4 h	3	6
Heroin	Usually 2–4 h	Very short[d]	6
Fentanyl (Sublimaze)	Minutes	4	6
Codeine	2–4 h (oral)	3[d]	6
Meperidine (Demerol)	2–4 h	2.5	6
Pentazocine (Talwin)	2–4 h	2	6
Dextromethorphan	2–4 h (oral)	6–29	4

Note: Generally, if patients remain asymptomatic 6 h after the administration of naloxone, they may be discharged.

[a] About 1/2 of dose is metabolized to norproxyphene, an active metabolite with a $t_{1/2}$ of 30–36 h.
[b] Single dose.
[c] Repeated dosing.
[d] Rapidly deacetylated to morphine.

Comment: Naloxone is easily administered via the IV, IM, intratracheal,[105] intralingual,[106] or even the intranasal[56] routes. The intravenous route is preferred since it allows more exact titration and because it provides for a rapid onset of action (about 1 min) and predictable delivery of drug. The intramuscular route (1.0 to 2.0 mg) usually works within minutes, but makes titration more difficult and takes longer to work (5 to 10 min). It may be advantageous in the prehospital setting. The intralingual route, with antidote given near the venous plexus on the ventral lateral tongue, may work as rapidly as the intravenous route, but does not allow for titration of dosage.

f. Aspiration: Guard against aspiration.

5. Flumazenil

a. Caution: Because of a higher incidence of severe adverse effects flumazenil should be used only under the limited circumstances described previously.

b. Restraint: Consider restraining and disrobing the patient prior to administering antidote.

c. Antidote: If a pure benzodiazepine overdose is suspected, treat hypoxia, hypotension, acidosis, and arrhythmias and check a 12-lead electrocardiogram (ECG) for QRS widening. If the ECG is normal, and the patient has no known seizure disorders, *and* is not taking proconvulsant medications, flumazenil may be administered.

    Comment: Generally flumazenil should be used only to reverse serious respiratory depression. Its use is not advised to waken a stable, mildly somnolent patient. If serious respiratory depression does exist, consider endotracheal intubation and mechanical ventilation as an alternative to flumazenil.

    Comment: In a study of 50 patients treated with flunitrazepam ($t_{1/2}$ = 20 to 29 h) Claeys et al.[107] showed that 90 min after administration of flumazenil significant recurrent sedation was observed in healthy patients undergoing orthopedic surgery. Because the binding of flumazenil to the benzodiazepine-receptor complex is competitive, and because flumazenil has a much shorter duration of action ($t_{1/2}$ = 40 to 80 min) than most benzodiazepines, patients should be closely monitored for resedation.

d. Dose: Give flumazenil 0.2 mg over 30 s, to be followed 30 s later by 0.3 mg if the patient does not respond. Subsequent doses of 0.5 mg may also be given although most patients respond to less than 1.0 mg.[108] Although the manufacturers recommend the administration of up to 3 mg we recommend a maximal dosage of 1.0 mg in the drug-abusing patient at high risk for withdrawal.

    Comment: As long as flumazenil is administered slowly with a total dose of less than 1 mg, only 50% of benzodiazepine receptors will be occupied by the drug.[109] In theory, this should prevent the severe manifestations of withdrawal associated with higher doses.[17]

9.1.2.2 Secondary Interventions

1. Reassess: If the patient remains comatose, stuporous, or lethargic despite antidotes, reassess for underlying medical causes (meningitis, trauma, epilepsy, etc.) and admit to hospital.

2. Monitor: Maintain continuous monitoring (cardiac status, oxygen saturation, blood pressure) at all times.

Comment: This is particularly important since the duration of action of most narcotics and benzodiazepines of abuse is much longer than the duration of action of their respective antidote.

3. CT/lumbar puncture: Consider CT and lumbar puncture if the patient is febrile or has persistently decreased level of consciousness or focal neurological findings.

4. ECG: Perform an ECG on all elderly patients.

5. Laboratory data: For patients who respond to antidotes and return to their baseline mental status within an observation period of several hours, no laboratory testing may be necessary given a normal physical examination on reassessment. If the patient remains persistently altered or has significantly abnormal vital signs check electrolytes, CBC, CPK, CPK-MB, renal function, and possibly hepatic function. While toxicology screens of blood and urine are generally overutilized,[5] they are recommended if the diagnosis remains questionable.

6. Disposition

Admission: All patients who have required more than one dose of antidote to maintain their mental status should be admitted for further evaluation and therapy including possible infusion of naloxone or flumazenil.

Comment: Infusions should be maintained in an *intensive care setting* and patients should be closely monitored any time the infusion is stopped. Duration of observation depends on the route of drug administration, the drug ingested, the presence or absence of liver dysfunction, and the possibility of ongoing drug absorption from the gastrointestinal tract. Usually 6 h is adequate.

Flumazenil infusion: Infuse 0.2 to 0.5 h in maintenance fluids (D5W, D51/2NS, 1/2NS, NS), adjusting rate to provide the desired level of arousal. Hojer et al.[110] demonstrated that infusions of 0.5 mg/h were well tolerated and that this dose prevented patients with severe benzodiazepine poisoning from relapsing into coma after arousal with a single bolus injection.

Naloxone infusion: Goldfrank et al.[111] suggest taking two-thirds the amount of naloxone required for the patient to initially wake up and administering that amount at an hourly rate in the patient's maintenance IV (D5W, D51/2NS, 1/2NS, NS). Based on the half-life of naloxone this regimen will maintain the plasma naloxone levels at or greater than those that would have existed 30 min after the bolus dose.[111,112]

Example: The patient responds to 3 mg of naloxone initially. Add 20 mg naloxone to 1 L maintenance fluids and run at 100 cc/h thus delivering 2 mg naloxone/h (e.g., 2/3 the initial dose per hour).

7. Discharge: Stable patients who have regained normal mental status and have normal (or near normal) laboratory data may be observed for a period of time, which depends on the drug ingested (see Table 9.1 for recommended observation period after opioid overdose) and underlying conditions. Usually if the patient is awake and alert *6 h* after administration of antidote, the patient may be safely discharged if there is no further drug absorption from the gastrointestinal tract.

9.2 AGITATION, DELIRIUM, AND PSYCHOSIS

9.2.1 General Comments

Confounders: Rapid control of drug-induced agitation, delirium, or psychosis is one of the most difficult skills to master when dealing with complications of drug abuse. The use of sedation and restraints is fraught with a host of ethical and legal issues.[113–116] Safety issues for the patient as well as the medical staff must be considered. Numerous reports of injuries to emergency department personnel[117,118] exist. Diagnostic confusion may occur since agitation or delirium may be the result of a drug overdose alone, or may be from a medical problem combined with drug intoxication (i.e., myocardial infarction from cocaine abuse), or simply a medical problem masquerading as drug abuse (i.e., meningitis). Finally, failing to understand the differences between agitation, psychosis, and delirium (see following discussion) often leads to incorrect management schemes. Regardless of the cause, effective, compassionate, and rapid control of agitation is necessary to decrease the incidence of serious complications and to provide a thorough evaluation of the patient. One can never safely say that the patient was "too agitated" or "too uncooperative" to assess.

Delirium vs. psychosis with and without agitation: Altered sensorium (disorientation and confusion) and visual hallucinations are characteristic of *delirium*. In contrast, *psychosis* is associated with paranoia, auditory hallucinations, and usually an intact sensorium.[5] *Agitation* (physical or psychic perturbation) may complicate either delirium or psychosis and is commonly seen in patients with stimulant overdose. Differentiating between delirium and psychosis with or without agitation and agitation alone is useful because it may suggest specific groups of drugs and potentially, specific treatment.[5] For example, a patient with anticholinergic poisoning from Jimson weed typically has delirium with confusion and disorientation, while an amphetamine- or cocaine-intoxicated person usually has paranoid psychosis with agitation, but is oriented. Physostigmine is useful in the diagnosis of anticholinergic syndrome,[119] but would not be helpful for amphetamine- or cocaine-induced agitation. Agitation from stimulants should be treated with benzodiazepines, while psychosis alone can be treated with haloperidol with or without benzodiazepines.

Benzodiazepines vs. neuroleptics: There is significant controversy regarding the optimal choice of sedating agents. Much research has dealt directly with agitated patients in the psychiatric setting,[120–122] but no controlled clinical studies of benzodiazepines or neuroleptic medications in treating strictly drug-induced agitation have been described. Animal research[123–125] and human experience[126] support the use of *benzodiazepines* for cocaine-induced agitation as well as generalized anxiety.[127,128] Neuroleptics (e.g., haloperidol) have been shown to decrease the lethal effects of amphetamines in rats[129–131] and chlorpromazine was found to be effective in treating a series of 22 children with severe amphetamine poisoning.[132] Many of the children exhibited seizures before receiving chlorpromazine, but ongoing motor activity was reduced in all cases. These data are consistent with the observation that chlorpromazine antagonizes cocaine-induced seizures in dogs.[123] Callaway et al.[133] argue that neuroleptics have been used safely in other patient populations at risk for seizures, such as the treatment of alcoholic hallucinosis during alcohol withdrawal.[134] Concerns about neuroleptics potentiating drug-induced seizures may therefore be exaggerated. Butyrophenone neuroleptics such as haloperidol have less effect on seizure thresholds than do phenothiazines such as chlorpromazine[135] and also produce less interference with sweat-mediated evaporative cooling (e.g., anticholinergic effect) in cases of drug-induced hyperthermia.[133] Hoffman[136] has argued against the use of haloperidol for cocaine intoxication on the basis of controlled animal studies showing haloperidol failed to improve survival, and *possibly* increased lethality.[137] He also argues that haloperidol causes a variety of physiologic responses that limit heat loss. These include (1) presynaptic dopamine-2 (D_2) receptor blockage, causing a loss of inhibition of norepinephrine release and increased central and peripheral adrenergic activity; (2) hypothalamic D_2 blockade causing direct inhibition of central heat dissipating mechanisms; and (3) anticholinergic effects causing loss of evaporative cooling via loss of sweat. The risk of a dystonic reaction, which has been associated with fatal laryngospasm[138,139] and rhabdomyolysis,[140] is also of concern. Acute dystonia, which is more common in young males,[141] could severely impair a resuscitation attempt and may aggravate hyperthermia. Interestingly, the incidence of dystonic reactions from neuroleptic agents has been shown to be dramatically reduced when benzodiazepines are coadministered.[142] Recently the use of the atypical antipsychotic agent ziprazidone has been recommended for controlling acute psychotic agitation. Although study populations are mixed, they are primarily composed of psychiatric patients with functional, as opposed to drug-induced psychosis. Nevertheless, ziprazidone has not been associated with hyperthermia, dystonia, nor the anticholinergic effects of haloperidol. Studies suggest beneficial effects similar to lorazepam or haloperidol with less sedation.[143–145]

Recommendations: Because of the complex neuropharmacology associated with agitation, delirium, and psychosis in the drug abusing patient our preference is a selective approach based on symptom complex:

Severe agitation: In cases of severe agitation, regardless of underlying delirium or psychosis, we recommend starting with benzodiazepines due to their proven safety and known ability to increase the seizure threshold. They should be given in incremental doses until the patient is appropriately sedated and large doses should not be withheld as long as the blood pressure remains stable and the airway is secure. If respiratory depression occurs, the patient should be endotracheally intubated and mechanically ventilated.[136]

Psychosis: If severe agitation includes marked psychotic features or there is known amphetamine or amphetamine-derivative overdose (i.e., 3,4-methylenedioxymethamphetamine or MDMA), or if the major symptom complex has psychotic features, then haloperidol may be used. Due to synergistic effects[122] and to decrease the incidence of dystonic reactions,[142] haloperidol should be administered in combination with a benzodiazepine. Anticholinergic agents (i.e., benztropine) reduce the incidence of dystonic reactions;[146] however, because of the potential to confuse an anticholinergic syndrome with psychosis[147] and because anticholinergic agents limit heat dissipation, they are not routinely recommended.

Delirium: As long as agitation is not prominent the administration of low dose benzodiazepines, or observation alone, is usually adequate to control symptoms of mild delirium until drug effects wear off. Intramuscular ziprazidone may also be considered in this setting. In selected anticholinergic poisonings involving uncontrollable agitation or severe hyperthermia, physostigmine (0.5 to 1.0 mg slow IV push) should be considered.[148] Physostigmine may potentiate the effects of depolarizing neuromuscular-blocking agents (e.g., succinylcholine decamethonium)[149,150] and may have additive depressant effects on cardiac conduction in patients with cyclic antidepressant overdose.[151,152] Its use is therefore contraindicated in patients with tricyclic antidepressant poisoning and poisoning that impairs cardiac conduction. Physostigmine may induce arousal in patients with benzodiazepine or sedative-hypnotic intoxication[153] due to its nonspecific analeptic effects.

A word of caution: Control of agitation, delirium, and psychosis is important, but even more important is the treatment of the underlying cause. Algorithms for detecting hypoxia, hypotension, and hypoglycemia still apply. In the mentally unstable patient, who will not allow evaluation or examination, physical restraint and the liberal use of benzodiazepines (see below) may be necessary.

9.2.2 Stepwise Approach to Management

9.2.2.1 Immediate Interventions

1. Airway, Breathing, Circulation: Maintain the airway and assist ventilation if necessary. Administer supplemental oxygen. Treat hypotension, and resuscitate as per previous reviews.[90]

2. Antidotes: Administer appropriate antidotes, including 25 g dextrose IV if the patient is hypoglycemic, as per the section on coma. If the patient does not allow assessment and stabilization, proceed as follows (once the patient is under control, reassess the need for antidotes).

3. Reduction of environmental stimuli: If possible attempt calming the patient by eliminating excessive noise, light, and physical stimulation. Generally, this is all that is necessary for the treatment of panic attacks from mild cocaine overdose, or from certain hallucinogens such as LSD or marijuana.[148,154] Talk to the patient and attempt to address the patient's immediate needs (minor pain, anxiety, need to use the bathroom). An offer of food or water may calm the patient and avoid further confrontation. Gay et al.[154] from the Haight-Ashbury Free Medical Clinics, in San Francisco, have described the "ART" technique as a way of establishing credibility with the intoxicated patient:

Table 9.2   Patient Management with Use of Restraints

A. Rehearse strategies before employing these techniques.

B. Use restraints sooner rather than later and thoroughly document all actions.

C. Remember universal precautions (see Table 9.3).

D. Use restraints appropriately. The use of overwhelming force will often be all that is necessary to preclude a fight.
1. When it is time to subdue the patient, approach him or her with at least five persons, each with a prearranged task.
2. Grasp the clothing and the large joints to attempt to "sandwich" the patient between two mattresses.
3. Place the patient on the stretcher face down to reduce leverage and to make it difficult for the patient to lash out.
4. Remove the patient's shoes or boots.
5. In exceptional circumstances, as when the patient is biting, grasp the hair firmly.
6. Avoid pressure to the chest, throat, or neck.

E. The specific type of restraint used (hands, cloth, leather, etc.) is determined by the amount of force needed to subdue (i.e., use hard restraints for PCP-induced psychoses).

F. Keep in mind, when using physical restraints, that the minimum amount of force necessary is the maximum that ethical practice allows. The goal is to restrain, not to injure. Restraining ties should be adequate but not painfully constricting when applied (being able to slip your finger underneath is a good standard). The restrained patient should be observed in a safe, quiet room away from the other patients; however, the patient must be reevaluated frequently, as the physical condition of restrained patients could deteriorate.

Source: From Wasserberger, J. et al., *Top. Emerg. Med.,* 14, 71, 1992. With permission.

A = Acceptance. Acceptance disarms patients who may already be experiencing fear of their surroundings or paranoid ideation.

R = Reduction of stimuli, rest, and reassurance. If patients are stable and symptoms are mild, place them in a quiet surrounding, and reassure them that they are going to be all right as you proceed to assess them. If patients are dangerous or seriously ill, control them with physical and/or medical restraints (see following section). When stable, proceed to eliminate any source of obvious distraction or distress (too many people in the resuscitation room, bright lights, loud noises, etc.).

T = Talkdown technique. Use verbal sincerity, concern, and a gentle approach since drug abusers can misinterpret insincere and/or abrupt actions as being hostile. If patients are obviously beyond reason or dangerous *do not attempt to "talk them down."* Generally, this step should be restricted to patients who are oriented and simply frightened. It is also *not* recommended for patients who have taken phencyclidine (PCP) due to the unpredictable effects of this drug.[155] Staff members should be careful to never position themselves with a potentially violent or distraught patient between them and the door.

4. Sedation: Medical management may be necessary if the patient remains uncooperative. Explain to the patient your intention to use medications.

5. Paralysis: If significant hyperthermia occurs as a result of excessive muscular hyperactivity, or if significant risk for spinal injury is present, consider early skeletal muscle paralysis (see discussion under hyperthermia). Procedures for the rapid sequence induction for airway management and paralysis are reviewed elsewhere.[2]

6. Physical restraints: Restraint has proven efficacy in reducing injury and agitation.[156] If the patient continues to be uncooperative, rapidly gain control of the individual using several trained staff and physical restraints (Table 9.2 on restraining technique and Table 9.3 on universal precautions). Empty the room of all extraneous and/or potentially dangerous objects and apply the restraints in a humane and professional manner.[157] The method of restraint should be the least restrictive necessary for the protection of the patient and others.[113]

9.2.2.2 Secondary Interventions

1. Insert IV, monitor: Once the patient is restrained insert an intravenous line, and assess vital signs.

Table 9.3   Universal Precautions

1. Appropriate barrier precautions should be routinely used when contact with blood or other body fluids is anticipated. Wear gloves. Masks and eye protection are indicated if mucous membranes of the mouth, eyes, and nose may be exposed to drops of blood or other body fluids. Gowns should be worn if splashes of blood are likely.
2. Hands and skin should be washed immediately if contaminated. Wash hands as soon as gloves are removed.
3. Exercise care in handling all sharps during procedures, when cleaning them, and during disposal. Never recap or bend needles. Carefully dispose of sharps in specially designed containers.
4. Use a bag-valve-mask to prevent the need for mouth-to-mouth resuscitation. Such devices should be readily available.
5. Health care workers with weeping dermatitis should avoid direct patient care until the condition resolves.
6. Because of the risk of perinatal HIV transmission, pregnant health care workers should strictly adhere to all universal precautions.

Note: In its 1987 recommendations, the Centers for Disease Control (CDC) stated that universal precautions "should be used in the care of all patients, especially including those in emergency-care settings in which the risk of blood exposure is increased and the infection status of the patient is usually unknown." The CDC stipulated the six basic universal precautions above.

2. Assess underlying medical conditions: Draw blood and assess for serious medical conditions. Rule out metabolic disturbances (e.g., hypoxia, hypoglycemia, hyponatremia, thyrotoxicosis, uremia), alcohol or sedative-hypnotic withdrawal, CNS infection (e.g., meningitis, encephalitis) or tumor, hyperthermia, postictal state, trauma, etc.

3. Frequent reassessment: Any patient left in physical restraints must have frequent reassessments of vital signs, neurological status, and physical examination.[113] Sudden death, and asphyxiation, have occurred in individuals while in restraints.[115,158–160]

4. Documentation: The patient's danger to him- or herself, degree of agitation, specific threats, and verbal hostilities should all be documented in case of future charges by the patient that the patient was improperly restrained against his or her will (i.e., battery). Documentation should include the reasons for, and means of, restraint and the periodic assessment (minimum of every 20 min) of the restrained patient. Legal doctrines pertinent to involuntary treatment have been reviewed elsewhere.[116]

5. Medications: Sedation is necessary for patients struggling vigorously against restraints, or for patients who are persistently agitated, hyperthermic, panicking, or hyperadrenergic. Consider one of the following sedatives or combinations. See previous discussion under general comments.

Lorazepam	0.05–0.10 mg (2–7 mg) IM or IV initially over 1–2 min	May repeat doses every 5 min until sedation is achieved
Diazepam	Up to 0.20 mg/kg (5–10 mg) IV initially over 1–2 min	May repeat doses every 5 min until sedation is achieved Diazepam is not recommended in patients >60 years old due to prolonged duration of action in this group
Haloperidol	0.1–0.2 mg/kg (5–10 mg) IM or IV initially over 1–2 min	May repeat dosing 5 mg every 15 min until sedation is achieved Probably safe in most overdoses although more studies are necessary to confirm
Ziprasidone	10–20 mg IM	Studies still pending for use in patients with drug-induced agitation

6. Reassess medical condition: For persistently altered mental status perform CT of the head and consider lumbar puncture. Cases involving body packers[161–163] or stuffers[164] with ongoing absorption of drug, or certain drugs with delayed absorption (i.e., belladonna alkaloids in Jimson weed[165]) may have prolonged duration of symptoms.

7. Laboratory data: Electrolytes, CBC, BUN, Cr, CPK, CPK with MB fraction if myocardial infarction or ischemia is suspected. Consider liver function studies including PT/ PTT in severely ill patients. Rule out coagulopathy with a disseminated intravascular coagulation (DIC) panel.

Obtain blood and urine cultures if hyperthermic. While toxicology screens of blood and urine are generally overutilized,[5] they are recommended if the diagnosis remains questionable.

8. Disposition: Consider discharging patients who meet all the following criteria after an appropriate period of observation:

   a. Normal vital signs and mental status
   b. Normal or near normal laboratory data

Patients who have a chronically altered mental status, e.g., schizophrenia, or organic psychosis, and who are not a risk to themselves or others may be considered for discharge with appropriate psychological counseling and follow up. Patients with true delirium, or escalating agitation, or abnormal vital signs must be either admitted to the hospital or observed for further improvement.

9.3 SEIZURES

9.3.1 General Comments

Seizures from drug abuse have been known to be lethal[166–168] or cause permanent neurological injury.[169–171] Primate studies using baboons[172] have shown that 82 min of induced status epilepticus produced visible neuropathological injury in nonparalyzed ventilated animals. Results were similar if the baboons were paralyzed and ventilated first. In addition to the potential for direct brain injury, prolonged seizure activity may cause or aggravate hyperthermia, which can cause further injury to the brain and produce rhabdomyolysis.

Mechanisms: Drugs may precipitate seizures through several distinct mechanisms (Table 9.4). A direct CNS stimulant effect is probably the mechanism in most cocaine-, phencyclidine-, and amphetamine-induced seizures.[173,174] Seizures from these drugs generally occur *at the time of use* while seizures associated with other drugs such as alcohol, benzodiazepines, and barbiturates generally occur during *a time of withdrawal* from chronic, high doses of the drug.[173] Other *indirect* causes of seizures exist. Cerebral infarction or hemorrhage may precipitate seizures in patients abusing cocaine or amphetamines.[175,176] Vasculitis has been associated with amphetamine and cocaine abuse and may result in seizures.[177] Intravenous drug-abusing (IVDA) patients with acquired immune deficiency syndrome (AIDS) are susceptible to CNS infections such as toxoplasmosis, cryptococcus, viral encephalitis, and syphilis or lymphoma, which can precipitate seizures. IVDA also is frequently complicated by bacterial endocarditis, septic cerebral emboli, and seizures. Foreign material (e.g., talc or cotton) emboli and toxic drug by-products or expanders have been implicated[178] (Table 9.5 through Table 9.7) as well as brain trauma or closed head injury. Finally, chronic alcohol abuse often leads to systemic medical problems such as hypoglycemia, liver failure, sepsis, or meningitis, all of which may precipitate seizure activity.

Table 9.4   Mechanisms of Drug-Related Seizures

1. Direct CNS toxicity: Cocaine, phencyclidine, amphetamines
2. CNS hyperactivity after cessation of drug: Alcohol, barbiturates, benzodiazepines
3. Indirect CNS toxicity
   a. Trauma: subdural, epidural hematoma due to blunt force
   b. Stroke: cerebral infarct, hemorrhage, or vasculitis
   c. Infection of CNS
   d. Foreign materials (e.g., talc), other drug adulterants (see Tables 9.5 to 9.7)
   e. Systemic metabolic problems (e.g., hypoglycemia, liver or renal failure)
   f. Post-traumatic epilepsy, or epilepsy exacerbated by drug abuse
   g. Epilepsy additional to drug use

Table 9.5   Cocaine Additives

Pharmacologically Active	Inert
Lidocaine	Inositol
Cyproheptidine	Mannitol
Methephedrine	Lactose
Diphenhydramine	Dextrose
Benzocaine	Starch
Mepivacaine	Sucrose
Aminopyrine	Sodium bicarbonate
Methapyrilene	Barium carbonate
Tetracaine	Mannose
Nicotinamide	
Ephedrine	**Volatile Compounds**
Phenylpropanolamine	
Acetaminophen	Benzene
Procaine base	Methyl ethyl ketone
Caffeine	Ether
Acetophenetidin	Acetone
1-(1-Phenylcyclohexyl)pyrrolidine	
Methaqualone	
Dyclonine	
Pyridoxine	
Codeine	
Stearic acid	
Piracetum	
Rosin (colophonum)	
Fencanfamine	
Benzoic acid	
Phenothiazines	
L-Threonine	
Heroin	
Boric acid	
Aspirin	
Dibucaine	
Propoxyphene	
Heroin[a]	
Amphetamine[a]	
Methamphetamine[a]	

[a] Considered frequent additives/coinjectants; absolute frequency unknown.

Source: Shesser, R. et al., *Am. J. Emerg. Med.* 9, 336, 1991. With permission.

Table 9.6   Phencyclidine Additives

Active	Inert
Phenylpropanolamine	Magnesium sulfate
Benzocaine	Ammonium chloride
Procaine	Ammonium hydroxide
Ephedrine	Phenyllithium halide
Caffeine	Phenylmagnesium halide
Piperidine	
PCC (1-piperidinocyclohexanecarbonitrile)	**Volatile**
TCP (1-[1-(2-thienyl)cyclohexyl]-piperdine)	
PCE (cyclohexamine)	Ethyl ether
PHP (phenylcyclohexylpyrrolidine)	Toluene
Ketamine	Cyclohexanol
	Isopropanol

Source: Shesser, R. et al., *Am. J. Emerg. Med.* 9, 336, 1991. With permission.

Table 9.7 Heroin Additives

Alkaloids	Inert
Thebaine	Starch
Acetylcodeine	Sugar
Papaverine	Calcium tartrate
Noscapine	Calcium carbonate
Narceine	Sodium carbonate
Active nonalkaloids	Sucrose
Tolmectin	Dextrin
Quinine	Magnesium sulfate
Phenobarbital	Dextrose
Methaqualone	Lactose
Lidocaine	Barium sulfate
Phenolphthalein	Silicon dioxide
Caffeine	Vitamin C
Dextromoramide	
Chloroquine	**Volatile**
Diazepam	
Nicotinamide	Rosin
N-Phenyl-2-naphthylamine	Toluene
Phenacetin	Methanol
Acetaminophen	Acetaldehyde
Fentanyl	Ethanol
Doxepin	Acetone
Naproxen	Diethyl ether
Promazine	Chloroform
Piracetem	Acetic acid
Procaine	
Diphenhydramine	
Aminopyrine	
Allobarbital	
Indomethacin	
Glutethimide	
Scopolamine	
Sulfonamide	
Arsenic	
Strychnine	
Cocaine[a]	
Amphetamine[a]	
Methamphetamine[a]	

[a] Considered frequent additives/coinjectants; absolute frequency unknown.
Source: Shesser, R. et al., *Am. J. Emerg. Med.* 9, 336, 1991. With permission.

Benzodiazepines: Benzodiazepines are the preferred choice for the initial control of the actively seizing patient.[179] Accordingly, pharmacological studies demonstrated that cocaine-induced seizures were efficiently inhibited by $GABA_A$ receptor agonists and NMDA receptor antagonists, whereas sodium and calcium channel blockers were ineffective.[174] Benzodiazepines, unlike MNDA receptor antagonists, are readily available, require no prolonged loading, and are quite safe from a cardio-vascular standpoint.[180–182] The main disadvantages are excessive sedation and respiratory depression, especially when given with barbiturates such as phenobarbital. Lorazepam is also quite viscous and must be refrigerated and diluted before infusion.[179] Diazepam is irritating to veins and after intramuscular dosing absorption is unpredictable.

Which benzodiazepine?: Of the benzodiazepines lorazepam has the longest anticonvulsant activity[183] (4 to 6 h) and is considered the agent of first choice. Lorazepam has a tendency to persist in the brain while agents like diazepam and midazolam both redistribute out of the brain more rapidly and thus have a shorter protective effect.[184] Leppik et al.[185] found no significant statistical difference between diazepam and lorazepam in clinical efficacy for initial control of convulsive status. It was found, however, that lorazepam provided seizure control in 78% of patients with the first intravenous dose while diazepam provided seizure control after the first injection only 58% of the time. Levy and Kroll[186] found that the average dose of lorazepam to control status epilepticus in a study of 21 patients was 4 mg and all patients responded within 15 min. Chiulli et al. reported on a retrospective study of 142 equally matched children given benzodiazepines and phenytoin for control of seizures.[530] The intubation rate for those given lorazepam (mean dose 2.7 mg) was 27% while 73% of those given diazepam (mean dose 5.2 mg) had to be intubated. This study had an overall intubation rate that was quite high (45%), raising the question why so many children needed to be intubated.[179] Interestingly, lorazepam is not FDA-approved for seizure control. Midazolam may be used alternatively and has the advantage of rapid IM absorption in patients without venous access. In one study it was found to have a stronger influence on electroencephalographic measures,[187] and may be more effective in status epilepticus than diazepam or lorazepam.[188]

Barbiturates: Barbiturates are associated with a higher incidence of hypotension than benzo-diazepines,[189–191] and as a result should not be administered in the hypotensive patient. Furthermore, they require time-consuming loading (greater than 30 min). Although phenobarbital may be administered at an IV rate of 100 mg/min (requiring only 10 min to fully load a 70-kg patient with 15 mg/kg) most nursing protocols require the physician to institute phenobarbital loading or to give no more than 60 mg/min IV.[179] Finally, barbiturates frequently cause prolonged sedation (especially after the co-administration of benzodiazepines) thus hindering the ability of the physician to perform serial examinations. Barbiturates do have an advantage of lowering intracranial pressure[190] in the head-injured patient and are helpful for treating withdrawal symptoms in patients with sedative–hypnotic addiction.[192,193] Barbiturates (i.e., phenobarbital) are considered second-line agents after the use of benzodiazepines (i.e., lorazepam) for seizures caused by drugs of abuse.

Fosphenytoin: Phenytoin is a poorly soluble anticonvulsant that is mixed with propylene glycol to enhance its solubility. The propylene glycol, not the phenytoin, is a cardiac depressant and may cause hypotension and cardiovascular collapse if administered too rapidly. Fosphenytoin was recently introduced to eliminate the poor aqueous solubility and irritant properties of intra-venous phenytoin and to eliminate the need for the propylene glycol solvent. Fosphenytoin is rapidly converted to phenytoin after intravenous or intramuscular administration and unlike pheny-toin does not require prolonged administration of a loading dose on a cardiac monitor. In clinical studies, this prodrug showed minimal evidence of adverse events and no serious cardiovascular or respiratory adverse reactions.[194] Unlike phenobarbital and benzodiazepines, which elevate the seizure threshold, phenytoin exerts its anticonvulsant effects mainly by limiting the spread of seizure activity and reducing seizure propagation. Because phenytoin does not elevate the seizure threshold, it is less effective against drug-induced seizures.[195] Animal models[196] of cocaine-induced seizures and human studies[197] of alcohol withdrawal seizures have supported this claim. Cardiac toxicity of phenytoin was suggested by Callaham et al.[198] who showed an increased incidence of ventricular tachycardia in dogs intoxicated with amitriptyline treated with phenytoin. Fosphenytoin and phenytoin are thus considered third-line agents for drug-induced seizures. They may be considered more useful for the drug-abusing patient with epilepsy whose seizures have responded to phenytoin in the past.

General anesthesia: Pentobarbital or thiopental anesthesia may be used as a last resort, usually with the aid of an anesthesiologist, to induce general anesthesia.[199,200] If paralysis is used, the patient must be intubated and mechanically ventilated. It is important to remember that when patients having seizures are paralyzed with neuromuscular blockers such that seizure activity is not readily apparent, they may continue to have electrical seizure activity, which results in persistent cerebral hypermetabolism and the continued risk of brain injury.[172] Munn and Farrell[201] reported on a 14-year-old girl who was pharmacologically paralyzed during 14 h of unrecognized status epilepticus. The originally healthy girl suffered persistent, serious cognitive impairment and subsequent epilepsy. An EEG should be used to monitor in all patients paralyzed for a seizure disorder to determine the need for further anticonvulsant therapy.

9.3.2 Stepwise Approach to Management

9.3.2.1 Immediate Interventions

1. Airway, Breathing, Circulation: Maintain the airway and assist ventilation if necessary. Administer supplemental oxygen. Treat hypotension, and resuscitate as per previous reviews.[90]

2. Antidotes: Administer appropriate antidotes, including 25 g dextrose IV if the patient is hypoglycemic. Administer naloxone only if seizures are thought to be caused by hypoxia resulting from narcotic-associated respiratory depression.

3. Anticonvulsants: Administer one of the drugs listed in the tabulation below.

Comment: As noted above the authors have a strong preference for benzodiazepines (i.e., lorazepam). If lorazepam is chosen, most seizures stop after 2 to 4 mg, but there are no clear dose–response data available.[179] Some authorities stop if 4 mg is unsuccessful, but it seems reasonable to give up to 10 to 12 mg of lorazepam before switching to an alternative therapy. Neurologists generally recommend the aggressive use of a single drug before switching to another drug. Switching too quickly frequently results in the underdosing of both drugs. Respiratory depression should not keep one from using large doses of benzodiazepines[179] (as has been done safely with delirium tremens[202]), especially in the drug-abusing patient with status epilepticus. If large doses of benzodiazepines are used, patients frequently require intubation and mechanical ventilation.

Drugs Used for Seizure Control

Lorazepam	0.05–0.10 mg/kg IV over 2 min	May repeat as necessary, may give intramuscularly (IM) although IV route preferred
Midazolam	0.05 mg/kg IV over 2 min	May repeat as necessary
Diazepam	0.10 mg/kg IV over 2 min	May repeat as necessary
Phenobarbital	15–20 mg/kg IV over 20 min	Watch for hypotension, prolonged sedation
Fosphenytoin	15–20 mg/kg IV given at 100–150 mg/min (7–14 min)	Generally not as effective as benzodiazepines or barbiturates, may give IM although IV route preferred
Pentobarbital	5–6 mg/kg IV, slow infusion over 8–10 min, then continuous infusion at 0.5–3.0 mg/kg/h titrated to effect	Use as inducing agent for general anesthesia, watch for hypotension, continuous EEG monitoring necessary after general anesthesia

4. Reassess temperature: Immediately check the rectal temperature and cool the patient rapidly if the temperature is above 40°C (104°F) (see Section 9.4 on hyperthermia).

5. Lumbar puncture: Perform lumbar puncture if the patient is febrile to rule out meningitis. Do not wait for CT results or laboratory analysis of cerebral spinal fluid (CSF) to initiate therapy with appropriate antibiotics (i.e., a third-generation cephalosporin) if meningitis is suspected. Perform CT prior to lumbar puncture if the patient is at risk for having a CNS mass lesion.

6. Gastric decontamination: Consider gastrointestinal decontamination if the patient is a body packer or stuffer or if the patient has ingested large quantities of drug (see Section 9.9, gastric decontamination).

7. Laboratory data: Electrolytes, glucose, calcium, magnesium, and biochemical screens for liver and renal disease are generally recommended.[173] Check creatine kinase levels to detect evidence of rhabdomyolysis. Although urine and blood toxicologic screens are generally overutilized,[5] they are recommended in the case of new-onset seizures to avoid an inappropriate diagnosis of idiopathic epilepsy.

9.3.2.2 Secondary Interventions

1. Computerized tomography (CT): Earnest et al.[178] documented a 16% incidence of "important intracranial lesions on CT scan" in a series of 259 patients with first alcohol-related seizures,

Table 9.8   High-Risk Seizures

Neurological deficit
Evidence of head trauma
Prolonged postictal state
Focal seizures or focal onset with secondary generalization[a]
Seizures occurring after a period of prolonged abstinence[a]
Onset of seizures before age 30 if alcohol only involved
Mental illness or inability to fully evaluate the patient's baseline mental function

[a] High risk for having a positive CT result requiring intervention.

and Pascual-Leone et al.[203] found CT scan lesions in 16% ($n = 44$) of cocaine-induced seizures. Cocaine-induced thrombosis and hypertension have been implicated as the cause of stroke in patients with seizures.[204–206] Considering these studies and also the high incidence of traumatic, hemorrhagic, and infectious injuries associated with drug abuse, a CT of the brain (with contrast) is recommended for new-onset seizures or for any high-risk seizures (Table 9.8). In a smaller study Holland et al.[207] performed a retrospective review of 37 cocaine-associated seizures and concluded that CT scanning was not necessary regardless of the patient's previous seizure history if the patient suffered a brief, generalized, tonic–clonic seizure and had normal vital signs, physical examination, and a postictal state lasting 30 min or less. We await larger studies to confirm the Holland et al. findings prior to making similar recommendations.

2. Monitor: Monitor neurological and cardiovascular status as well as hydration and electrolyte balance.

3. Anticonvulsant therapy: Chronic anticonvulsant or other specific treatment of alcohol- or drug-related seizures rarely is indicated. For patients who present with multiple seizures, status epilepticus, or high-risk seizures (Table 9.8) continued outpatient therapy may be indicated.

4. Disposition: Only patients with normal vital signs and physical examination after a brief isolated seizure, with a normal evaluation (i.e., CT scan, laboratory data, etc.), should be considered for discharge from the emergency department.

9.4 HYPERTHERMIA/HEAT STROKE

9.4.1   General Comments

While mild hyperthermia is usually benign, in the setting of drug overdose it may be a sign of impending disaster. Severe hyperthermia (>40.5°C) is a well-recognized cause of major morbidity and mortality, regardless of the cause. Classic heat stroke, for example, characterized by a core temperature of 40.5°C or higher, and severe CNS dysfunction has been associated with mortality rates of up to 80% as well as with a high likelihood of disabling neurologic sequelae.[208] Although no study has documented the incidence of death as it relates to drug abuse per se, a case series by Rosenberg et al.[209] described 12 patients who presented with temperatures 40.5°C or greater for at least 1 h. Five of 12 patients died and four had severe permanent neurologic sequelae. Clinical signs common to patients who went on to develop severe hyperthermia were increased muscular activity and absence of sweating.

Classic vs. drug-induced heat stroke: If a patient with apparent environmental heat illness has a continuing rise in temperature even after removal from ambient heat and ongoing exertion, drug-induced hyperthermia must be strongly considered. Rosenberg et al. reported a 3 to 12 h delay to the onset of severe hyperthermia in 7 of 12 patients with drug-induced hyperthermia.[209] A variety of drugs[133,210–213] and toxins[171] can cause hyperthermia, and this may initially be overlooked while the more familiar manifestations (i.e., seizures) of the intoxication are being managed. Patients with hyperthermia and altered mental status may be diagnosed as having environmental or exertional heat stroke while the potential contribution of drugs is neglected.[209] Clues to drug-induced hyperthermia from the history and physical examination must be aggressively pursued.

Mechanisms: Mechanisms of drug-induced hyperthermia are varied. Most commonly, excessive heat production results from muscular hyperactivity (sympathomimetic and epileptogenic agents) or metabolic hyperactivity (salicylates). Heat dissipation is often impaired by inhibition of sweating (anticholinergic agents), cutaneous vasoconstriction (sympathomimetic agents), and/or by interference with central thermoregulation (phenothiazines, cocaine, amphetamines).[209,214–216] When healthy, cocaine-naive persons are subjected to passive heating, pretreatment with even a small dose of intranasal cocaine impairs sweating and cutaneous vasodilation (the major autonomic adjustments to thermal stress) and heat perception (the key trigger for behavioral adjustments).[217] The combined serotonin-releasing and dopamine-releasing drug MDMA produces lethal hyperthermia more potently than amphetamine,[218] supporting a synergistic role for serotonergic with dopamine in drug-induced hyperthermia.[133] *Phencyclidine* is a sympathetic nervous system stimulant, and may also have anticholinergic properties,[219] which inhibit sweating. This property plus the tendency to generate unrestrained outbursts of violent activity and seizures have resulted in hyperthermia and rhabdomyolysis and death.[220] Of 1000 cases of PCP intoxication reviewed by McCarron et al.[221] 26 had temperatures over 38.9°C and four had temperatures over 41°C. Large overdoses of *LSD* have been associated with severe hyperthermia.[222,223] This has been suggested to be due to its serotonergic effects[210] and a tendency to provoke panic. A patient restrained in a straitjacket after becoming violent after LSD ingestion developed hyperthermia to 41.6°C, hypotension, rhabdomyolysis, renal failure, and died.[224] Specific mechanisms may dictate the specific form of hyperthermic syndrome although classically five syndromes are described: malignant hyperthermia, neuroleptic malignant syndrome, anticholinergic poisoning, sympathomimetic poisoning, and serotonin syndrome.

Malignant hyperthermia: Less commonly, drug-induced hyperthermia may develop as a form of malignant hyperthermia. Although hyperthermia associated with cocaine and PCP have been ascribed this diagnosis,[225,226] malignant hyperthermia is a rare complication that is usually associated with exposure to volatile anesthetic agents or depolarizing muscle relaxants.[171] The primary defect is felt to be an alteration in cellular permeability, which results in an inability to regulate calcium concentrations *within* the skeletal muscle fibers.[227] As a result neuromuscular paralysis (acting at the *neuromuscular junction*) is not effective in controlling the severe muscular rigidity and heat generation seen with malignant hyperthermia. Dantrolene (1 to 2 mg/kg rapidly IV) is the most effective treatment for malignant hyperthermia. While dantrolene has been suggested to diminish hyperthermia associated with amphetamine[228,229] and LSD[230] overdose, it has not been shown in any controlled study to be effective and confirmation of its usefulness for these indications requires further evaluation.

Neuroleptic malignant syndrome: Neuroleptic malignant syndrome (NMS) is another uncommon cause of drug-induced hyperthermia associated with the use of haloperidol and certain other neuroleptic agents. It has been reviewed in depth elsewhere.[212,231,232] Muscular rigidity, autonomic instability, and metabolic disturbances are presumed to occur due to neurotransmitter imbalances. Neuromuscular paralysis and routine external cooling measures are generally effective for treatment of the severe rigidity and hyperthermia in this condition. In case reports NMS has been attributed to cocaine[233,234] and LSD,[230] although exertional hyperthermia seems a more probable diagnosis in these instances. Treatment includes the use of bromocriptine (5.0 mg per nasogastric tube every 6 h),[235] and supportive care.

Serotonin syndrome: A clinical syndrome associated with increased free serotonin levels, usually the result of a prescription drug interaction such as selective serotonin-reuptake inhibitor with cocaine or amphetamines. Muscle rigidity is not as prominent as with NMS and sweating and gastrointestinal complaints are much more common. Symptoms of hyperthermia, hyperreflexia, agitation, and an exaggerated tremor predominate.[214–216]

Importance of paralysis and cooling: Zalis et al.[236,237] showed that hyperthermia was directly related to mortality in mongrel dogs with *amphetamine* overdose. Paralysis was shown to stop muscle hyperactivity, reduce hyperthermia, and decrease mortality.[238] Davis et al.[239] showed that dogs treated with toxic doses of *PCP* exhibited toxicity, which was diminished by paralysis and cooling measures.[239] Animal studies also indicate a key role for hyperthermia in complications associated with *cocaine* overdosage. Catravas and Waters[123] demonstrated that dogs given otherwise lethal *cocaine* infusions survived if severe hyperthermia was prevented. In this study temperature correlated better with survival than did pulse or blood pressure. Measures to prevent hyperthermia have included paralysis with pancuronium, sedation with chlorpromazine or diazepam, and external cooling.

Prognosis: Prognosis for severe hyperthermia depends on the *duration of temperature elevation*, the *maximum temperature* reached, and the affected individual's *underlying health*.[240] *Coagulopathy* was reported to be associated with death in four of five cases in one report[209] and has been shown to correlate with mortality in other studies.[241] *Seizures* are also associated with a poor prognosis.[209] This may in part be because they are often resistant to treatment in the hyperthermic individual. Any *delay in cooling* has been associated with a significantly increased incidence of mortality as well.[242]

9.4.2 Stepwise Approach to Management

It does not take long either to boil an egg or to cook neurons.[243]

9.4.2.1 Immediate Interventions

1. Airway, Breathing, Circulation: Maintain the airway and assist ventilation if necessary. Administer supplemental oxygen. Treat hypotension, and resuscitate as per previous reviews.[1–3]

2. Antidotes: Administer appropriate antidotes, including 25 g dextrose IV if the patient is hypoglycemic, as per the section on coma.

3. Control seizures and muscular hyperactivity: See Section 9.3, seizures, and Section 9.2, agitation.

4. Cooling: The fastest cooling techniques reported in the literature have usually been implemented in a research laboratory environment, utilizing animal models and equipment and techniques that are not universally available. In clinical practice, a technique that allows easy patient access and is readily available is preferable to a technique that may be more effective, but is difficult to perform. A comparison of the cooling rates achieved in several animal and human models with various cooling techniques is shown in Table 9.9. The advantages and disadvantages are summarized in Table 9.10. We favor evaporative cooling as the technique of choice. Evaporative cooling combines the advantages of simplicity and noninvasiveness with the most rapid cooling rates that can be achieved with any external techniques.[244] Some authors advocate the use of strategically placed ice packs although there are no controlled studies demonstrating their effectiveness and ice packs may contribute to shivering, which may further increase heat generation. In the authors' experience with exercise-induced heat stroke, ice packs placed at the groin and axillae do not causing shivering if they are used when the temperature is high (>40°C) and removed as the patient cools. Gastric lavage with cold water or saline is an effective and rapid central cooling technique that can be used in combination with evaporation in severe cases. Neuromuscular paralysis is recommended in all severe cases in which temperature is persistently greater than 40°C. Cooling technique is as follows:

a. Completely remove *all* clothing.
b. Place cardiac monitor leads on the patient's back so that they adhere to the skin during the cooling process.
c. Wet the skin with lukewarm tap water with a sponge or spray bottle (plastic spray bottles work the best).
d. Position *large high-speed fan(s)* close to the patient and turn them on.

Table 9.9   Cooling Rates Achieved with Various Cooling Techniques

Technique	Author/Year	Species	Rate °C/min
Evaporative	Weiner/1980[520]	Human	0.31
	Barner/1984[521]	Human	0.04
	Al-Aska/1987[522]	Human	0.09
	Kielblock/1986[523]	Human	0.034
	Wyndam/1959[524]	Human	0.23
	White/1987[525]	Dog	0.14
	Daily/1948[526]	Rat	0.93
Immersion (ice water)	Weiner/1980[520]	Human	0.14
	Wyndam/1959[524]	Human	0.14
	Magazanik/1980[527]	Dog	0.27
	Daily/1948[526]	Rat	1.86
Ice packing (whole body)	Kielblock/1986[523]	Human	0.034
	Bynum/1978[528]	Dog	0.11
Strategic ice packs	Kielblock/1986[523]	Human	0.028
Evaporative and strategic ice packs	Kielblock/1986[523]	Human	0.036
Cold gastric lavage	Syverud/1985[529]	Dog	0.15
	White/1987[525]	Dog	0.06
Cold peritoneal lavage	Bynum/1978[528]	Dog	0.56

Source: Helmrich, D.E., Syverud, S.A., Roberts, J.R. and Hedges, J.R., Eds., *Clinical Procedures in Emergency Medicine,* 2nd ed. Philadelphia: WB Saunders, 1991. With permission.

Table 9.10   Various Cooling Techniques

Technique	Advantages	Disadvantages
Evaporative	Simple, readily available Noninvasive Easy monitoring and patient access Relatively more rapid	Constant moistening of skin surface required to maximize heat loss Cumbersome
Immersion	Noninvasive Relatively more rapid	Patient monitoring and access difficult — inability to defibrillate Shivering Poorly tolerated by conscious patients
Ice packing	Noninvasive Readily available	Shivering Poorly tolerated by conscious patients
Strategic ice packs	Noninvasive Readily available Can be combined with other techniques	Relatively slower Shivering Poorly tolerated by conscious patients
Cold gastric lavage	Can be combined with other techniques	Relatively slower Invasive May require airway protection Human experience limited Invasive
Cold peritoneal lavage	Very rapid	Invasive Human experience limited

Source: Helmrich, D.E., Syverud, S.A., Roberts, J.R. and Hedges, J.R., Eds., *Clinical Procedures in Emergency Medicine,* 2nd ed. Philadelphia: WB Saunders, 1991. With permission.

e. Place ice pack to the groin and axillae (optional).

f. If shivering occurs, treat with diazepam, 0.1 to 0.2 mg/kg IV, or midazolam, 0.05 mg/kg IV.

g. Treat continued muscular hyperactivity, i.e., either severe shivering, rigidity, or agitation, with neuromuscular paralysis (vecuronium, 0.1 mg/kg IVP) with endotracheal intubation and mechanical ventilation.

h. Employ vigorous fluid replacement to correct volume depletion and to facilitate thermoregulation by sweating.

i. If the patient continues to exhibit muscle rigidity despite administration of neuromuscular blockers, give dantrolene, 1 mg/kg rapid IV push. Repeat as necessary up to 10 mg/kg.

j. Place a Foley catheter and monitor urine output closely.
k. Monitor the rectal or esophageal temperature and discontinue cooling when the temperature reaches 38.5°C to avoid hypothermia.

Comments:

Immersion: Immersion in an ice water bath is also a highly effective measure to reduce core temperatures, but limits the health care provider's access to the patient, and requires more equipment and preparation.

Thermometry: Unfortunately, most standard measurements of body temperature differ substantially from actual core temperature. Oral thermometry is affected by mouth breathing and is a poor approximation of core temperature. Rectal thermometry is less variable, but responds to changes in core temperature slowly. Thermistors that are inserted 15 cm into the rectum offer continuous monitoring of temperature with less variability and, although slower to respond to changes in core temperature than tympanic temperature readings, are not biased by head skin temperature. Temperatures taken using infrared thermometers that scan the tympanic membrane are of variable reliability and reproducibility.[245–248] Studies have shown that infrared tympanic membrane thermometers may be influenced by patient age,[249] measuring technique,[250] the presence or absence of cerumen,[245,251] and head skin temperature as noted above.[252] If a patient has a Swan-Ganz catheter, pulmonary arterial temperature may be measured precisely with a thermistor catheter. An esophageal thermistor positioned adjacent to the heart closely correlates with core temperature as well. It is the least invasive, most accurate method available in the emergency department and is recommended (although rectal thermistors will suffice for most cases). Thermistors attached to urinary catheters may work equally well.

Circulatory support: Usually, fluid requirements are modest, averaging 1200 ml of Ringer's lactate or saline solution in the first 4 h.[253,254] This is because a major factor in the hypotensive state is peripheral vasodilation.[171] With cooling there may be a sudden rise in systemic vascular resistance, and pulmonary edema may be caused, or exacerbated, by overzealous fluid administration.[255,256] Insertion of a Swan-Ganz catheter or central venous pressure monitor is indicated whenever necessary to guide fluid therapy. Patients with low cardiac output and hypotension should not be treated with α-adrenergic agents since these drugs promote vasoconstriction without improving cardiac output or perfusion, decrease cutaneous heat exchange, and perhaps enhance ischemic renal and hepatic damage.[257] One case report described excellent results using low-dose continuous isoproterenol infusion (1 μg/min).[253]

Shivering: Since shivering may occur with rapid cooling, and thus generate more heat, some authors[257,258] recommend chlorpromazine as an adjunct measure. Chlorpromazine is felt to act as a muscle relaxant and vasodilator promoting heat exchange at the skin surface. Phenothiazines, however, *may* aggravate hypotension, and have anticholinergic properties. They are also associated with serious dystonic reactions that may exacerbate hyperthermia. Distinct subtypes of dopamine receptors have been identified, including D_1 and D_2 receptors. Chlorpromazine and haloperidol are *D_2 receptor antagonists* and rat studies have shown that specific *D_1 receptor antagonists*, but not D_2 receptor antagonists reduced the hyperthermic response to cocaine infusion.[259] Dopamine is also known to participate in core temperature regulation, but it is unclear whether a predominance of D_1 or D_2 receptor activation results in hyperthermia or hypothermia.[260] Until more is understood about the exact role of the dopaminergic system in hyperthermia, the use of chlorpromazine and other dopamine blockers in the management of hyperthermia victims is not recommended.

Other pharmacologic interventions: Pharmacologic interventions aimed specifically at hyperthermia (i.e., dantrolene) have been suggested for such drugs as MDMA (i.e., ecstasy)[228] but have not been proven to be of any benefit.[229,261] Antipyretics are of no specific benefit[262] and salicylates may aggravate bleeding tendencies.[263] Alcohol sponge baths are not recommended, particularly in small children, since alcohol may be absorbed through dilated cutaneous blood vessels and inhaled, producing isopropanol poisoning and coma.[264]

9.4.2.2 Secondary Interventions

1. Laboratory data: Send blood for complete blood count, platelet count, PT, PTT, electrolytes, calcium, CPK, cardiac enzymes, BUN, creatinine, and liver function tests. Type and cross-match blood and send blood cultures. For severely ill patients send lactic acid level, and ABG. Check serum CPK and urine for myoglobin. If rhabdomyolysis is suspected, see Section 9.5 on rhabdomyolysis. Although urine and blood toxicologic screens are generally overutilized,[5] they should be sent if the diagnosis is in question. Send salicylate levels on all cases with an unknown cause of hyperthermia.

2. CT: Consider CT of brain for persistently altered mental status, focal neurological deficit.

3. Lumbar puncture: Perform lumbar puncture and send cerebral spinal fluid for analysis if patient has signs or symptoms of meningitis. Do not wait for results before administering empiric antibiotics.

4. Cardiac evaluation: ECG, CXR.

5. Disposition: All patients with serious hyperthermia or heat stroke should be admitted to the hospital. Patients with normal or mildly abnormal laboratory values who become normothermic in the emergency department may be admitted to the medical floor. All others require intensive monitoring.

9.5 RHABDOMYOLYSIS

9.5.1 General Comments

Rhabdomyolysis is defined as a syndrome of skeletal muscle injury or necrosis with release of muscle cell contents into the blood.[265] It has been associated with all drugs of abuse.[133,224,266–277] Since the classic signs and symptoms of nausea, vomiting, myalgias, muscle swelling, tenderness, and weakness are present in only a minority of cases (13% in one study[278]), the diagnosis depends on laboratory evaluation and a high clinical suspicion. Elevated levels of serum CK, in the absence of CK from other sources (brain or heart), is the most sensitive indicator of muscle injury[265] with most authors recognizing a CK level of more than fivefold that of the upper limit of normal as diagnostic. The diagnosis may also be suspected with a positive urine dipstick for heme: if no red blood cells are present on the urine microscopic examination, the positive orthotolidine reaction may be attributed to myoglobin (or hemoglobin). Because myoglobin is cleared from the plasma in 1 to 6 h by renal excretion and by metabolism to bilirubin,[265] the urine dipstick test for myoglobin may occasionally be negative due to rapid clearance.[279,280] Gabow et al.[265] reported that in the absence of hematuria, only 50% of patients with rhabdomyolysis had urine that was orthotolidine-positive.

The diagnosis of rhabdomyolysis is important because it may produce life-threatening hyperkalemia and myoglobinuric renal failure; it is often associated with disseminated intravascular coagulation (DIC), and acute cardiomyopathy from serious underlying conditions such as heat stroke or severe acidosis.[265,277,280–282] Myoglobinuric renal failure may frequently be prevented by vigorous treatment.

Case in point: In 1984, Ron and colleagues[283] described seven patients at very high risk for developing renal failure as a result of extensive crush injuries, severe rhabdomyolysis, and gross myoglobinurea following the collapse of a building. Their treatment goal was to rapidly obtain a urine pH of 6.5 and to maintain diuresis of 300 ml/h or more. Crystalloid infusions were begun at the scene and continued during transport to the hospital. If urine output did not rise to 300 ml/h and the central venous pressure rose by more than 4 cm H_2O, the infusion was halted and 1 g mannitol/kg body weight as a 20% solution was administered IV. Sodium bicarbonate (44 mEq) was added to every other bottle of 500-ml crystalloid solution. The electrolyte composition of IV solutions was adjusted to maintain a serum sodium concentration of 135 to 145 mmol/L and a serum potassium concentration between 3.5 and 4.5 mmol/L. Repeated doses of mannitol (1 g/kg body wt) were given if the urine output fell below 300 ml/h for 2 consecutive hours and if the central venous pressure rose by more than 4 cm H_2O. Further doses of bicarbonate were given if the urine pH fell below 6.5. Acetazolamide was given intravenously if plasma pH approached 7.45. Despite peak creatinine kinase (CK) levels exceeding 30,000 IU/dl none of the seven patients developed renal failure.

Assessing risk for developing acute renal failure: Several heterogeneous studies have attempted to identify which patients will progress to myoglobinuric renal failure based on their laboratory values. Unfortunately, there are no prospective studies with standardized treatment regimens to determine which patients are at risk. A study of 200 victims of severe beatings in South Africa found that base deficit, delay in treatment, and CK levels were significant risk factors for the development of ARD and death.[284] Ward et al.,[284] in another retrospective study ($n = 157$), found that the factors predictive of renal failure included (1) a peak CK level greater than 16,000 IU/dl (58% of patients with CK above 16,000 IU/dl vs. 11% of patients with CK below 16,000 IU/dl developed renal failure), (2) a history of hypotension, (3) *dehydration*, (4) older age, (5) sepsis, and (6) hyperkalemia. A retrospective review of 93 patients with "severe" rhabdomyolysis (serum CK greater than 5000 U/L) found that patients with a peak CK level of greater than 15,000 U/L had significantly higher rates of acute renal dysfunction (72% vs. 38%).[285] A recent analysis of 372 patients with crush syndrome after the 1995 earthquake in Kobe, Japan, demonstrated that patients with a peak CK level greater than 75,000 U/L had a higher rate of acute renal failure and mortality than those with a peak CK less than 75,000 U/L (84% vs. 39% and 4% vs. 17%, respectively).[286] Eneas et al.[287] found that only patients with a peak CK greater than 20,000 U/L failed to respond to a mannitol–bicarbonate diuresis and went on to require dialysis. The nonresponders also had significantly higher serum phosphate levels and hematocrit readings upon admission, indicative of more severe muscle injury and hemoconcentration. Several studies have attempted to predict the development of renal failure using serum or urine myoglobin levels. A prospective study of eight patients by Feinfeld[288] found that four of five patients with urine myoglobin levels greater than 1000 ng/ml (normal = <10 ng/ml) developed acute renal dysfunction, while none of the three patients with urine myoglobin levels less than 300 ng/ml developed it. Another report found that elevated urine myoglobin levels greater than 20,000 ng/ml were associated with a significantly increased risk of renal dysfunction.[289]

Prognosis: Approximately 10% of patients with rhabdomyolysis presenting to hospitals develop myoglobinuric renal failure[277] and major reports of patient series indicate that approximately 5% of patients with serious rhabdomyolysis die.[265,268,280,281,290] Death is often due not to rhabdomyolysis or one of its complications but to a complication of the primary disorder associated with the rhabdomyolysis (i.e., traumatic injury, or sepsis). With temporary support from hemodialysis acute myoglobinuric renal failure has a good prognosis, and full recovery should be expected.[280,281,291]

Crystalloids: Less controversy exists behind the need for volume replacement in the setting of rhabdomyolysis than it does for the use of bicarbonate, mannitol, or furosemide. In reviews of myoglobinuric renal failure,[265,268,280,283,292–295] hypovolemia is a consistent finding among all evaluated risk factors. Myoglobinuric renal failure seen in military recruits and bodybuilders has an especially strong association with dehydration.[296–298] Recently, Zurovsky et al.[299] demonstrated that, in rats, mortality and renal failure increased from both chronic dehydration (24 to 72 h) and acute dehydration from sucrose-induced diuresis or hemorrhage. The role of dehydration appears to implicate renal ischemia and perhaps acidosis and/or aciduria as necessary cofactors in the development of myoglobinuric acute renal failure.[300]

Alkalinization: The purpose of alkalinization of urine is to prevent the dissociation of myoglobin into globin and hematin.[277] Dissociation has been shown to occur below a pH of 5.6.[301] The nephrotoxic effect of hematin has been ascribed to the production of free hydroxy radicals.[302] Dog studies have shown that the infusion of free hematin causes significantly greater renal dysfunction than does myoglobin.[303] Furthermore, in urine below pH 5.0, the solubility of myoglobin decreases markedly causing myoglobin cast formation and an increase in the percentage of myoglobin retained in renal tubules. This process has been shown to have a high correlation with the development of acute renal failure.[304] Rabbit studies by Perri et al.[305] showed that animals with a urinary pH of less than 6 invariably develop renal failure after infusions of myoglobin, whereas those with a urine pH of more than 6 do not develop renal insufficiency. Despite well-performed animal studies, no controlled human studies have evaluated the effectiveness of alkalinization for rhabdomyolysis. For this reason, as well as certain concerns about hypernatremia, hypervolemia, and hypocalcemia, some authors[306] do not recommend bicarbonate therapy. We feel that the preponderance of evidence favors the use of bicarbonate and that with adequate monitoring of volume, electrolyte, and calcium levels bicarbonate therapy is safe and is likely to be of benefit.

Mannitol: Three major mechanisms have been proposed to explain the protective action of mannitol. The first suggests that a diuresis may simply dilute nephrotoxic agents in urine (e.g., hematin, urate) and "flush out" partially obstructed tubules.[307] Knochel points out that renal tubular oxygen consumption is closely coupled to sodium reabsorption[282] and by preventing sodium reabsorption, mannitol or furosemide may decrease oxygen requirements of renal tubules. This may allow the tubules to survive the metabolic insult produced by hematin.[277] Finally, mannitol may simply convert oliguric renal failure to nonoliguric renal failure. Studies have demonstrated a lower morbidity and mortality in nonoliguric renal failure than in oliguric renal failure.[308,309] Wilson et al.[310] showed that mannitol plus saline almost totally prevented the development of azotemia after glycerol-induced rhabdomyolysis in rats. As with bicarbonate, mannitol has not been shown to be more effective in prospective, controlled trials than saline alone. In selected cases in which urinary output is low (see following recommendations) and where hemodynamic status is stable, we believe the potential benefits of mannitol administration outweigh the potential risks.

Furosemide: Loop diuretics such as furosemide have also been used in an attempt to prevent acute renal failure. As with mannitol and bicarbonate no controlled human studies on its efficacy have been done. Furosemide may work similarly to mannitol to decrease sodium reabsorption and thus conserve renal tubule energy expenditure, thus decreasing the risk of ischemia. It may also simply convert oliguric renal failure to nonoliguric renal failure. Furosemide has the advantage of not increasing serum osmolality to the extent that mannitol does, but may exacerbate hypovolemia if not used with caution.

Recommendation: Based on the report by Ron and co-workers,[283] animal studies, and personal experience with the treatment of more than 100 cases of documented rhabdomyolysis, Curry et al.[277] proposed a treatment regimen that we recommend with adjustments under a stepwise approach to management. Using this treatment approach Curry et al. report only two instances of myoglobinuric renal failure out of 100 patients presenting with evidence of rhabdomyolysis. One was in a woman with severe salicylate poisoning who had established renal failure and anuria at the time of admission. The second was a woman who had sepsis and anoxic encephalopathy after seizures and cardiac arrest from IV cocaine.[277] While this regimen has not been tested prospectively it has suggestive benefit and if volume, serum osmolarity, and electrolyte status are monitored it is quite safe. Patients lacking nephrotoxic risk factors such as dehydration and acidosis, with only mild elevations of CK (<16,000 IU/dl) and no ongoing muscle injury may not require the full course of therapy recommended here. Any patient not treated by the full protocol should have CK levels monitored closely (i.e., every 12 h) and should be able to drink large amounts of fluids to maintain a brisk *urine output*.

9.5.2 Stepwise Approach to Management

9.5.2.1 Immediate Interventions

1. Airway, Breathing, Circulation, Antidotes: Maintain the airway and assist ventilation if necessary. Administer supplemental oxygen. Treat hypotension, and resuscitate as per previous reviews.[3] Administer appropriate antidotes, including 25 g dextrose IV if the patient is hypoglycemic, as per the section on coma.

2. Crystalloid: If cardiac/volume status is stable, initiate a fluid bolus of 1 L normal saline and continue until hypovolemia is corrected. Assuming that larger volumes are not needed for other reasons, crystalloid infusion is then administered at a rate of 2.5 ml/kg body weight per hour. Monitor urine output closely.

3. Bicarbonate: If urinary pH is <5.6 (the pH at which myoglobin dissociates into globin and hematin), administer sodium bicarbonate IV in boluses of 1 mmol/kg body weight until the arterial blood pH is about 7.45 or the urinary pH rises to 5.6.

Comment: *Urinary* pH, not arterial pH, has been found to correlate with precipitation of myoglobin within renal tubules,[304,305] and as a result the primary concern should be to increase urinary pH. Because of metabolic complications that may exist at a higher arterial pH (hypokalemia, and the shifting of the oxygen-hemoglobin saturation curve to the left), bicarbonate should not be used if serum pH is already >7.45.

9.5.2.2 Secondary Interventions

1. Reassess: Check serum sodium and potassium concentrations, and urine pH frequently.

Comment: If large volumes of normal saline are required for resuscitation, or sodium bicarbonate is used, check sodium every 6 to 8 h; otherwise check every 12 to 24 h. Check arterial pH every few hours if the patient is significantly acidotic (pH < 7.3) or if large amounts of sodium bicarbonate are used.

2. Potassium: Potassium may help to maintain a more alkaline urine. If urine pH falls below 5.6 in the presence of alkalemia and serum potassium is less than 4.0 mEq/L, then administer additional potassium until the urine pH rises above 6.0 or until the serum potassium concentration reaches 5 mmol/L.

Comment: The kidneys of patients with hypokalemia will spare potassium and excrete hydrogen ions resulting in a decrease of urinary bicarbonate, thus maintaining aciduria. Acidic urine increases myoglobin precipitation and increases the risk of myoglobinuric renal failure. There are no controlled studies demonstrating the role of potassium in the treatment of rhabdomyolysis, but it is of little harm and may be beneficial. One study showed that during active work, potassium may act as a vasodilator and increase blood flow to working muscle.[311] Knochel et al.[312] have presented data demonstrating that skeletal muscle of potassium-depleted dogs releases very little potassium during exertion and that exertion is not accompanied by an increase in blood flow. This may result in localized muscle ischemia and persistent rhabdomyolysis.

3. Acetazolamide: Acetazolamide, like potassium, may assist in producing a more alkaline urine. If the patient is persistently aciduric despite alkalemia and normal serum potassium concentrations, Curry et al.[277] recommend the use of 250 mg of acetazolamide IV to increase urinary pH. There is, however, no evidence that acetazolamide is efficacious for treatment of rhabdomyolysis.

Comment: In general, acetazolamide should not be given to a patient suffering from salicylate poisoning since it acidifies blood and alkalinizes CSF, increasing the volume of distribution of salicylate and trapping salicylate in the CNS.[313–315] In animal models of salicylate poisoning, the administration of acetazolamide markedly increases mortality rate.[315]

4. Decreased urine output below 1.5 to 2.0 ml/kg/h with objective hemodynamic parameters of either normovolemia or hypovolemia: Administer more crystalloid (500 cc fluid bolus) and consider increasing crystalloid infusion rate to 3.5 cc/kg/h.

5. Decreased urine output below 1.5 to 2.0 ml/kg/h with objective hemodynamic parameters of hypervolemia (mannitol): Give a single dose of 1 g/kg body weight IV over 30 min, administer any additional doses 0.5 g/kg IV over 15 min. Monitor serum osmolality if repeated doses are required. Mannitol may be administered every 6 h if serum osmolality remains below 300 mOsm/L.

Comment: Watch for pulmonary edema and monitor serum osmolality. Mannitol should also not be used in the presence of hemorrhagic shock or hypovolemia.

6. Furosemide: If urine output does not respond to fluids or mannitol, then administer furosemide. Start with 10 mg IVP.

7. Discontinuation of therapy: Continue the above treatment protocol until the urine is consistently orthotolidine-negative, laboratory signs of continued rhabdomyolysis are no longer present, and renal function is improving or normal. Stop fluids, mannitol, and bicarbonate if oliguria or anuria are refractory to therapy.

8. Hemodialysis: Those who do go on to develop acute tubular necrosis may require hemodialysis or peritoneal dialyses for several days or weeks until renal function returns.[265,277,280,281] Indications for hemodialysis include serious electrolyte abnormalities (e.g., hyperkalemia), clinically significant acidosis resistant to conventional therapy, and volume overload. A moderate elevation of BUN and creatinine levels without other clinical effects is not an indication for dialysis.[306]

9. Hyperkalemia: Sodium bicarbonate, glucose and insulin, sodium polystyrene, calcium, and dialysis may be required in severe cases.[265,281]

10. Hypocalcemia: Hypocalcemia is common in patients with severe rhabdomyolysis[277] but even with calcium levels less than 8.0 mEq/L, hypocalcemia rarely causes symptoms.[282,316,317] Treatment of asymptomatic hypocalcemia has been discouraged because it theoretically could increase deposition of calcium due to precipitation with phosphate in damaged muscle, further augmenting rhabdomyolysis.[316]

11. Laboratory data: CBC, electrolytes, BUN, creatinine, calcium, phosphorus, urinalysis, urine dip for blood (orthotolidine test), CK (MM and MB fractions), and arterial blood gas (if sodium bicarbonate to be used) (Figure 9.1).

12. Disposition: Patients with drug overdose who present with mild elevations of their CK (less than 3000 U/L) may be considered for discharge if all of the following conditions are met:

a. The patient must have normal vital signs.
b. There is no evidence of ongoing muscle injury.
c. The patient has normal renal function.
d. The patient is well hydrated and not acidotic, with normal electrolytes.
e. The patient can take fluids by mouth and is not at risk for dehydration.
f. Follow up is easily arranged for repeat CK in 12 to 24 h.
g. A repeat serum CK level 6 to 8 h after the first shows a decreasing trend.

All other patients should be admitted to the hospital for aggressive fluid therapy as described above.

9.6 HYPERTENSIVE EMERGENCIES

9.6.1 General Comments

Hypertension: Drug-induced hypertension is of concern because it can cause stroke (usually cerebral hemorrhage), acute myocardial infarction, pulmonary edema, dissecting aneurysm, and/or hypertensive encephalopathy.[319-321] Phenylpropanolamine, in particular, has been associated with cerebral hemorrhage when blood pressure was not rapidly lowered.[322-324] In patients with hypertension associated with amphetamines or cocaine, benzodiazepines may be successful in controlling the hypertension (and possibly dysrhythmias) by reducing the central sympathetic stimulus[123-125] and related catecholamine release.[325,326] If a stable, previously normotensive patient, without evidence of end organ damage, has extremely high blood pressure (>120 mm Hg diastolic) despite sedation, one should consider the use of a vasodilator such as nitroglycerin or phentolamine, or possibly a calcium channel blocker.[327] In contrast to patients with chronic hypertension, most young patients with drug-induced hypertension do not have chronic compensatory changes in their cerebral and cardiovascular system. For this reason blood pressure in previously normotensive individuals may be reduced rapidly to normal levels.[328]

Hypertensive emergencies: Hypertensive emergencies, defined as an increase in blood pressure that causes functional disturbances of the CNS, the heart, or the kidneys,[329] require a more aggressive

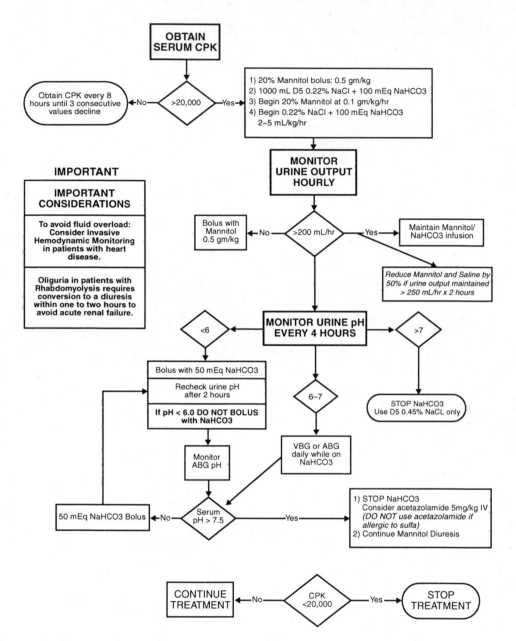

Figure 9.1   Treatment algorithm by Malinoski et al.,[318] which is a slightly more aggressive alternative to the protocol recommended above, advocating the use of mannitol and sodium bicarbonate in all patients.

approach.[330–332] Evidence of hypertensive encephalopathy, acute heart failure, aortic dissection, or coronary insufficiency requires rapid reduction of blood pressure (usually within 60 min) in a controlled fashion. Direct arteriolar dilating agents such as nitroglycerin, or nitroprusside, a pure alpha-adrenergic blocking agent such as phentolamine, or a calcium antagonist[333] may be used.

Stroke: Hypertension in the presence of a stroke is a more complicated issue, since hypertension may be a homeostatic response to maintain intracerebral blood flow in the presence of intracranial hypertension.[334] In this case blood pressure should not be lowered, or, if there is ongoing evidence of sympathomimetic drug intoxication, lowered gradually to a diastolic blood pressure no less than the 100 to 110 mm Hg range.

Beta-blockers: In animal models of cocaine intoxication associated with hemodynamic dysfunction and mortality, propanolol has been shown to be protective,[335] to have no effect,[336] or to increase mortality.[337,338] The reasons for the differences in these experimental results are unclear but may be related to the different doses of cocaine or the type of beta-adrenergic antagonist utilized.[339] Human studies, however, have been more consistent. In a randomized, double-blinded, placebo-controlled trial, Lange et al.[340] administered intranasal cocaine to 30 stable volunteers referred for cardiac catheterization. In this study it was found that intracoronary propranolol administration caused no change in arterial blood pressure but decreased coronary sinus blood flow and increased coronary vascular resistance. Several case reports have also documented an aggravation of hypertension when nonselective beta-adrenergic antagonists have been used in the treatment of acute cocaine intoxication.[341–343]

Labetalol: The exacerbation of hypertension and coronary vasospasm when nonselective beta-adrenergic antagonists are administered to cocaine-intoxicated patients may result from blockade of beta-2 receptor-induced vasodilation causing an "unopposed" peripheral alpha-adrenergic vasoconstriction.[339] It has therefore been suggested that labetalol, which has both alpha-adrenergic and beta-adrenergic antagonist activity, may be safer.[154,342] Controversy exists since the beta-adrenergic antagonist potency of labetalol is seven times greater than its relatively weak alpha antagonist potency,[344] and studies of hypertension in cocaine-intoxicated animals are conflicting: some have shown hemodynamic improvement[345] while others show no hemodynamic effect.[346] Mortality data are difficult to decipher as studies have shown decreased mortality,[335] increased mortality,[337,338] or no change in mortality.[336] The human experience (case reports) with labetalol has been better than with propanolol,[342,347,348] but in two unusual cases involving catecholamine excess that physiologically resemble cocaine intoxication (one involving pheochromocytoma,[349] and the other an accidental epinephrine overdosage[350]), hypertension was exacerbated by the administration of labetalol. In a study similar to that of Lange et al.,[351] Boehrer et al.[352] evaluated 15 patients referred for cardiac catheterization and found that while labetalol reversed the cocaine-induced rise in mean arterial pressure *it did not* alleviate cocaine-induced coronary vasoconstriction. An interesting case report described the induction of life-threatening hyperkalemia in a dialysis patient with hypertensive emergency treated with labetalol.[353]

Esmolol: Esmolol, an ultra-short-acting ($t_{1/2}$ = 9 min), easily titrated, beta-1 selective, adrenoreceptor blocking agent, has been used successfully in the treatment of cocaine-induced adrenergic crises.[126,343,354] However, the effects of esmolol on coronary vasoconstriction have not been evaluated. Its use may be most appropriate to control heart rate in the setting of acute aortic dissection[355] induced by hypertension from stimulant abuse. If esmolol is used, it is recommended that vasodilators such as nitroglycerin be given simultaneously since nitroglycerin is known to alleviate stimulant-induced vasoconstriction.[356] Pollan et al.[354] reported a case of a 64-year-old man who became hypertensive and tachycardic after the administration of cocaine for nasal polyp removal. This patient had *resolution* of ST segment depression after the administration of 20 mg IV of esmolol with good control of hemodynamic parameters. Esmolol has also been used in the management of pheochromocytoma with a rapid decrease in systolic blood pressure without effect on diastolic pressure.[357,358]

9.6.2 Stepwise Approach to Management

9.6.2.1 Immediate Interventions

1. Airway, Breathing, Circulation: Maintain the airway and assist ventilation if necessary. Administer supplemental oxygen. Resuscitate as per previous reviews.[3]

2. Antidotes: Administer appropriate antidotes, including 25 g dextrose IV if the patient is hypoglycemic, as per Section 9.1.

3. Agitation or seizures: Administer a benzodiazepine such as lorazepam (0.05 to 0.10 mg/kg) and control agitation as described under Section 9.2.

4. Medications: If the patient is persistently hypertensive and a hypertensive emergency exists, then administer one of the following drugs:

Treatment for Drug-Induced, Hypertensive Emergency

Drug	Dose	Onset	Mechanism of Action
Sodium nitroprusside	0.25–10 µg/kg/min as IV infusion	2–5 min	Direct arterial and venous vasodilator
Nitroglycerin	5–100 µg as IV infusion	2–5 min	Direct arterial and venous vasodilator
Esmolol	Load with 500 µg/kg/min over 1 min Maintenance infusion: 50–200 µg/kg/min	2–5 min	B_1 adrenoreceptor blocker
Phentolamine	5–10 mg IVP	2–5 min	Alpha-adrenergic blocker

The treatment goal is to lower the blood pressure to a level that is "normal" for that patient within 30 to 60 min in a controlled, graded manner.[329] Although there is a broad range of normal blood pressures for an individual, if the patient's normal blood pressure is unknown, the diastolic blood pressure should be lowered to a minimum of 120 mm Hg or until there is no evidence of ongoing organ injury. The use of nitroprusside generally requires continuous intra-arterial blood pressure monitoring.

Comment: Phenylpropanolamine, an indirect sympathomimetic and direct alpha agonist, is frequently substituted for stimulants such as amphetamine and cocaine. The combination of severe hypertension with reflex bradycardia is a clue to vasoconstriction from the direct alpha-stimulation from phenylpropanolamine. Hypertension from phenylpropanolamine is usually best treated with phentolamine.

5. Laboratory data/imaging: For patients with hypertensive emergencies: Draw electrolytes, CK, CK-MB, BUN, creatinine, and PT/PTT. Perform EKG, and CXR. For apparently uncomplicated hypertension: Laboratory data may be done at the discretion of the physician. An ECG is recommended to rule out silent ischemia.

9.6.2.2 Secondary Interventions

1. Monitoring: Continue close monitoring of patient's blood pressure and cardiac status with frequent manual blood pressure readings. Consider placing an arterial line for better monitoring in patients with persistently labile hypertension or for those who have hypertension that is difficult to control.

2. CT of brain: Patients with severe headaches that do not resolve after the control of hypertension should undergo CT of the head to rule out intracranial bleeding.

3. Lumbar puncture: If CT of the head is negative and the patient continues to have symptoms of severe headache and/or nuchal rigidity, perform lumbar puncture to rule out small subarachnoid hemorrhage.

4. Disposition: All patients that meet the following conditions may be considered for discharge from the emergency department:

a. Moderate uncomplicated hypertension controlled with sedation or a single dose of antihypertensive agents
b. Normal vital signs after a period of observation of 4 to 6 h
c. Normal ECG
d. Normal physical examination

All patients with hypertensive emergencies should be admitted to the hospital regardless of response to initial therapy.

9.7 CARDIAC CARE

9.7.1 General Comments

Almost all drugs of abuse can be associated with acute cardiac complications ranging from benign supraventricular tachycardia to ventricular fibrillation, sudden death, and myocardial infarction. Cocaine is a prototype cardiac toxin among drugs of abuse. As such, most of this section pertains directly to cocaine. Other stimulants (i.e., amphetamines,[359,360] phenylpropanolamine,[361,362] and methylphenidate[363,364]) may be associated with cardiac complications as well, and management should proceed in a fashion similar to that of the cocaine-intoxicated patient. One should also consider the likely possibility that cocaine has been mixed with or substituted for other stimulants (see Table 9.5 to Table 9.7).[365] If cardiac complications occur from drugs of abuse other than stimulants (i.e., heroin, barbiturates) cardiac care parallels current advanced cardiac life support guidelines,[366] with a few exceptions.

Mechanisms: The ability of cocaine to increase myocardial oxygen demand secondary to induction of hypertension and tachycardia, while decreasing coronary blood flow through vasoconstriction, and induction of coronary thromboses (the latter due to enhancement of platelet aggregation) makes it an ideal precipitant of myocardial ischemia and infarction.[367,368]

Benzodiazepines: In experiments in animals, benzodiazepines attenuate the cardiac and CNS toxicity of cocaine.[123,124,369] Perhaps through their anxiolytic effects, benzodiazepines reduce blood pressure and heart rate, thereby decreasing myocardial oxygen demand.[367] They are recommended as first-line agents for treatment of cocaine-intoxicated patients with myocardial ischemia who are anxious, have tachycardia, and/or are hypertensive.

Aspirin: Aspirin should be administered to help prevent the formation of thrombi in patients with suspected ischemia. This recommendation is based on theoretical considerations (e.g., decreasing platelet aggregation),[370–372] the drug's good safety profile, and the extensive investigation of aspirin in patients with ischemic heart disease unrelated to cocaine. There are, however, no clinical data on the use of aspirin in patients with cocaine-associated myocardial ischemia.[367]

Nitroglycerin: Nitroglycerin is recommended as first-line therapy for cocaine-induced cardiac ischemia based on studies that show a reversal of cocaine-induced coronary artery vasoconstriction[356] and reports of its ability to relieve cocaine-associated chest pain.[373]

Calcium-channel blockers: In studies of cocaine intoxication in animals, calcium-channel blockers prevent malignant arrhythmias,[374] blunt negative ionotropic effects,[375] limit the increase in systemic vascular resistance,[375] and protect against myocardial infarction.[336] However, one study by Derlet et al.[376] showed that calcium-channel blockers may increase CNS toxicity and mortality.[376] This study, which was performed on rats, has been criticized on the basis that the cocaine was administered intraperitoneally and that pretreatment with a calcium antagonist might have accelerated peritoneal absorption.[377] Another study by Nahas et al.[378] showed that nitrendipine (a calcium antagonist with good CNS penetration) protected rats against cocaine-induced seizures and lethality. Verapamil reverses cocaine-induced coronary artery vasoconstriction[379] and may play a role in the treatment of refractory myocardial ischemia secondary to cocaine use.

Phentolamine: Phentolamine, an alpha-adrenergic antagonist, reverses cocaine-induced coronary artery vasoconstriction,[351] and electrocardiographic resolution of ischemia has been documented in some patients.[367] The use of a low dose (1 mg) may avoid the hypotensive effects of the drug while maintaining the anti-ischemic effects.[380]

Beta-blockers: Because of their association with coronary vasoconstriction and conflicting animal studies (see previous section on hypertension), beta-adrenergic blockers are not routinely recommended for the treatment of cocaine-associated ischemic chest pain. However, esmolol is indicated for severe adrenergic crisis associated with tachycardia and hypertension. Esmolol or metoprolol may play a role in the treatment of cocaine-induced malignant ventricular ectopy if lidocaine and defibrillation fail[380] (see section below on arrhythmias).

Thrombolytic therapy: Biogenic amines such as serotonin and epinephrine, which are released in large quantities by drugs such as cocaine, stimulate platelet aggregation. Stimulated platelets release thromboxane A2, which exacerbates ischemia by increasing vasoconstriction. The activation of the coagulation cascade and the formation of thrombin clot may follow. Thus, thrombolytic therapy seems rational in the setting of cocaine-induced myocardial infarction. However, the safety of thrombolysis has been questioned by Bush[381] after one patient died of an intracerebral hemorrhage. A larger study by Hollander et al.[382] noted no such complications among 36 patients who received thrombolytic therapy. Although thrombolytic agents may be safe, several concerns persist among clinicians: First, the mortality from cocaine-associated myocardial infarction is extremely low in patients who reach the hospital alive (0/136 patients in one study).[383] Second, the clinical benefit of thrombolytic therapy in cocaine-induced coronary thrombosis has not been demonstrated.[382] Finally, young patients with cocaine-associated chest pain have a high incidence of early repolarization (a variant of the normal ECG[384,385]); as a result they may inadvertently receive thrombolysis when it is not necessary.[381,384,385] Because of these concerns as well as the belief by some[386] that the major mechanism of cocaine-mediated infarction is vasospasm, thrombolytic therapy is only recommended under the following circumstances: (1) when percutaneous coronary intervention and angioplasty is not available; (2) in acute myocardial infarction with an electrocardiogram with >2 mm ST-segment elevation in two or more contiguous *precordial leads*, or >1 mm ST-segment elevation in two or more contiguous *limb leads*; and (3) when no contraindications to thrombolytic therapy exist (Table 9.11). It is interesting to note that studies have shown significant coronary artery disease (i.e., stenosis > 50%) is present in up to 77% of patients with cocaine-induced myocardial infarction.[387]

Lidocaine: Lidocaine, a sodium channel blocker, was initially thought to increase the risk of arrhythmias and seizures in patients with cocaine intoxication, based on studies in Sprague-Dawley rats.[388] Recent evidence from dog[389] and guinea pig hearts[390] suggests that lidocaine competes with cocaine for binding sites at the sodium channels and is then rapidly released from the sodium channel without harmful effects. A retrospective review of 29 patients who received lidocaine in the context of cocaine-associated dysrhythmias showed no adverse outcomes.[391] Cautious use of lidocaine to treat ventricular arrhythmias occurring after cocaine use therefore seems reasonable. Ventricular arrhythmias that occur within a few hours after the use of cocaine may be the result of sodium channel blockade (e.g., quinidine-like effects) or from excessive levels of circulating catecholamines. For this reason cardioselective beta-blockers and/or sodium bicarbonate may be effective as well.[392]

Arrhythmias: Arrhythmias that occur after cocaine abuse may be associated with myocardial infarction, excessive catecholinergic surge, and/or sodium channel blockade (e.g., "quinidine-like" effects).[393]

> **Supraventricular arrhythmias:** Supraventricular arrhythmias due to cocaine include paroxysmal supraventricular tachycardia, rapid atrial fibrillation, and atrial flutter.[394] These arrhythmias are usually short-lived and if the patient is hemodynamically stable do not require immediate therapy.[395–397] Benzodiazepines modulate the stimulatory effects of cocaine on the CNS[154,170,398] and may blunt the hypersympathetic state driving the arrhythmia. Patients with persistent supraventricular arrhythmias should be treated initially with a benzodiazepine (i.e., lorazepam or diazepam), and then if necessary with a cardioselective beta-blocker such as esmolol (see discussion under stepwise approach to management). Unstable supraventricular rhythms should be managed in accordance with the American Heart Association's American Cardiac Life Support (ACLS) protocols.
>
> **Ventricular arrhythmias (stable):** As with supraventricular arrhythmias from cocaine, ventricular ectopy and short runs of ventricular tachycardia (VT) are usually transient, and most often resolve with

Table 9.11   Contraindications to Thrombolytic Therapy

Absolute Contraindications

Active internal bleeding
Altered consciousness
Cerebrovascular accident (CVA) in the past 6 months or *any* history of hemorrhagic CVA
Intracranial or intraspinal surgery within the previous 2 months
Intracranial or intraspinal neoplasm, aneurysm, or arteriovenous malformation
Known bleeding disorder
Persistent, severe hypertension (systolic BP > 200 mm Hg and/or diastolic BP > 120 mm Hg)
Pregnancy
Previous allergy to a streptokinase product (this does not contraindicate tPA administration)
Recent (within 1 month) head trauma
Suspected aortic dissection
Suspected pericarditis
Trauma or surgery within 2 weeks that could result in bleeding into a closed space

Relative Contraindications

Active peptic ulcer disease
Cardiopulmonary resuscitation for > 10 min
Current use of oral anticoagulants
Hemorrhagic ophthalmic conditions
History of chronic, uncontrolled hypertension (diastolic BP > 100 mm Hg), treated or untreated
History of ischemic or embolic CVA > 6 months ago
Significant trauma or major surgery > 2 weeks ago but < 2 months ago
Subclavian or internal jugular venous cannulation

Source: Adapted from National Heart Attack Alert Program Coordinating Committee 60 Minutes to Treatment Working Group, NIH Publication No. 93-3278. September 1993, p. 19.

careful observation supplemented by titrated doses of a benzodiazepine.[366] In cases with persistent ventricular ectopy, cardioselective beta-blockers (i.e., metoprolol or esmolol) may reverse excessive catecholaminergic stimulation and suppress the ectopy. Lidocaine may also be of benefit.[123,399,400]

Ventricular arrhythmias (unstable): Ventricular fibrillation (VF) and malignant VT (VT) with hypotension, or evidence of congestive heart failure, or ischemia, should initially be treated as recommended by the ACLS algorithm. Lidocaine (1.0 to 1.5 mg/kg) may be given with caution as previously discussed. Defibrillation should proceed as usual.[366]

Epinephrine: Concerns about epinephrine have been raised since it has similar cardiovascular effects as cocaine and may even mediate many of its effects. There is, however, no good evidence to suggest eliminating the initial epinephrine dose in treating cocaine-induced VF. Clinicians should, however, increase the interval between subsequent doses of epinephrine to every 5 to 10 min and avoid high-dose epinephrine (greater than 1 mg per dose) in refractory patients.[366]

Propranolol or other beta-blocker: Propranolol continues to be recommended by the Committee on Emergency Cardiac Care for the treatment of malignant cocaine-induced VF and VT. This recommendation is based on animal data and empiric reports but is not supported by any human studies.[154,369,401,402] The risk of beta-blockade in cocaine toxicity is that of unopposed alpha-stimulation resulting in severe hypertension, as well as coronary vasoconstriction.[341] This is of less concern with the use of a cardioselective beta-blocker such as esmolol or metoprolol.

9.7.2   Stepwise Approach to Management

9.7.2.1   Immediate Interventions

1. Airway, Breathing, Circulation: Maintain the airway and assist ventilation if necessary. Administer supplemental oxygen. Treat hypotension, and resuscitate as per previous reviews.[3,366]

2. Antidotes: Administer appropriate antidotes, including 25 g dextrose IV if the patient is hypoglycemic, as per Section 9.1 on coma.

3. IV, monitor, O$_2$: Administer oxygen by nasal cannula at 4 L/min, monitor cardiac status (obtain ECG), and start a peripheral intravenous line. Hang normal saline to keep vein open.

4. Benzodiazepines: Administer a benzodiazepine (i.e., 0.25 to 0.5 mg, or 2 to 4 mg IVP lorazepam) if the patient is anxious, hypertensive, or is experiencing cardiac chest pain or transient arrhythmias.

5. Sublingual and transdermal nitroglycerin/aspirin: If hemodynamically stable but chest pain persists, administer nitroglycerin sublingually (up to three tablets or three sprays of 0.4 mg each). Apply a nitroglycerin paste, 1 in., to the chest. Give one aspirin (325 mg) by mouth.

6. IV nitroglycerin: If chest pain is present and the patient is hemodynamically stable, begin a nitroglycerin drip starting at 8 to 10 µg/min. Titrate upward to control of pain if blood pressure remains stable.

7. Calcium-channel blocker: Consider the use of a calcium-channel blocker such as verapamil (5.0 mg IV over 2 min, with a repeat 5 mg dose IV if symptoms persist) or diltiazem (0.25 mg/kg IV over 2 min, with repeat dose of 0.35 mg/kg IV over 2 min if symptoms persist) for resistant myocardial ischemia. Consider administration of **morphine sulfate** for chest pain if hemodynamically stable (2.0 mg IVP with additional doses titrated to control pain and anxiety).

8. Phentolamine: Use phentolamine, 1.0 to 5.0 mg IVP for resistant chest pain.

9. Thrombolytics: If ECG shows new ST segment elevation (greater than 2 mm in two consecutive leads) that persists despite nitrates or calcium-channel blockers, no contraindications exist (Table 9.11), and percutaneous coronary intervention is not readily available, administer a thrombolytic agent (Table 9.12, dosing). See previous reviews for comprehensive guide to thrombolytics.[403–406]

Table 9.12   Current Thrombolytic Agents and Their Dosing in the Acute MI Patient

Drug	Dose	Comments
Streptokinase (SK) (Cost $300)[a]	1.5 million units IV over 60 min	SK is antigenic; allergic reaction and rarely anaphylaxis (<1% incidence) may occur. Administration may cause hypotension, necessitating a slower infusion rate than that recommended. SK may not be effective if administered 5 days to 6 months after prior SK therapy or 12 months after APSAC therapy or a streptococcal infection.
APSAC (Anistreplase) (Cost $1675)[a]	30 units IV over 2–5 min	APSAC is also antigenic and its administration may be complicated by hypotension (see above). APSAC may not be effective if administered 5 days to 12 months after prior SK or APSAC therapy or a streptococcal infection.
Reteplase (Retavase) (Cost $3200)[a]	10 units IV over 2 min, followed by a second dose of 10 units IV over 2 min, 30 min after the first dose	Fast, convenient double-bolus dosing. Unlike SK and APSAC, reteplase is not antigenic. Hypotension complicating infusion is less likely than with either SK or APSAC. A slightly higher incidence of cerebral hemorrhage has been noted compared with SK.
tPA (Alteplase) (Cost $3200)[a]	"Front-loaded" dosing: 15 mg IV over 2 min, followed by 0.75 mg/kg (50 mg maximum) IV over 30 min, followed by 0.5 mg/kg (35 mg maximum) IV over 60 min	Do not exceed the maximum dose of 100 mg. Unlike SK and APSAC, tPA is not antigenic. Hypotension complicating infusion is less likely than with either SK or APSAC. A slightly higher incidence of cerebral hemorrhage has been noted compared with SK.
Tenecteplase (TNKase) (Cost $2850)	A single bolus dose should be administered over 5 s based on patient weight (30–50 mg)	Ease of administration, but may not stop infusion once given. Similar efficacy and complication rate as tPA.

[a] Average wholesale price to the pharmacy.

Comment: Establish two peripheral IVs, and perform a 12-lead ECG q 30 min until infusion completed. Avoid all unnecessary venous and arterial sticks and beware that automated blood pressure cuffs, nasogastric tubes, Foley catheters, and central lines are associated with increased bleeding.[407]

10. Arrhythmias:

Supraventricular arrhythmias: See discussion above. Generally, treatment parallels ACLS guidelines with the use of benzodiazepines and beta-blockers in the doses recommended below.

Ventricular arrhythmias: If stable ventricular tachycardia does not respond to benzodiazepines (i.e., lorazepam 0.25 to 0.50 mg/kg or 2 to 4 mg IVP) it should be treated with lidocaine (1.5 mg/kg IVP) and/or beta-blockers (metoprolol 5.0 mg IV every 5 min, to a total of 15 mg; or esmolol, load with 500 µg/kg/min over 1 min and run a maintenance infusion at 50 to 200 µg/kg/min; or propranolol, 1.0 mg IV every 5 min to a total of 3 mg). Esmolol has the advantage of being a beta-1, cardioselective agent with a short half-life ($t_{1/2}$ = 9 min) allowing it to be rapidly discontinued in the event of an adverse reaction. Unstable ventricular tachycardia should be treated with immediate cardioversion or defibrillation (see ACLS recommendations on VT, VF) along with the administration of lidocaine, beta-blockers, and benzodiazepines. Patients should be reshocked after each administration of lidocaine or beta-blocker.[366] The quinidine-like effects of cocaine are manifested by a wide complex sinus rhythm and frequently respond to boluses of sodium bicarbonate (50 mEq IV, repeat every 5 min to a total of 150 mEq). A bicarbonate drip (made by adding two to three ampoules of sodium bicarbonate in one liter of D5W) may be run simultaneously at 200 cc/h.

Comment: Caution should be taken to avoid hypernatremia or hypervolemia and resulting pulmonary edema from overzealous sodium bicarbonate administration. Also, class IA and IC antiarrhythmic agents (i.e., procainamide, dysopyramide, quinidine, propafenone) are contraindicated in the setting of drug-induced conduction blockade as is occasionally seen with cocaine.[390,392,408]

9.7.2.2 Secondary Interventions

1. Repeat ECG: Repeat ECG if chest pain worsens or recurs.

2. Chest radiograph: To further assess for congestive heart failure or evidence of cardiomyopathy; also to assess for pneumothorax, or pneumomediastinum.

3. Monitoring: A minimum of 12 h of cardiac monitoring is recommended for patients with chest pain associated with cocaine use (see section on disposition).

4. Coronary stress testing: Because patients with cocaine-associated chest pain have a 1-year survival of 98% and an incidence of late myocardial infarction of only 1%, urgent cardiac evaluation is probably not necessary for patients in whom acute myocardial infarction has been ruled out.[367] However, keep in mind that patients who rule in for cocaine-induced myocardial infarction, despite an average age of 32 to 38 years, have a 31 to 67% incidence of significant underlying coronary artery disease.

5. Laboratory data: Baseline laboratory data should include a CBC, PT/PTT, cardiac isoenzymes including creatine kinase MB, troponin T, as well as electrolytes. Repeat isoenzymes every 8 to 12 h.

Comment: Rhabdomyolysis may complicate cocaine intoxication and as a result increased concentrations of myoglobin, creatine kinase, and creatine kinase MB may occur even in the absence of myocardial infarction.[409] After using cocaine, approximately 50% of patients have elevations in the serum creatine kinase concentration whether or not they are experiencing a myocardial infarction.[410] If the patient has a continuously rising enzyme concentration this is much more likely to represent a true myocardial infarction.[383,410] The immunoassay for cardiac troponin I has no detectable cross-reactivity with human skeletal muscle troponin I, making it a more specific test than that for creatine kinase MB in assessing myocardial injury when skeletal-muscle injury also exists.[411,412] However, troponin I is a late marker for myocardial infarction with improved sensitivity after 12 h (95 to 100%) vs. CK-MB, which is usually elevated within 6 to 8 h.[413]

6. Disposition

a. **Intensive care unit**: All patients with evidence of acute myocardial infarction, or any unstable patient.

b. **Telemetry:** Hemodynamically stable patients without ongoing chest pain, ECG changes, or elevated cardiac isoenzymes to a monitored observation unit for a minimum of 12 h of monitoring and serial creatine kinase MB measurements and repeat ECGs. Patients who have no evidence of ongoing chest pain with normal ECG and cardiac isoenzymes after 12 h may be discharged.

c. **Home:** Selected patients who have normal ECG, cardiac enzymes, and no evidence of ongoing ischemia may be discharged after a period of 9 to 12 h.

Comment: Observation periods of 9 to 12 h to rule out myocardial infarction in low-risk patients with chest pain unrelated to cocaine use have become more common.[414–416] Similar observation periods may be appropriate for many patients with cocaine-associated chest discomfort since these patients appear to have a low incidence of cardiovascular complications, whether or not they have myocardial infarction.[417] Of patients with cocaine-associated chest pain, approximately 6% will have a myocardial infarction.[384,410,418] Of those patients with cocaine-associated myocardial infarction, 36% will go on to develop cardiovascular complications.[383] Of those who develop cardiovascular complications 94–100% can be detected by the use of ECG, serial creatine kinase MB measurements, and observation for 12 h.[383]

9.8 STROKE

9.8.1 General Comments

Any physician treating a patient who has suffered a stroke must consider drug abuse in the differential diagnosis, especially if the patient is young.[419–424] In a study done at San Francisco General Hospital, drug abuse was identified as the most common predisposing condition among patients under 35 years of age presenting with stroke.[425] Most patients had either infective endocarditis (13/73) or stroke occurring soon after the use of a stimulant (34/73). Kaku and Lowenstein[425] estimated that the relative risk for stroke among drug abusers after controlling for other stroke risk factors was 6.5.

Mechanism: Acute stroke associated with drugs of abuse may result from hemorrhage, vasoconstriction, severe hypertension, hypotension, embolism of foreign materials (i.e., talc, ground up tablets, etc.; see Table 9.5 through Table 9.7) via a patent foramen ovale, vasculitis, cardiac thrombi, endocarditis, and opportunistic infection.[426] Among patients with stroke from cocaine abuse about 50% have cerebral hemorrhage, 30% subarachnoid hemorrhage, and 20% have ischemic stroke.[427,428] The pathophysiologic mechanisms involved are thus much different than for the general population, where the overwhelming majority of strokes are ischemic (80%) in origin and only 10% result from hemorrhage.[429] This difference makes the treatment of drug-induced stroke significantly different. Instead of anticoagulation or internal carotid artery surgery, the drug-abusing patient may be more appropriately treated with steroids for vasculitis, antibiotics for endocarditis, or calcium-channel blockers for vasospasm.

Thrombolytics: There is substantial disagreement in the literature regarding the safety and efficacy of thrombolytic therapy for ischemic strokes. Data from the five completed randomized trials evaluating the use of intravenous thrombolytics in the treatment of ischemic strokes (ECASS,[430] MAST-I,[431] NINDS,[432] MAST-E,[433] and ASK[434]) involve a total of more than 2500 patients, but these studies used two different thrombolytic agents — tissue plasminogen activator (tPA) and streptokinase (SK) — that were given at different doses, with different adjunctive treatments, and with very different inclusion criteria. Thus it is impossible to pool the data for meta-analysis. Analyzing the studies individually, however, reveals that all three of the SK trials found excess mortality in the SK group that was both statistically and clinically significant, as did one of the two studies that used tPA. The fifth study, the NINDS trial, is the only one of the five to find outcome benefit in treated patients. The patients in the NINDS study all received thrombolytics within a 3-h time interval, which required rapid CT and radiologist review of the results before treatment could begin. These strict exclusion criteria would result in the treatment of only a very small percentage of stroke victims[434a] (less than 5%). Furthermore, the increased risk of bleeding associated with thrombolytics would be imposed upon a number of patients who did not require treatment. Libman and colleagues[435] reported that about 20% of the time when members of the trained acute stroke intervention team at their institution diagnosed stroke on clinical grounds prior to CT scan, the ultimate diagnosis proved to be different. Although treatment depended on CT results, in over half of the patients misdiagnosed clinically the CT scan also returned a result entirely compatible with stroke. Of these, 13 patients were postictal, 13 had systemic infections as the cause of their "stoke mimic," and 10 had an ultimate diagnosis of toxic-metabolic cause. Because of the controversy surrounding ischemic strokes, and because of the increased risk of intracerebral hemorrhage (from uncontrolled hypertension, seizures, cerebral aneurysms, and vasculitis), thrombolytics are not recommended at this time for the treatment of drug-induced stroke.

Heparin: Although heparin has been recommended for the treatment of crescendo transient ischemic attacks (TIAs), strokes with a cardioembolic source, and posterior circulation strokes,[436–438] it should be used with extreme caution in patients with drug-induced strokes because of the higher potential for hemorrhage (i.e., ~50%).

Antibiotics: Stroke complicates approximately 20% of all cases of endocarditis, with an overall mortality rate for endocarditis-associated strokes of 20%.[439,440] Fortunately, the risk of recurrent embolism is low when infection is controlled (0.3%/day),[440] obviating the need for anticoagulation despite that most endocarditis-related stokes are due to embolism from cardiac vegetations.[439,440] Present recommendations for empiric antibiotic treatment are nafcillin 2.0 g q 4 h IV + gentamicin 1.0 mg/kg q 8 h IM or IV. If the patient is penicillin allergic give vancomycin 1.0 g q 12 h IV + gentamicin 1.0 mg/kg q 8 h IM or IV.

Surgery: Foreign body emboli most often have followed injection of crushed tablet preparations meant for oral use, especially methylphenidate (Ritalin) and pentazocine plus tripelennamine ("T's and Blues").[441,442] Patients dissolve tablets or capsules in water and filter them to varying extents, and then inject them. Showers of insoluble fillers (principally talc) enter the circulation[419] and lodge in the lung, forming granulomas. Granulomas may also form in the lung and brain (possibly due to the passage of foreign materials through a patent foramen ovale), and may require surgical intervention. Surgery may also be required for decompression of cerebral hematomas, repair of ruptured aneurysms, and the removal of abscesses.

Nimodipine: Cocaine is known to decrease reuptake of serotonin, which is believed to play a role in cocaine-induced headaches and may be associated with cocaine-induced vasoconstriction.[443–445] Rothrock et al.[446] reported on three cases of amphetamine-related stroke: in one case a 35-year-old abuser had 20 episodes of transient right hemiparesis occurring within minutes of inhaling methamphetamine; later he developed permanent right hemiparesis. In animal studies, intravenous methamphetamine administration has resulted in narrowing of the middle cerebral artery branches within 19 min.[447] While the pharmacologic approaches to cerebral vasospasm are varied, the calcium-channel blocker nimodipine has been used widely with proven efficacy in preventing vasospasm associated with hemorrhagic stroke.[448,449] No studies looking at this issue in the setting of drug-induced hemorrhagic stroke exist. Although two animal studies[450,451] found that nimodipine potentiated the toxicity of cocaine and amphetamines in rats, it is felt that in selected patients the risk–benefit ratio may favor nimodipine administration. Such populations may include the drug-abusing patient who is experiencing transient ischemic attacks closely temporally related to substance abuse or who has had a documented subarachnoid hemorrhage associated with cerebral vasospasm. Recent reports suggest no benefit of nifedipine in ischemic strokes of any type.[452]

Glucocorticoids/cyclophosphamide (vasculitis): Vasculitis has been associated with nearly every drug of abuse (ephedrine,[453] pentazocine and tripelennamine,[442] amphetamines,[447,454,455] phenylpropanolamine,[456] heroin,[457,458] methylphenidate,[459] pseudoephedrine,[323] and cocaine[460–463]). In the case of drug-induced vasculitis, removal and discontinuance of the offending agent is essential. While not considered emergency therapy, the combination of cyclophosphamide and prednisone may be of benefit in the treatment of drug-induced vasculitis and resulting stroke. Salanova[464] and Glick[323] reported on two cases of amphetamine- and phenylpropanolamine-induced vasculitis that had improvement documented angiographically with combination cyclophosphamide and prednisone. This combination therapy is also recommended for the treatment of other life-threatening vasculitides including polyarteritis nodosa (PAN) and Wegener's granulomatosis.[464]

Comment: Many reports of drug-induced vasculitis are based on angiographic findings of segmental narrowing and dilations of distal intracerebral arteries. Although such signs are characteristic of cerebral vasculitis, they are nonspecific features of vascular injury, and can also be caused by vasospasm (secondary to a drug's action or to subarachnoid hemorrhage), fibromuscular dysplasia, atherosclerosis, and cerebral emboli.[465] Biopsy is recommended to determine which patients should receive appropriate therapy.

Acute hypertension: Acute, severe hypertension from stimulants such as cocaine and amphetamines can increase vascular intraluminal pressures, cause turbulent blood flow, and weaken the endothelium, leading to hemorrhage and thrombosis. Severe hypertension should therefore be controlled (see Section 9.6 on hypertension). Moderate hypertension, however, may be a homeostatic response designed to maintain intracerebral blood flow in the presence of intracranial hypertension. In this case, blood pressure should not be lowered, or, if there is ongoing evidence of sympathomimetic drug intoxication, it should be lowered gradually to a diastolic blood pressure in the 100 to 110 mm Hg range. Clinical judgment should be used in this setting since decreasing blood flow to "watershed" areas or borderline ischemic zones with poor collateral circulation may lead to larger neurological deficits.[466–468]

9.8.2 Stepwise Approach to Management

9.8.2.1 Immediate Interventions

1. Airway, breathing, circulation: Maintain the airway and assist ventilation if necessary. Administer supplemental oxygen. Treat hypotension, and resuscitate as per previous reviews.[3,366] If the patient requires rapid sequence intubation consider using an agent such as pentobarbital, 5 mg/kg, or thiopental, 3 to 5 mg/kg, that will both lower intracranial pressure and decrease risk of seizures. Do not give barbiturates to a hypotensive patient. Lidocaine, 100 mg, prior to intubation is helpful in attenuating the rise in intracranial pressure seen with laryngoscopy.[469,470]

2. Antidotes: Administer appropriate antidotes, including 25 g dextrose IV if the patient is hypoglycemic, as per Section 9.1 on coma. Even focal findings may be caused by hypoglycemia; a focal neurologic finding occurs in about 2.5% of hypoglycemic patients.[471]

3. IV, monitor, O_2: Administer oxygen by nasal cannula at 4 L/min. Monitor cardiac status (obtain ECG) and start a peripheral intravenous line. Hang normal saline to keep vein open.

4. Herniation and increased intracranial pressure: Hyperventilation (to a pCO_2 of 30 to 35 mm Hg), mannitol (0.5 g/kg over 20 min IV), and possibly furosemide (10 mg IV) are indicated for evidence of *progressive* mass effect, shift, or herniation. Limit IV fluids to avoid cerebral edema.

5. Control agitation: An agitated patient with ongoing sympathomimetic effects of stimulants (delirium, psychosis, and agitation) should be sedated with benzodiazepines as discussed in Section 9.2. Straining, struggling, or arguing could elevate intracranial pressure and increase the risk of exacerbating a hemorrhagic stroke. Neuromuscular paralysis with endotracheal intubation and mechanical ventilation may be necessary.

6. Control seizure activity: Due to their ability to lower intracranial pressure barbiturates may be preferred for seizure control if the patient has evidence of increased intracranial pressure. Benzodiazepines are still recommended for the rapid initial management (Section 9.3, seizures).

7. Control nausea and vomiting: For the same reasons discussed above. Use something that will not lower the seizure threshold such as prochlorperizine. Instead, try metoclopramide 10 to 50 mg IVP.

8. Hypertension: Antihypertensive therapy is not usually necessary in the emergency department. Exceptions may be patients in whom acute ongoing drug intoxication is apparent. It should be kept in mind that the more severe the stroke, the greater the homeostatic, hypertensive response.

9. CT of the brain: Perform a CT of the brain without contrast on all the following patients:

a. Patients with focal neurological deficits
b. Patients with altered mental status that does not rapidly return to normal after a brief period of observation
c. Patients who complain of severe rapid onset of headache that persists after sedation, and minor pain medications

10. Laboratory data: Baseline laboratory data should include CBC, platelets, PT/PTT, electrolytes, and sedimentation rate. Perform CPK isoenzymes if the patient has chest pain, or is obtunded to rule out myocardial infarction. Draw blood cultures if endocarditis is suspected. While toxicology screens of blood and urine are generally overutilized,[5] they are recommended if diagnosis remains questionable.

9.8.2.2 Secondary Interventions

1. Monitor and reassess: Closely monitor neurological status for signs of deterioration.

2. ECG: Perform ECG to determine underlying cardiac rhythm.

3. Seizure prophylaxis: Phenobarbital 15 mg/kg IV over 20 min, as prophylaxis in hemorrhagic strokes. Fosphenytoin may be considered as an alternative although it is considered less effective for drug-related seizures.

4. Autonomic instability: Extreme fluctuations in blood pressure and heart rate are often the result of excessive autonomic discharge associated with hemorrhagic stroke and may, in severe cases, be treated with esmolol or labetalol (see hypertension).

5. Echocardiogram, blood cultures: Transthoracic echocardiography is a useful noninvasive diagnostic test for endocarditis, which is approximately 80% sensitive in finding vegetations on native and bioprosthetic valves.[472] Transesophogeal echocardiography (not usually available in the emergency department) is preferred for the detection of valvular vegetations due to increased sensitivity, especially if the patient has mechanical prosthetic valves that may produce artifact from the metallic components.[473] Obtain three blood cultures to increase sensitivity to greater than 95% in the febrile patient.[474]

6. Thrombolytics/heparin: Avoid thrombolytics and use heparin sparingly (e.g., only in those patients with evidence of cressendo transient ischemia in consultation with a neurologist, in patients who have had hemorrhagic stroke ruled out).

7. Angiogram: If the stroke is hemorrhagic or if the patient has evidence of endocarditis, consider performing a cerebral angiogram to rule out vasculitis/aneurysm.

8. Nimodipine: Nimodipine, 60 mg PO q 6 h should be considered in all patients with subarachnoid hemorrhage and others with evidence of recent drug abuse and stuttering onset or progression of symptoms suggestive of acute vasospasm.

9. Biopsy: Surgical biopsy should be performed when the diagnosis of *vasculitis* is suggested by angiogram and yet still remains in question. Alternatively, if the patient requires surgery for any other reason (i.e., intracerebral hematoma) a biopsy can be done at that time. Because there seems to be discernible histological differences between drug-induced and primary CNS vasculitis, leptomeningeal biopsy may be the definitive means of differentiating these two entities.[323]

10. Disposition: All patients with drug-induced stroke should be admitted to the hospital for thorough evaluation. Likewise all patients with drug-induced TIAs should be admitted to the hospital.

9.9 INGESTIONS AND DECONTAMINATION

9.9.1 General Comments

Ingestion vs. "packing" or "stuffing": Definitions of the terms ingestion, packing, and stuffing are required to understand the different approaches to decontamination that are recommended here. *Ingestions* occur when drugs of abuse are taken orally as a method of inducing a "high" or as a suicidal attempt. *Body packing* refers to the use of the human gastrointestinal (GI) tract for purposes of drug smuggling.[475–477] Smugglers or "mules" ingest a drug, usually cocaine or heroin, in carefully wrapped high-grade latex, aluminum foil, or condoms designed to prevent leakage. Case reports even describe the use of children who are forced to consume large numbers of drug-containing packets.[478] Each packet typically contains potentially lethal amounts of drug (a typical packet of cocaine contains 5 to 7 g; lethal dose = 1.0 to 1.2 g in a human). *Body stuffing* refers to the act of swallowing poorly wrapped "baggies," vials, or other packages filled with illegal drugs in an attempt to conceal them from the police. Baggies or vials may or may not contain lethal amounts of drug. A variant of body stuffing is the ingestion of drugs to produce an acute medical condition that could necessitate medical intervention, thereby deferring incarceration[479] (see Table 9.13).

Methods of decontamination:

> **Gastric lavage:** Gastric lavage has been a widely accepted medical treatment for ingested poisons.[480] Opposed to this practice are four large prospective, randomized, controlled studies in humans involving a total of 2476 patients, which have consistently failed to support the routine use of gut

Table 9.13   Comparison of Body Packers and Body Stuffers

	Body Packer	Body Stuffer
Profile	Returning from trip abroad; found in airports or at border crossings	Encountered on street or in drug raid, often arrested for dealing or other charge; may be chronic drug abuser or known drug dealer
How brought to attention	Deny drug ingestion; serious symptoms (seizure, respiratory arrest) or asymptomatic; diagnosis by radiograph or physical examination; likely to have a diagnostic radiograph or rectal examination	Seen taking drugs, or found symptomatic in jail; radiograph tends to be of little diagnostic help
Drugs involved	High-profit drug (e.g., cocaine or heroin)	Any drug sold on street, including hallucinogens or sedatives; often involves more than one drug
Packaging material	High-grade latex, aluminum foil, or condoms designed to prevent leakage Large amount of drugs per package	Loosely wrapped in paper or foil; single doses or free drug
Treatment	Usually observation; surgery for intestinal obstruction; value of charcoal or cathartic unknown; treat if symptoms develop	Gastric emptying and activated charcoal and cathartic; observe and treat symptomatically
Clinical course	Rupture of single package may be fatal because of the large amount of drug per package; specific toxic syndromes may be present, e.g., narcotic or cocaine toxicity	Variable symptoms, often from a mixed drug overdose; may have acute laryngeal obstruction

emptying. Kulig et al.[481] demonstrated that poisoned patients receiving charcoal alone without prior gut emptying had no significant difference in clinical outcome compared to patients who were treated with both gastric lavage and activated charcoal. The exception was a small subset ($n = 16$) of patients who were obtunded on presentation and were lavaged within 1 h of ingestion. Albertson et al.[482] compared the clinical effectiveness of syrup of ipecac and activated charcoal to that of activated charcoal alone in the treatment of 200 patients with mild to moderate toxic ingestions. Patients receiving only activated charcoal were discharged from the emergency department in significantly less time than those receiving both syrup of ipecac plus activated charcoal. Merigian et al.[483] evaluated 808 patients with ingestions and found no benefit from gastric emptying with administration of activated charcoal compared to activated charcoal alone. Moreover, gastric lavage was associated with a higher incidence of medical intensive care unit admissions and aspiration pneumonia in this study. Most recently, Pond et al.[484] performed a prospective, controlled study of 876 patients and concluded that gastric emptying is unnecessary in the treatment of acute overdose regardless of severity of intoxication and promptness of presentation.

Recommendation: Based on these studies, there is little support for routine use of gastric lavage in the drug abusing patient who presents to the emergency department after an ingestion. An exception may be the patient who has swallowed an extremely large quantity of drug and presents within 30 to 60 min.

Activated charcoal: Activated charcoal given orally has been proved to be as effective as gastric emptying followed by activated charcoal in the studies described above. In other studies involving volunteers, activated charcoal was shown to be superior to ipecac-induced emesis, or gastric lavage.[485,486] A dose of 50 to 100 g of activated charcoal is generally sufficient to bind the drug and prevent absorption, although this may vary depending on the drug and the amount that was taken. This 50 to 100 g dose was based on a study in which healthy volunteers were given up to 5 g of para-aminosalicylate (PAS).[487] The fraction of unadsorbed PAS decreased from 55 to 3% as the charcoal-to-PAS ratio increased from 1:1 to 10:1. Activated charcoal is relatively safe, although vomiting and diarrhea are seen commonly when cathartics such as sorbitol are added, and constipation can result if cathartics are withheld. Serious adverse effects include pulmonary aspiration of activated charcoal along with gastric contents;[488–490] significant morbidity from spillage of activated charcoal in the peritoneum after perforation from gastric lavage;[491] and intestinal obstruction and pseudo-obstruction,[492–494] especially following repeated doses of activated charcoal in the presence of dehydration.

Recommendation: Activated charcoal is recommended in all cases of orally administered drug intoxication except if the drug is not bound by charcoal (e.g., lithium, iron, alcohols).

Multiple-dose activated charcoal: Multiple-dose activated charcoal (MDAC), sometimes referred to as "gastrointestinal dialysis," is thought to produce its beneficial effect by interrupting the enteroenteric and in some cases, the enterohepatic re-circulation of drugs.[495] In addition, any remaining unabsorbed drug may be adsorbed to the repeated doses of activated charcoal. Phenobarbital is the only drug of abuse for which there is evidence from both clinical and experimental studies in animals and volunteers that drug elimination is increased by the use of MDAC.[495] Pharmacokinetic data would also support the use of MDAC for carbamazepine, theophylline, aspirin, dapsone, and quinine ingestions.[495] Pond et al.[496] performed a controlled trial of ten comatose patients who overdosed on phenobarbital. In this study, the control and treatment groups both received 50 g activated charcoal on presentation and, in addition, patients in the treatment group were given 17 g activated charcoal together with sorbitol every 4 h until they could be extubated. Although the mean elimination half-life of phenobarbital was shortened (36 ± 13 h vs. 93 ± 52 h), the length of time the patients in each group required mechanical ventilation or stayed in the hospital did not differ significantly. This study suggested that acute tolerance to the effects of the drug obviated the benefit of faster drug elimination. Another study looking at a series of six patients given charcoal in larger doses and without cathartic showed enhanced elimination of phenobarbital, and also decreased time to recovery.[497] Beware of inducing aspiration with MDAC. Other adverse effects including obstipation and appendicitis have been described with MDAC.[498]

Recommendation: MDAC is recommended in cases in which there may be large quantities of drug in the intestinal tract (i.e., body packers or body stuffers) and in selected cases of phenobarbital overdose (i.e., comatose patients who have not received hemoperfusion).

Whole bowel irrigation: Whole bowel irrigation (WBI) involves the administration of large volumes (2 L/h in an adult, 0.5 L/h in a child) of polyethylene glycol electrolyte lavage solution (PEG-ELS) per nasogastric tube to flush out the gastrointestinal tract and decrease the time available for drug to be absorbed. It has been used effectively in the management of iron,[499–501] sustained-release theophylline,[502] sustained-release verapamil,[503,504] sustained-release fenfluramine,[505] zinc sulfate,[504] and lead,[506] and for body packers.[475,507] Because of its balanced electrolyte content and iso-osmolor nature, PEG-ELS use results in minimal net water and electrolyte shifts, and is safe and effective under the right circumstances. In the case of body packers, the excellent bowel cleansing from WBI may reduce morbidity should bowel perforation occur or surgery be required.[475] In a case described by Utecht et al.[507] 10-g packets of heroin wrapped in electrician's tape appeared to be dissolved by 8 L of PEG-ELS solution. Endoscopy showed this patient to have only electrician's tape left in his stomach after WBI, suggesting the heroin initially present had been dissolved by the WBI solution. Polyethylene glycols are used extensively in pharmaceutical manufacturing as solubilizing agents and it has been shown that PEG 4000, a water-soluble polymer comparable to the polymer used in PEG-ELS, can increase the dissolution rates of poorly water-soluble drugs.[508] Alkaloidal heroin is poorly water soluble; 1 g dissolves in 1700 ml of water.[509] Therefore, the large amount of heroin, 10 g in each package, would not have been solubilized in the stomach by water alone. The patient had continuing absorption of heroin despite the administration of multiple doses of activated charcoal. Rosenberg[510] has shown that the antidotal efficacy of oral activated charcoal was markedly diminished by PEG-ELS in volunteers treated with aspirin. Tenenbein[511] likewise reported that PEG-ELS binds to charcoal and that this interferes with aspirin adsorption by activated charcoal.

Recommendation: WBI is recommended in cases involving body packers. WBI is also recommended in situations in which large amounts of drug may still be present in the gastrointestinal tract due to concretions (common with gluthethimide, and meprobamate) or when a sustained-release preparation (i.e., sustained release morphine) has been ingested. Because WBI may solubilize heroin and may diminish the efficacy of activated charcoal the use of activated charcoal and cathartics is preferred over WBI for treatment of heroin body packers.

9.9.2 Stepwise Approach to Management

9.9.2.1 Immediate Interventions

1. Airway, breathing, circulation: Maintain the airway and assist ventilation if necessary. Administer supplemental oxygen. Treat hypotension, and resuscitate as per previous reviews.[3,90]

2. IV, monitor, O_2: Administer oxygen by nasal cannula at 4 L/min, monitor cardiac status (obtain ECG), and start a peripheral intravenous line. Hang normal saline to keep vein open.

3. Gastric lavage: Not recommended unless patient has ingested massive quantities and arrives within 30 min to 1 h of ingestion.

4. Activated charcoal: Administer activated charcoal 50 to 100 g PO. Try to obtain a 10:1 ratio of activated charcoal to drug by weight if possible. If unable to administer enough activated charcoal on the first dose repeat the dose in 4 h. Multiple-dose activated charcoal: give 12.5 g/h or 25 g every 3 to 4 h. Studies have shown that the administration of hourly activated charcoal produces a shorter half-life than less frequent dosing, even though the same dose was administered over the same treatment period.[512,513]

Comment: Administer MDAC for (1) the rare phenobarbital overdoses (as discussed above), (2) for the body packer or body stuffer (see below), and (3) for the patient suspected of taking a sustained release preparation. If the patient has difficulty tolerating activated charcoal because of drug-induced vomiting, smaller doses of activated charcoal administered more frequently may reduce the likelihood of vomiting. It may, however, be necessary to give either IV metoclopramide (10 to 50 mg IVP) or ondansetron (4 to 8 mg IVP) to ensure satisfactory administration of charcoal.[495]

5. Guard against aspiration: Do not force patients who are nauseated to take activated charcoal. If nausea exists, treat with metoclopramide as above. Patients who do not have a gag reflex should have their airways protected with endotracheal intubation (although this does not guarantee protection) and elevation of the head of the bed to 45°.

6. Laboratory data: Baseline laboratory data should be guided by clinical presentation. If the patient is asymptomatic no laboratory is immediately essential. Perform a CBC, and electrolytes with CPK isoenzymes if the patient is obtunded or has chest pain, to rule out occult metabolic/infectious disease and/or myocardial infarction. While toxicology screens of blood and urine are generally overutilized,[5] they are recommended if diagnosis remains questionable.

Comment: The use of urine toxicology screening may be particularly misleading in the case of a body packer or stuffer and should not be used to determine if the patient ingested any drugs. Recreational use of the drug prior to "stuffing" could lead to a false positive test. On the other hand, no prior drug usage without rupture of packets could lead to a false negative test. In one study of 50 body packers 64% had positive urine toxicology screens for drugs of abuse.[514]

9.9.2.2 Secondary Interventions

1. The body stuffer: Some authors recommend that the asymptomatic body packer or stuffer should be observed for a period of at least 48 to 72 h and treated with repeated dose-activated charcoal and cathartics.[479] This approach may be better suited to the treatment of body packers who have a lethal amount of drug in their intestinal tract. In the asymptomatic body stuffer the administration of activated charcoal and observation seems more appropriate but has not been carefully studied. In a series of more than 100 cocaine body packers, those who went on to develop serious complications became symptomatic within 6 h.[515] A recommended treatment approach follows:

    a. **Activated charcoal:** Give activated charcoal, 1 g/kg.
    b. **Observation:** If asymptomatic, observe for 6 h and repeat activated charcoal.
    c. **Discharge:** At this time it is felt that there is too little evidence to guide a well-supported recommendation for the release of these patients from the hospital. Clinical judgment should be used based on the type and the amount of drug ingested. Some recommend discharge after an observation period of greater than 6 h if the patient is asymptomatic.
    d. **WBI:** If symptomatic and large amount of drug has been ingested or sustained-release preparations are involved, consider whole bowel irrigation with 2 L/h of polyethylene glycol (PEG) after the first dose of activated charcoal.

2. The body packer: Treatment is as per the body stuffer and it is wise to admit these patients until all packets are passed and accounted for.

    a. **X-rays:** A plain upright abdominal film can detect a large percentage of packets (e.g., false negative rate of 17 to 19% in two series[516,517]) and is recommended to determine location and amount of drug ingested. However, a negative x-ray does not rule out body packing.
    b. **WBI:** The use of electrolyte bowel preparation solutions such as polyethylene glycol (e.g., GO-LYTELY) has aided foreign body passage[475,518] and is recommended in all cases except those involving heroin. Give 2 L/h for adults and 500 cc/h for children.
    c. **Cathartic:** An alternative to whole bowel irrigation is a cathartic, such as 3% sodium sulfate solution (250 to 500 ml), given orally with the activated charcoal. Cathartics such as sodium sulfate do not eliminate packets as rapidly as WBI. This may allow more time for the packets to dissolve. Conversely, a gentler approach with less risk of damage to the packets is provided. Use of cathartics without WBI is recommended in uncooperative patients (unless a court order is obtained), those who body-pack heroin (due to the reported possibility of increasing solubility of heroin in polyethylene glycol[507]), and in those known to have packets that are weakly wrapped (due to theoretical concerns about breaking open packets with vigorous irrigation and increased peristalsis[507]). Further studies are needed to validate these recommendations.

    d. Enemas: If foreign bodies are located in the colon, low-volume phosphasoda enemas or high-volume normal saline enemas may be helpful.[507]

    e. Suppository: One Dulcolax suppository per rectum to empty the rectum.

    f. Gastrointestinal series: Following the passage of the "last" packet, a Gastrograffin upper gastrointestinal series with small bowel follow-through may be performed to ensure that the gut has been purged of all containers.[519]

    g. Surgery: In the presence of a leaking or a ruptured package, decisions about surgical removal should be made on an individual basis; laparotomy is indicated if this is an intestinal obstruction.

Comment: Because of risk of packet rupture avoid attempts to remove packages via gastroscopy or colonoscopy.[519] Syrup of ipecac or gastric lavage are ineffective due to the large size of the packets, and may cause packages to break.

3. Disposition: Patients may be discharged from the emergency department if they meet the following criteria:

    a. Normal vital signs
    b. Normal physical exam, including the presence of bowel sounds
    c. Normal or near normal laboratory data
    d. Ingestion known to be nontoxic
    e. Psychiatric referral
    f. Stable family environment

Comment: As noted previously more studies are needed to support any recommendations for the safe discharge of body stuffers.

9.10 MANAGEMENT OF SPECIFIC DRUGS OF ABUSE

9.10.1 Psychostimulants

Drug	Unique Characteristics	Key Management Issues
Cocaine	Stimulant associated with more serious complications than any other; affects all organ systems; no longer confined to affluent sectors of society	Adrenergic crisis, hyperthermia, hypertension, cardiac ischemia and arrhythmias, seizures, stroke, panic attacks, psychosis, rhabdomyolysis
Amphetamines and methamphetamine	Frequently associated with paranoid psychosis after chronic abuse Lead poisoning has been described (lead is used as a reagent in illicit laboratories)	Same as cocaine with lower incidence of cardiac ischemia, stroke
MDMA, MDEA/MDA ("Ecstasy")	Designer amphetamine widely used at dance parties or "raves"; affects serotonin more than other amphetamines, leading to hallucinations; possibly linked to the serotonin syndrome	Same as cocaine with lower incidence of cardiac ischemia, stroke; severe hyperthermia in dehydrated dancers has led to death Rehydrate and control hyperthermia
Methcathinone ("CAT")	Designer amphetamine with intoxicating effects that may last up to 6 days; more common in former Soviet Union	Same as amphetamines
Pemoline/methyl-phenidate	Principal therapeutic use is in children and adults with attention-deficit disorder; commonly associated with abnormal involuntary movements	Same as amphetamines

Continued.

Drug	Unique Characteristics	Key Management Issues
DOB	Strong hallucinogenic effects that are long-lasting (up to 10 h); may have an ergot-like effect	Same as amphetamines; severe hypertension, or evidence of ischemia (digital, mesenteric) should be treated with phentolamine and anticoagulation
TMA-2, DOM/STP	Designer amphetamines with less sympathetic stimulation in usual doses; prominent hallucinogenic effects	Adequate treatment is usually possible by calming hallucinations with benzodiazepines and removal to a quiet setting
Ephedrine	Recently removed from over-the-counter sale; amphetamine-like substance less potent than amphetamines	Same as amphetamines
Phenylpropanol-amine	Primarily a β-adrenergic agonist, as a result hypertension with reflex bradycardia is common, also associated with cerebral hemorrhage	May treat hypertension with a β-blocker such as phentolamine; do not treat bradycardia with atropine since this will exacerbate hypertension
Mescaline	Phenylethylamine derivative found in peyote cactus, associated with strong hallucinogenic properties due to effects on the serotonergic system	Adequate treatment is usually possible by calming hallucinations with benzodiazepines and removal to a quiet setting
PCP, PHP, and derivatives	Associated with erratic, violent behavior; intoxicated patients prone to sustaining significant injuries due to dissociative, anesthetic properties	As with other psychostimulants with greater emphasis on controlling behavioral toxicity since this is the major cause of death

Abbreviations: MDMA-3,4-methylenedioxymethamphetamine; MDEA-3,4 methylenedioxy-N-ethylamphetamine; MDA-3,4-methylenedioxyamphetamine; DOB-4-bromo-2,5-dimethoxyamphetamine; TMP-2-2,4,5-trimethoxyam-phetamine; DOM/STP-4-methyl-2,5-dimethoxyamphetamine; PCP-phencyclidine; PHP-phenylcyclohexlpyrrolidine.

Contraindications: Nonselective beta-blockers should not be administered to patients with chest pain if a psychostimulant has been ingested although cardioselective beta-blockers may be used for certain tachyarrhythmias. Acidification of urine may slightly hasten the elimination of PCP and amphetamines but it is not recommended due to an increased risk of myoglobinuric renal failure.

9.10.2 Opiates

Drug	Unique Characteristics	Key Management Issues
Diacetylmorphine (heroin)	Prototype opiate of abuse, rapidly metabolized to morphine, more lipid soluble	Respiratory depression, coma, anoxic encephalopathy, pulmonary edema, withdrawal, compartment syndromes
Methadone (Dolophine)	Slow onset and long duration of action (half-life 15–72 h)	As with heroin; may require a naloxone infusion (see below) and prolonged monitoring
Designer Opiates: Fentanyl (Sublimaze), Sufentanil (Sufenta), Alfentanil (Alfenta)	Most potent opiates (16–700× morphine), with rapid onset and short duration of action (minutes)	As with heroin. May accumulate in body fat necessitating observation periods similar to heroin overdose (12 h); may see negative screen for opiates
Propoxyphene (Darvon)	High mortality, sudden death reported, convulsions and cardiac arrhythmias due to metabolite (norpropoxyphene), fat soluble so may have prolonged duration of action	As with heroin. Prolonged observation required after overdose (see Table 9.1). Wide complex tachycardia may respond to bicarbonate, may be resistant to naloxone, check acetaminophen level

Continued.

Drug	Unique Characteristics	Key Management Issues
Pentazocine (Talwin)	Agonist-antagonist, dysphoria, no cases of pulmonary edema reported	As with heroin May be resistant to naloxone
Dextromethorphan/ codeine	Less respiratory depression, possible serotonin-releasing effects	As with heroin Usually less serious in overdose than other opiates, check acetaminophen level if codeine ingested
Meperidine (Demerol)	Synthetic opiate associated with seizures in large doses due to metabolite (normeperidine)	As with heroin
Hydromorphone (Dilaudid)	Similar to morphine but more potent and shorter duration of action	As with heroin
Morphine (MS-contin)	Sustained-release, oral chewing converts to rapidly acting agents	As with heroin Prolonged observation required after overdose (see Table 9.1)

Contraindications: Administration of high dose (>2.0 mg) naloxone in any patient at risk for opiate withdrawal.

Naloxone infusion: Take two-thirds the amount of naloxone required for the patient to initially wake up and give that amount at an hourly rate. Mix the naloxone in the patient's maintenance IV (D5W, D51/2NS, 1/2NS, NS, etc.). Infusions should be maintained in an intensive care setting. Patients should be closely watched any time the infusion is stopped. Duration of observation depends on the route of drug administration, the drug ingested, the presence or absence of liver dysfunction, and the possibility of ongoing drug absorption from the gastrointestinal tract. Usually 6 h is adequate.

9.10.3 Sedative–Hypnotic Agents

Drug	Unique Characteristics	Key Management Issues
Benzodiazepines	High therapeutic index makes death unlikely unless coingestions involved; memory impairment common	Respiratory depression, coma, compartment syndromes; severe withdrawal; use flumazenil in selected cases only; supportive care usually all that is required
GHB	Common at "raves," associated with profound coma that rapidly resolves within 2 h, increased muscle tone with jerking	Supportive care, rarely requires endotracheal intubation, guard against aspiration
Long-lasting barbiturates (i.e., phenobarbital); duration of action = 10–12 h	Phenobarbital ($t_{1/2}$ = 24–140 h) may induce prolonged deep coma (5–7 days) mimicking death; pneumonia is a common complication due to prolonged coma; hypothermia	As with benzodiazepines, although cardiac depression and hypotension are more common and may necessitate cardiac support; alkalinization of urine may increase elimination; MDAC in selected cases (see discussion); hemoperfusion in selected cases
Other barbiturates: Intermediate acting (i.e., amobarbital) Short acting (i.e., secobarbital) Ultrashort acting (i.e., thiopental)	Commonly abused barbiturates; chronic drowsiness, psychomotor retardation; hypothermia	As above, although alkalinization, MDAC not helpful; hemoperfusion in selected cases; major withdrawal may necessitate hospitalization
Ethchlorvynol (Placidyl)	Pungent odor sometimes described as pearlike, gastric fluid often has a pink or green color, noncardiac pulmonary edema	See barbiturates

Continued.

Drug	Unique Characteristics	Key Management Issues
Glutethimide (Doriden)	Prominent anticholinergic side effects including mydriasis Prolonged cyclic or fluctuating coma (average 36–38 h); often mixed with codeine as a heroin substitute	See barbiturates
Meprobamate (Miltown)	Forms concretions, hypotension is more common than with other sedative-hypnotics, prolonged coma (average 38–40 h)	If concretions suspected, WBI or gastroscopic or surgical removal of drug may be necessary; hemoperfusion useful in severe cases
Methqualone (Quaalude)	Muscular hypertonicity, clonus, and hyperpyrexia, popular as an "aphrodisiac" or "cocaine downer"; no longer manufactured in the U.S.	Charcoal hemoperfusion increases clearance and may be useful in severe cases; diazepam may be necessary to treat severe muscular hypertonicity or "seizures"
Chloral hydrate	Metabolized to trichloroethanol which may sensitize the myocardium to the effects of catecholamines, resulting in cardiac arrhythmias	Tachyarrhythmias may respond to propranolol, 1–2 mg IV, or esmolol; flumazenil has been reported to produce dramatic reversal of coma in one case; amenable to hemodialysis

Note: Catecholamines (especially dopamine and epinephrine) are relatively contraindicated in cases of chloral hydrate-induced tachyarrhythmias.

Abbreviations: GHB, gammahydroxybuterate; MDAC, multiple-dose activated charcoal; WBI, whole bowel irrigation.

9.10.4 Hallucinogens

Drug	Unique Characteristics	Key Management Issues
LSD	Potent agent associated with panic attacks, acute psychotic reaction, and flashbacks in chronic users; vital signs are usually relatively normal; hallucinations for 1–8 h	Patients usually respond to benzodiazepines and seclusion in a quiet environment; toxicology screen negative; in extremely agitated patients watch for hyperthermia, rhabdomyolysis
Marijuana	Commonly used, associated with conjunctival injection, stimulation of appetite, orthostatic hypotension, and mild tachycardia; duration of effect: 3 h	Usually respond to simple reassurance and possible adjunctive benzodiazepine
Ketamine	Dissociative anesthetic with hallucinations characterized by profound analgesia, amnesia, and catalepsy Increasingly common as drug of abuse; duration of effect: 1–3 hours	Provide supportive care until drug effects wear off; cardiovascular parameters are usually well preserved
Atropine, hycosyamine, scopolamine (*Datura stramonium* or Jimson weed)	Anticholinergic syndrome with true delirium, symptoms may continue for 24–48 h because of delayed GI motility	Usually supportive care only, consider activated charcoal; physostigmine for uncontrolled agitation, hyperthermia
Solvents	Products of petroleum distillation abused by spraying them into a plastic bag or soaking a cloth and then deeply inhaling; cardiac sensitization may result in malignant arrhythmias, low viscosity agents (i.e., gasoline) are associated with aspiration); chronic exposure associated with hepatitis and renal failure	Usually hallucinogenic effects are short lived; removing the patient from the offending agent and providing fresh air are all that is necessary; treat aspiration by supporting airway; arrhythmias may respond to beta-blockers, epinephrine may worsen arrhythmias

Continued.

Drug	Unique Characteristics	Key Management Issues
Psilocybin	From the Stropharia and Conocybe mushrooms; suppresses serotonergic neurons, less potent than LSD with hallucinations that last from 2–8 h, patients may exhibit destructive behavior; hallucinations for 1–6 h	As with LSD

Note: Epinephrine is contraindicated in cases of solvent-induced tachyarrhythmias.

Abbreviations: LSD, lysergic acid diethylamide, GI, gastrointestinal.

REFERENCES

1. Barnes, T.A., et al., Cardiopulmonary resuscitation and emergency cardiovascular care. Airway devices. *Ann Emerg Med*, 2001. 37(4 Suppl): p. S145–51.
2. Blanda, M. and U.E. Gallo, Emergency airway management. *Emerg Med Clin North Am*, 2003. 21(1): p. 1–26.
3. Kern, K.B., H.R. Halperin, and J. Field, New guidelines for cardiopulmonary resuscitation and emergency cardiac care: changes in the management of cardiac arrest. *JAMA*, 2001. 285(10): p. 1267–9.
4. Krenzelok, E.P. and J.B. Leikin, Approach to the poisoned patient. *Dis Mon*, 1996. 42(9): p. 509–607.
5. Olson, K.R., P.R. Pentel, and M.T. Kelley, Physical assessment and differential diagnosis of the poisoned patient. *Med Toxicol*, 1987. 2(1): p. 52–81.
6. Proudfoot, A., Practical management of the poisoned patient. *Ther Drug Monit*, 1998. 20(5): p. 498–501.
7. Riordan, M., G. Rylance, and K. Berry, Poisoning in children 1: general management. *Arch Dis Child*, 2002. 87(5): p. 392–6.
8. Mokhlesi, B., et al., Adult toxicology in critical care: part I: general approach to the intoxicated patient. *Chest*, 2003. 123(2): p. 577–92.
9. Peterson, J., Coma, in *Emergency Medicine, Concepts and Clinical Practice*, P. Rosen and R.M. Barkin, Eds. 1992, Mosby Year Book: St Louis. p. 1728–1751.
10. Guido, M.E., W. Brady, and D. DeBehnke, Reversible neurological deficits in a chronic alcohol abuser: a case report of Wernicke's encephalopathy. *Am J Emerg Med*, 1994. 12(2): p. 238–40.
11. Wrenn, K.D., F. Murphy, and C.M. Slovis, A toxicity study of parenteral thiamine hydrochloride. *Ann Emerg Med*, 1989. 18(8): p. 867–70.
12. Centerwall, B.S. and M.H. Criqui, Prevention of the Wernicke–Korsakoff syndrome: a cost-benefit analysis. *N Engl J Med*, 1978. 299(6): p. 285–9.
13. Kagansky, N., S. Levy, and H. Knobler, The role of hyperglycemia in acute stroke. *Arch Neurol*, 2001. 58(8): p. 1209–12.
14. Parsons, M.W., et al., Acute hyperglycemia adversely affects stroke outcome: a magnetic resonance imaging and spectroscopy study. *Ann Neurol*, 2002. 52(1): p. 20–8.
15. Lindsberg, P.J. and R.O. Roine, Hyperglycemia in acute stroke. *Stroke*, 2004. 35(2): p. 363–4.
16. Dietrich, W.D., O. Alonso, and R. Busto, Moderate hyperglycemia worsens acute blood–brain barrier injury after forebrain ischemia in rats. *Stroke*, 1993. 24(1): p. 111–6.
17. Hoffman, R.S. and L.R. Goldfrank, The poisoned patient with altered consciousness. Controversies in the use of a "coma cocktail." *JAMA*, 1995. 274(7): p. 562–9.
18. Fowkes, J. Opiates in the Emergency Department, in *Toxicology and Infectious Disease in Emergency Medicine*. 1992. Academic Press, San Diego, CA.
19. Osterwalder, J.J., Naloxone — for intoxications with intravenous heroin and heroin mixtures — harmless or hazardous? A prospective clinical study. *J Toxicol Clin Toxicol*, 1996. 34(4): p. 409–16.
20. Meissner, W. and K. Ullrich, Re: naloxone, constipation and analgesia. *J Pain Symptom Manage*, 2002. 24(3): p. 276–7; author reply 277–9.
21. Dole, V.P., et al., Arousal of ethanol-intoxicated comatose patients with naloxone. *Alcohol Clin Exp Res*, 1982. 6(2): p. 275–9.

22. Wedin, G.P. and L.J. Edwards, Clonidine poisoning treated with naloxone [letter]. *Am J Emerg Med*, 1989. 7(3): p. 343–4.

23. Alberto, G., et al., Central nervous system manifestations of a valproic acid overdose responsive to naloxone. *Ann Emerg Med*, 1989. 18(8): p. 889–91.

24. Varon, J. and S.R. Duncan, Naloxone reversal of hypotension due to captopril overdose. *Ann Emerg Med*, 1991. 20(10): p. 1125–7.

25. Harrington, L.W., Acute pulmonary edema following use of naloxone: a case study. *Crit Care Nurse*, 1988. 8(8): p. 69–73.

26. Schwartz, J.A. and M.D. Koenigsberg, Naloxone-induced pulmonary edema. *Ann Emerg Med*, 1987. 16(11): p. 1294–6.

27. Partridge, B.L. and C.F. Ward, Pulmonary edema following low-dose naloxone administration [letter]. *Anesthesiology*, 1986. 65(6): p. 709–10.

28. Prough, D.S., et al., Acute pulmonary edema in healthy teenagers following conservative doses of intravenous naloxone. *Anesthesiology*, 1984. 60(5): p. 485–6.

29. Taff, R.H., Pulmonary edema following naloxone administration in a patient without heart disease. *Anesthesiology*, 1983. 59(6): p. 576–7.

30. Flacke, J.W., W.E. Flacke, and G.D. Williams, Acute pulmonary edema following naloxone reversal of high-dose morphine anesthesia. *Anesthesiology*, 1977. 47(4): p. 376–8.

31. Wasserberger, J. and G.J. Ordog, Naloxone-induced hypertension in patients on clonidine [letter]. *Ann Emerg Med*, 1988. 17(5): p. 557.

32. Levin, E.R., et al., Severe hypertension induced by naloxone. *Am J Med Sci*, 1985. 290(2): p. 70–2.

33. Azar, I. and H. Turndorf, Severe hypertension and multiple atrial premature contractions following naloxone administration. *Anesth Analg*, 1979. 58(6): p. 524–5.

34. Mariani, P.J., Seizure associated with low-dose naloxone. *Am J Emerg Med*, 1989. 7(1): p. 127–9.

35. Michaelis, L.L., et al., Ventricular irritability associated with the use of naloxone hydrochloride. Two case reports and laboratory assessment of the effect of the drug on cardiac excitability. *Ann Thorac Surg*, 1974. 18(6): p. 608–14.

36. Cuss, F.M., C.B. Colaco, and J.H. Baron, Cardiac arrest after reversal of effects of opiates with naloxone. *Br Med J* (Clin Res Ed), 1984. 288(6414): p. 363–4.

37. Lubman, D., Z. Koutsogiannis, and I. Kronborg, Emergency management of inadvertent accelerated opiate withdrawal in dependent opiate users. *Drug Alcohol Rev*, 2003. 22(4): p. 433–6.

38. Gaddis, G.M. and W.A. Watson, Naloxone-associated patient violence: an overlooked toxicity? *Ann Pharmacother*, 1992. 26(2): p. 196–8.

39. Rock, P., et al., Efficacy and safety of naloxone in septic shock. *Crit Care Med*, 1985. 13(1): p. 28–33.

40. Groeger, J.S., G.C. Carlon, and W.S. Howland, Naloxone in septic shock. *Crit Care Med*, 1983. 11(8): p. 650–4.

41. Gurll, N.J., et al., Naloxone without transfusion prolongs survival and enhances cardiovascular function in hypovolemic shock. *J Pharmacol Exp Ther*, 1982. 220(3): p. 621–4.

42. Groeger, J.S. and C.E. Inturrisi, High-dose naloxone: pharmacokinetics in patients in septic shock. *Crit Care Med*, 1987. 15(8): p. 751–6.

43. Olinger, C.P., et al., High-dose intravenous naloxone for the treatment of acute ischemic stroke. *Stroke*, 1990. 21(5): p. 721–5.

44. Baskin, D.S., C.F. Kieck, and Y. Hosobuchi, Naloxone reversal and morphine exacerbation of neurologic deficits secondary to focal cerebral ischemia in baboons. *Brain Res*, 1984. 290(2): p. 289–96.

45. Baskin, D.S. and Y. Hosobuchi, Naloxone and focal cerebral ischemia [letter]. *J Neurosurg*, 1984. 60(6): p. 1328–31.

46. Baskin, D.S. and Y. Hosobuchi, Naloxone reversal of ischaemic neurological deficits in man. *Lancet*, 1981. 2(8241): p. 272–5.

47. Flamm, E.S., et al., A phase I trial of naloxone treatment in acute spinal cord injury. *J Neurosurg*, 1985. 63(3): p. 390–7.

48. Young, W., et al., Pharmacological therapy of acute spinal cord injury: studies of high dose methylprednisolone and naloxone. *Clin Neurosurg*, 1988. 34: p. 675–97.

49. Bracken, M.B., et al., A randomized, controlled trial of methylprednisolone or naloxone in the treatment of acute spinal-cord injury. Results of the Second National Acute Spinal Cord Injury Study [see comments]. *N Engl J Med*, 1990. 322(20): p. 1405–11.

50. Cohen, M.R., et al., High-dose naloxone infusions in normals. Dose-dependent behavioral, hormonal, and physiological responses. *Arch Gen Psychiatry*, 1983. 40(6): p. 613–9.
51. Cohen, R.M., et al., High-dose naloxone affects task performance in normal subjects. *Psychiatry Res*, 1983. 8(2): p. 127–36.
52. Gerra, G., et al., Clonidine and opiate receptor antagonists in the treatment of heroin addiction. *J Subst Abuse Treat*, 1995. 12(1): p. 35–41.
53. Stine, S.M. and T.R. Kosten, Use of drug combinations in treatment of opioid withdrawal. *J Clin Psychopharmacol*, 1992. 12(3): p. 203–9.
54. Creighton, F.J. and A.H. Ghodse, Naloxone applied to conjunctiva as a test for physical opiate dependence. *Lancet*, 1989. 1(8641): p. 748–50.
55. Loimer, N., P. Hofmann, and H.R. Chaudhry, Nasal administration of naloxone for detection of opiate dependence. *J Psychiatr Res*, 1992. 26(1): p. 39–43.
56. Kelly, A.M. and Z. Koutsogiannis, Intranasal naloxone for life threatening opioid toxicity. *Emerg Med J*, 2002. 19(4): p. 375.
57. Wilhelm, J.A., et al., Duration of opioid antagonism by nalmefene and naloxone in the dog. A nonparametric pharmacodynamic comparison based on generalized cross-validated spline estimation. *Int J Clin Pharmacol Ther*, 1995. 33(10): p. 540–5.
58. Barsan, W.G., et al., Duration of antagonistic effects of nalmefene and naloxone in opiate-induced sedation for emergency department procedures. *Am J Emerg Med*, 1989. 7(2): p. 155–61.
59. Kaplan, J.L. and J.A. Marx, Effectiveness and safety of intravenous nalmefene for emergency department patients with suspected narcotic overdose: a pilot study. *Ann Emerg Med*, 1993. 22(2): p. 187–90.
60. Ellenhorn, M., *Ellenhorn's Medical Toxicology.* 2nd ed., M. Ellenhorn, Ed. 1997, New York: Elsevier Science Publishing Company. p. 437–8.
61. Chumpa, A., et al., Nalmefene for elective reversal of procedural sedation in children. *Am J Emerg Med*, 2001. 19(7): p. 545–8.
62. Nalmefene for alcohol dependence. *Harv Ment Health Lett*, 2000. 16(9): p. 7.
63. Rosen, D.A., et al., Nalmefene to prevent epidural narcotic side effects in pediatric patients: a pharmacokinetic and safety study. *Pharmacotherapy*, 2000. 20(7): p. 745–9.
64. Kearney, T., Flumazenil, in *Poisoning and Drug Overdose*, Olson, K.R., Ed. 1994, Appleton & Lange: Englewood Cliffs, NJ. p. 340–1.
65. Dunton, A.W., et al., Flumazenil: U.S. clinical pharmacology studies. *Eur J Anaesthesiol Suppl*, 1988. 2: p. 81–95.
66. Jensen, S., L. Knudsen, and L. Kirkegaard, Flumazenil used in the antagonizing of diazepam and midazolam sedation in out-patients undergoing gastroscopy. *Eur J Anaesthesiol Suppl*, 1988. 2: p. 161–6.
67. Kirkegaard, L., et al., Benzodiazepine antagonist Ro 15-1788. Antagonism of diazepam sedation in outpatients undergoing gastroscopy. *Anaesthesia*, 1986. 41(12): p. 1184–8.
68. Sewing, K.F., The value of flumazenil in the reversal of midazolam-induced sedation for upper gastrointestinal endoscopy [letter; comment]. *Aliment Pharmacol Ther*, 1990. 4(3): p. 315.
69. Bartelsman, J.F., P.R. Sars, and G.N. Tytgat, Flumazenil used for reversal of midazolam-induced sedation in endoscopy outpatients. *Gastrointest Endosc*, 1990. 36(3 Suppl): p. S9–12.
70. Davies, C.A., et al., Reversal of midazolam sedation with flumazenil following conservative dentistry. *J Dent*, 1990. 18(2): p. 113–8.
71. Chern, T.L., et al., Diagnostic and therapeutic utility of flumazenil in comatose patients with drug overdose. *Am J Emerg Med*, 1993. 11(2): p. 122–4.
72. Weinbroum, A., P. Halpern, and E. Geller, The use of flumazenil in the management of acute drug poisoning — a review. *Intensive Care Med*, 1991. 17 (Suppl 1): p. S32–8.
73. Weinbroum, A., et al., Use of flumazenil in the treatment of drug overdose: a double-blind and open clinical study in 110 patients. *Crit Care Med*, 1996. 24(2): p. 199–206.
74. Thomas, P., C. Lebrun, and M. Chatel, De novo absence status epilepticus as a benzodiazepine withdrawal syndrome. *Epilepsia*, 1993. 34(2): p. 355–8.
75. Spivey, W.H., Flumazenil and seizures: analysis of 43 cases. *Clin Ther*, 1992. 14(2): p. 292–305.
76. Chern, T.L. and A. Kwan, Flumazenil-induced seizure accompanying benzodiazepine and baclofen intoxication [letter]. *Am J Emerg Med*, 1996. 14(2): p. 231–2.

77. McDuffee, A.T. and J.D. Tobias, Seizure after flumazenil administration in a pediatric patient. *Pediatr Emerg Care*, 1995. 11(3): p. 186–7.

78. Mordel, A., et al., Seizures after flumazenil administration in a case of combined benzodiazepine and tricyclic antidepressant overdose. *Crit Care Med*, 1992. 20(12): p. 1733–4.

79. Kim, J.S., et al., Flumazenil-induced ballism. *J Korean Med Sci*, 2003. 18(2): p. 299–300.

80. Lheureux, P., et al., Risks of flumazenil in mixed benzodiazepine-tricyclic antidepressant overdose: report of a preliminary study in the dog. *J Toxicol Clin Exp*, 1992. 12(1): p. 43–53.

81. Treatment of benzodiazepine overdose with flumazenil. The Flumazenil in Benzodiazepine Intoxication Multicenter Study Group. *Clin Ther*, 1992. 14(6): p. 978–95.

82. Haverkos, G.P., R.P. DiSalvo, and T.E. Imhoff, Fatal seizures after flumazenil administration in a patient with mixed overdose. *Ann Pharmacother*, 1994. 28(12): p. 1347–9.

83. Lim, A.G., Death after flumazenil [letter] [published erratum appears in BMJ 1989 Dec 16;299(6714):1531] [see comments]. *BMJ*, 1989. 299(6703): p. 858–9.

84. Serfaty, M. and G. Masterton, Fatal poisonings attributed to benzodiazepines in Britain during the 1980s [see comments]. *Br J Psychiatry*, 1993. 163: p. 386–93.

85. Greenblatt, D.J., et al., Acute overdosage with benzodiazepine derivatives. *Clin Pharmacol Ther*, 1977. 21(4): p. 497–514.

86. Guglielminotti, J., et al., Prolonged sedation requiring mechanical ventilation and continuous flumazenil infusion after routine doses of clorazepam for alcohol withdrawal syndrome. *Intensive Care Med*, 1999. 25(12): p. 1435–6.

87. Saltik, I.N. and H. Ozen, Role of flumazenil for paradoxical reaction to midazolam during endoscopic procedures in children. *Am J Gastroenterol*, 2000. 95(10): p. 3011–2.

88. Reichen, J., Review: flumazenil leads to clinical and electroencephalographic improvement in hepatic encephalopathy in patients with cirrhosis. *ACP J Club*, 2003. 138(1): p. 15.

89. Gerra, G., et al., Intravenous flumazenil versus oxazepam tapering in the treatment of benzodiazepine withdrawal: a randomized, placebo-controlled study. *Addict Biol*, 2002. 7(4): p. 385–95.

90. Proceedings of the Guidelines 2000 Conference for Cardiopulmonary Resuscitation and Emergency Cardiovascular Care: An International Consensus on Science. *Ann Emerg Med*, 2001. 37(4 Suppl): p. S1–200.

91. Harper, C., et al., An international perspective on the prevalence of the Wernicke–Korsakoff syndrome. *Metab Brain Dis*, 1995. 10(1): p. 17–24.

92. Peeters, A., et al., Wernicke's encephalopathy and central pontine myelinolysis induced by hyperemesis gravidarum. *Acta Neurol Belg*, 1993. 93(5): p. 276–82.

93. Boldorini, R., et al., Wernicke's encephalopathy: occurrence and pathological aspects in a series of 400 AIDS patients. *Acta Biomed Ateneo Parmense*, 1992. 63(1–2): p. 43–9.

94. Tate, J.R. and P.F. Nixon, Measurement of Michaelis constant for human erythrocyte transketolase and thiamin diphosphate. *Anal Biochem*, 1987. 160(1): p. 78–87.

95. Reuler, J.B., D.E. Girard, and T.G. Cooney, Current concepts. Wernicke's encephalopathy. *N Engl J Med*, 1985. 312(16): p. 1035–9.

96. Cheeley, R.D. and S.M. Joyce, A clinical comparison of the performance of four blood glucose reagent strips. *Am J Emerg Med*, 1990. 8(1): p. 11–5.

97. Jones, J.L., et al., Determination of prehospital blood glucose: a prospective, controlled study. *J Emerg Med*, 1992. 10(6): p. 679–82.

98. Wilkins, B.H. and D. Kalra, Comparison of blood glucose test strips in the detection of neonatal hypoglycaemia. *Arch Dis Child*, 1982. 57(12): p. 948–50.

99. Barreau, P.B. and J.E. Buttery, The effect of the haematocrit value on the determination of glucose levels by reagent-strip methods. *Med J Aust*, 1987. 147(6): p. 286–8.

100. Tanvetyanon, T., M.D. Walkenstein, and A. Marra, Inaccurate glucose determination by fingerstick in a patient with peripheral arterial disease. *Ann Intern Med*, 2002. 137(9): p. W1.

101. Atkin, S.H., et al., Fingerstick glucose determination in shock. *Ann Intern Med*, 1991. 114(12): p. 1020–4.

102. Fazel, A., et al., Influence of sample temperature on reflectance photometry and electrochemical glucometer measurements. *Diabetes Care*, 1996. 19(7): p. 771–4.

103. Boyle, P.J., et al., Plasma glucose concentrations at the onset of hypoglycemic symptoms in patients with poorly controlled diabetes and in nondiabetics. *N Engl J Med*, 1988. 318(23): p. 1487–92.

104. Hoffman, J.R., D.L. Schriger, and J.S. Luo, The empiric use of naloxone in patients with altered mental status: a reappraisal. *Ann Emerg Med*, 1991. 20(3): p. 246–52.

105. Weisman, R., Naloxone, in *Goldfrank's Toxicologic Emergencies*, Goldfrank, L.R., Lewin, N.A., et al., Eds. 1994, Appleton & Lange: Englewood Cliffs, NJ. p. 784.

106. Maio, R.F., B. Gaukel, and B. Freeman, Intralingual naloxone injection for narcotic-induced respiratory depression. *Ann Emerg Med*, 1987. 16(5): p. 572–3.

107. Claeys, M.A., et al., Reversal of flunitrazepam with flumazenil: duration of antagonist activity. *Eur J Anaesthesiol Suppl*, 1988. 2: p. 209–17.

108. Martens, F., et al., Clinical experience with the benzodiazepine antagonist flumazenil in suspected benzodiazepine or ethanol poisoning. *J Toxicol Clin Toxicol*, 1990. 28(3): p. 341–56.

109. Persson, A., et al., Imaging of [11C]-labelled Ro 15-1788 binding to benzodiazepine receptors in the human brain by positron emission tomography. *J Psychiatr Res*, 1985. 19(4): p. 609–22.

110. Hojer, J., et al., A placebo-controlled trial of flumazenil given by continuous infusion in severe benzodiazepine overdosage. *Acta Anaesthesiol Scand*, 1991. 35(7): p. 584–90.

111. Goldfrank, L., et al., A dosing nomogram for continuous infusion intravenous naloxone. *Ann Emerg Med*, 1986. 15(5): p. 566–70.

112. Mofenson, H.C. and T.R. Caraccio, Continuous infusion of intravenous naloxone [letter]. *Ann Emerg Med*, 1987. 16(5): p. 600.

113. Use of patient restraint. American College of Emergency Physicians. *Ann Emerg Med*, 1996. 28(3): p. 384.

114. Shanaberger, C.J., What price patient restraint? *Orwick v. Fox. J Emerg Med Serv JEMS*, 1993. 18(6): p. 69–71.

115. Stratton, S.J., C. Rogers, and K. Green, Sudden death in individuals in hobble restraints during paramedic transport. *Ann Emerg Med*, 1995. 25(5): p. 710–2.

116. Lavoie, F.W., Consent, involuntary treatment, and the use of force in an urban emergency department. *Ann Emerg Med*, 1992. 21(1): p. 25–32.

117. Gunnels, M., Violence in the emergency department: a daily challenge. *J Emerg Nurs*, 1993. 19(4): p. 277.

118. Cembrowicz, S.P. and J.P. Shepherd, Violence in the accident and emergency department. *Med Sci Law*, 1992. 32(2): p. 118–22.

119. Rumack, B.H., Editorial: Physostigmine: rational use. *JACEP*, 1976. 5(7): p. 541–2.

120. Lenox, R.H., et al., Adjunctive treatment of manic agitation with lorazepam versus haloperidol: a double-blind study. *J Clin Psychiatry*, 1992. 53(2): p. 47–52.

121. Cavanaugh, S.V., Psychiatric emergencies. *Med Clin North Am*, 1986. 70(5): p. 1185–202.

122. Stevens, A., et al., Haloperidol and lorazepam combined: clinical effects and drug plasma levels in the treatment of acute schizophrenic psychosis. *Pharmacopsychiatry*, 1992. 25(6): p. 273–7.

123. Catravas, J.D. and I.W. Waters, Acute cocaine intoxication in the conscious dog: studies on the mechanism of lethality. *J Pharmacol Exp Ther*, 1981. 217(2): p. 350–6.

124. Guinn, M.M., J.A. Bedford, and M.C. Wilson, Antagonism of intravenous cocaine lethality in non-human primates. *Clin Toxicol*, 1980. 16(4): p. 499–508.

125. Derlet, R.W. and T.E. Albertson, Diazepam in the prevention of seizures and death in cocaine-intoxicated rats. *Ann Emerg Med*, 1989. 18(5): p. 542–6.

126. Merigian, K.S., et al., Adrenergic crisis from crack cocaine ingestion: report of five cases. *J Emerg Med*, 1994. 12(4): p. 485–90.

127. Shephard, R.A., Behavioral effects of GABA agonists in relation to anxiety and benzodiazepine action. *Life Sci*, 1987. 40(25): p. 2429–36.

128. Norman, T.R. and G.D. Burrows, Anxiety and the benzodiazepine receptor. *Prog Brain Res*, 1986. 65: p. 73–90.

129. Derlet, R.W., T.E. Albertson, and P. Rice, The effect of haloperidol in cocaine and amphetamine intoxication. *J Emerg Med*, 1989. 7(6): p. 633–7.

130. Derlet, R.W., T.E. Albertson, and P. Rice, Antagonism of cocaine, amphetamine, and methamphetamine toxicity. *Pharmacol Biochem Behav*, 1990. 36(4): p. 745–9.

131. Derlet, R.W., T.E. Albertson, and P. Rice, Protection against d-amphetamine toxicity. *Am J Emerg Med*, 1990. 8(2): p. 105–8.

132. Espelin, D., Amphetamine poisoning: Effectiveness of clorpromazine. *N Engl J Med*, 1968. 278: p. 1361–5.

133. Callaway, C.W. and R.F. Clark, Hyperthermia in psychostimulant overdose. *Ann Emerg Med*, 1994. 24(1): p. 68–76.

134. Soyka, M., C. Botschev, and A. Volcker, Neuroleptic treatment in alcohol hallucinosis: no evidence for increased seizure risk. *J Clin Psychopharmacol*, 1992. 12: p. 66–7.

135. Lipka, L.J. and C.M. Lathers, Psychoactive agents, seizure production, and sudden death in epilepsy. *J Clin Pharmacol*, 1987. 27(3): p. 169–83.

136. Hoffman, R.S., Cocaine intoxication considerations, complications and strategies: point and counterpoint. *Emerg Med*, 1992. 1: p. 1–6.

137. Witkin, J., S.R. Godberg, and J.L. Katz, Lethal effects of cocaine are reduced by the dopamine-1 receptor antagonist SCH 23390 but not by haloperidol. *Life Sci*, 1989. 44: p. 1285–91.

138. Pollera, C.F., et al., Sudden death after acute dystonic reaction to high-dose metoclopramide [letter]. *Lancet*, 1984. 2(8400): p. 460–1.

139. Barach, E., et al., Dystonia presenting as upper airway obstruction. *J Emerg Med*, 1989. 7(3): p. 237–40.

140. Cavanaugh, J.J. and R.E. Finlayson, Rhabdomyolysis due to acute dystonic reaction to antipsychotic drugs. *J Clin Psychiatry*, 1984. 45(8): p. 356–7.

141. Addonizio, G. and G.S. Alexopoulos, Drug-induced dystonia in young and elderly patients. *Am J Psychiatry*, 1988. 145(7): p. 869–71.

142. Menza, M.A., et al., Controlled study of extrapyramidal reactions in the management of delirious, medically ill patients: intravenous haloperidol versus intravenous haloperidol plus benzodiazepines. *Heart Lung*, 1988. 17(3): p. 238–41.

143. Yildiz, A., G.S. Sachs, and A. Turgay, Pharmacological management of agitation in emergency settings. *Emerg Med J*, 2003. 20(4): p. 339–46.

144. Brook, S., J.V. Lucey, and K.P. Gunn, Intramuscular ziprasidone compared with intramuscular haloperidol in the treatment of acute psychosis. Ziprasidone I.M. Study Group. *J Clin Psychiatry*, 2000. 61(12): p. 933–41.

145. Brook, S., Intramuscular ziprasidone: moving beyond the conventional in the treatment of acute agitation in schizophrenia. *J Clin Psychiatry*, 2003. 64 (Suppl 19): p. 13–8.

146. Spina, E., et al., Prevalence of acute dystonic reactions associated with neuroleptic treatment with and without anticholinergic prophylaxis. *Int Clin Psychopharmacol*, 1993. 8(1): p. 21–4.

147. Shenoy, R.S., Pitfalls in the treatment of jimsonweed intoxication [letter]. *Am J Psychiatry*, 1994. 151(9): p. 1396–7.

148. Hurlbut, K.M., Drug-induced psychoses. *Emerg Med Clin North Am*, 1991. 9(1): p. 31–52.

149. Kopman, A.F., G. Strachovsky, and L. Lichtenstein, Prolonged response to succinylcholine following physostigmine. *Anesthesiology*, 1978. 49(2): p. 142–3.

150. Manoguerra, A.S. and R.W. Steiner, Prolonged neuromuscular blockade after administration of physostigmine and succinylcholine. *Clin Toxicol*, 1981. 18(7): p. 803–5.

151. Pentel, P. and C.D. Peterson, Asystole complicating physostigmine treatment of tricyclic antidepressant overdose. *Ann Emerg Med*, 1980. 9(11): p. 588–90.

152. Newton, R.W., Physostigmine salicylate in the treatment of tricyclic antidepressant overdosage. *JAMA*, 1975. 231(9): p. 941–3.

153. Nattel, S., L. Bayne, and J. Ruedy, Physostigmine in coma due to drug overdose. *Clin Pharmacol Ther*, 1979. 25(1): p. 96–102.

154. Gay, G.R., Clinical management of acute and chronic cocaine poisoning. *Ann Emerg Med*, 1982. 11(10): p. 562–72.

155. Khantzian, E.J. and G.J. McKenna, Acute toxic and withdrawal reactions associated with drug use and abuse. *Ann Intern Med*, 1979. 90(3): p. 361–72.

156. Fisher, W.A., Restraint and seclusion: a review of the literature. *Am J Psychiatry*, 1994. 151(11): p. 1584–91.

157. Splawn, G., Restraining potentially violent patients. *J Emerg Nurs*, 1991. 17(5): p. 316–7.

158. Wetli, C.V. and D.A. Fishbain, Cocaine-induced psychosis and sudden death in recreational cocaine users. *J Forensic Sci*, 1985. 30(3): p. 873–80.

159. O'Halloran, R.V. and L.V. Lewman, Restraint asphyxiation in excited delirium [see comments]. *Am J Forensic Med Pathol*, 1993. 14(4): p. 289–95.

160. Miles, S.H., Restraints and sudden death [letter; comment]. *J Am Geriatr Soc*, 1993. 41(9): p. 1013.

161. Introna, F., Jr. and J.E. Smialek, The "mini-packer" syndrome. Fatal ingestion of drug containers in Baltimore, Maryland. *Am J Forensic Med Pathol*, 1989. 10(1): p. 21–4.

162. Simon, L.C., The cocaine body packer syndrome. *West Indian Med J*, 1990. 39(4): p. 250–5.

163. Geyskens, P., L. Coenen, and J. Brouwers, The "cocaine body packer" syndrome. Case report and review of the literature. *Acta Chir Belg*, 1989. 89(4): p. 201–3.

164. Pollack, C.V., Jr., et al., Two crack cocaine body stuffers [clinical conference]. *Ann Emerg Med*, 1992. 21(11): p. 1370–80.

165. Jimson weed poisoning — Texas, New York, and California, 1994. *MMWR Morb Mortal Wkly Rep*, 1995. 44(3): p. 41–4.

166. Wetli, C.V. and R.K. Wright, Death caused by recreational cocaine use. *JAMA*, 1979. 241(23): p. 2519–22.

167. Simpson, D.L. and B.H. Rumack, Methylenedioxyamphetamine. Clinical description of overdose, death, and review of pharmacology. *Arch Intern Med*, 1981. 141(11): p. 1507–9.

168. Campbell, B.G., Cocaine abuse with hyperthermia, seizures and fatal complications. *Med J Aust*, 1988. 149(7): p. 387–9.

169. Olson, K.R., et al., Seizures associated with poisoning and drug overdose [corrected and republished article originally printed in *Am J Emerg Med* 1993 Nov;11(6):565–8]. *Am J Emerg Med*, 1994. 12(3): p. 392–5.

170. Jonsson, S., M. O'Meara, and J.B. Young, Acute cocaine poisoning. Importance of treating seizures and acidosis. *Am J Med*, 1983. 75(6): p. 1061–4.

171. Olson, K.R. and N.L. Benowitz, Environmental and drug-induced hyperthermia. Pathophysiology, recognition, and management. *Emerg Med Clin North Am*, 1984. 2(3): p. 459–74.

172. Meldrum, B.S., R.A. Vigouroux, and J.B. Brierley, Systemic factors and epileptic brain damage. Prolonged seizures in paralyzed, artificially ventilated baboons. *Arch Neurol*, 1973. 29(2): p. 82–7.

173. Earnest, M.P., Seizures. *Neurol Clin*, 1993. 11(3): p. 563–75.

174. Lason, W., Neurochemical and pharmacological aspects of cocaine-induced seizures. *Pol J Pharmacol*, 2001. 53(1): p. 57–60.

175. Jacobs, I.G., et al., Cocaine abuse: neurovascular complications. *Radiology*, 1989. 170(1 Pt 1): p. 223–7.

176. Auer, J., R. Berent, and B. Eber, Cardiovascular complications of cocaine use. *N Engl J Med*, 2001. 345(21): p. 1575; author reply 1576.

177. Rumbaugh, C.L., et al., Cerebral angiographic changes in the drug abuse patient. *Radiology*, 1971. 101(2): p. 335–44.

178. Earnest, M.P., et al., Neurocysticercosis in the United States: 35 cases and a review. *Rev Infect Dis*, 1987. 9(5): p. 961–79.

179. Roberts, J.R., Initial therapeutic strategies for the treatment of status epilepticus. *Emerg Med News*, 1996. 10: p. 2, 14–5.

180. Finder, R.L. and P.A. Moore, Benzodiazepines for intravenous conscious sedation: agonists and antagonists. *Compendium*, 1993. 14(8): p. 972, 974, 976–80 passim; quiz 984–6.

181. Roth, T. and T.A. Roehrs, A review of the safety profiles of benzodiazepine hypnotics. *J Clin Psychiatry*, 1991. 52 (Suppl): p. 38–41.

182. Dement, W.C., Overview of the efficacy and safety of benzodiazepine hypnotics using objective methods. *J Clin Psychiatry*, 1991. 52 (Suppl): p. 27–30.

183. Treiman, D.M., The role of benzodiazepines in the management of status epilepticus. *Neurology*, 1990. 40(5 Suppl 2): p. 32–42.

184. Kyriakopoulos, A.A., D.J. Greenblatt, and R.I. Shader, Clinical pharmacokinetics of lorazepam: a review. *J Clin Psychiatry*, 1978. 39(10 Pt 2): p. 16–23.

185. Leppik, I.E., et al., Double-blind study of lorazepam and diazepam in status epilepticus. *JAMA*, 1983. 249(11): p. 1452–4.

186. Levy, R.J. and R.L. Krall, Treatment of status epilepticus with lorazepam. *Arch Neurol*, 1984. 41(6): p. 605–11.

187. Bebin, M. and T.P. Bleck, New anticonvulsant drugs. Focus on flunarizine, fosphenytoin, midazolam and stiripentol. *Drugs*, 1994. 48(2): p. 153–71.

188. Kumar, A. and T.P. Bleck, Intravenous midazolam for the treatment of refractory status epilepticus. *Crit Care Med*, 1992. 20(4): p. 483–8.

189. Schalen, W., K. Messeter, and C.H. Nordstrom, Complications and side effects during thiopentone therapy in patients with severe head injuries. *Acta Anaesthesiol Scand*, 1992. 36(4): p. 369–77.

190. Singbartl, G. and G. Cunitz, Pathophysiologic principles, emergency medical aspects and anesthesiologic measures in severe brain trauma. *Anaesthesist*, 1987. 36(7): p. 321–32.

191. Lee, T.L., Pharmacology of propofol. *Ann Acad Med Singapore*, 1991. 20(1): p. 61–5.

192. Sellers, E.M., Alcohol, barbiturate and benzodiazepine withdrawal syndromes: clinical management. *Can Med Assoc J*, 1988. 139(2): p. 113–20.

193. Sullivan, J.T. and E.M. Seller, Treating alcohol, barbiturate, and benzodiazepine withdrawal. *Ration Drug Ther*, 1986. 20(2): p. 1–9.

194. Ramsay, R.E. and J. DeToledo, Intravenous administration of fosphenytoin: options for the management of seizures. *Neurology*, 1996. 46(6 Suppl 1): p. S17–9.

195. Staff, *Clinical Pharmacology: An Electronic Drug Reference and Teaching Guide*. 1.5 ed, S. Reents, Ed. 1995, Gainesville, FL: Gold Standard Multimedia.

196. Derlet, R.W. and T.E. Albertson, Anticonvulsant modification of cocaine-induced toxicity in the rat. *Neuropharmacology*, 1990. 29(3): p. 255–9.

197. Alldredge, B.K., D.H. Lowenstein, and R.P. Simon, Placebo-controlled trial of intravenous diphenylhydantoin for short-term treatment of alcohol withdrawal seizures. *Am J Med*, 1989. 87(6): p. 645–8.

198. Callaham, M., H. Schumaker, and P. Pentel, Phenytoin prophylaxis of cardiotoxicity in experimental amitriptyline poisoning. *J Pharmacol Exp Ther*, 1988. 245(1): p. 216–20.

199. Appleton, R., T. Martland, and B. Phillips, Drug management for acute tonic-clonic convulsions including convulsive status epilepticus in children. *Cochrane Database Syst Rev*, 2002(4): p. CD001905.

200. Lowenstein, D.H., Treatment options for status epilepticus. *Curr Opin Pharmacol*, 2003. 3(1): p. 6–11.

201. Munn, R.I. and K. Farrell, Failure to recognize status epilepticus in a paralyzed patient. *Can J Neurol Sci*, 1993. 20(3): p. 234–6.

202. Wolf, K.M., A.F. Shaughnessy, and D.B. Middleton, Prolonged delirium tremens requiring massive doses of medication [see comments]. *J Am Board Fam Pract*, 1993. 6(5): p. 502–4.

203. Pascual-Leone, A., et al., Cocaine-induced seizures. *Neurology*, 1990. 40(3 Pt 1): p. 404–7.

204. Brown, E., et al., CNS complications of cocaine abuse: prevalence, pathophysiology, and neuroradiology. *AJR Am J Roentgenol*, 1992. 159(1): p. 137–47.

205. Daras, M., A.J. Tuchman, and S. Marks, Central nervous system infarction related to cocaine abuse. *Stroke*, 1991. 22(10): p. 1320–5.

206. Tuchman, A.J. and M. Daras, Strokes associated with cocaine use [letter]. *Arch Neurol*, 1990. 47(11): p. 1170.

207. Holland, R.W.D., et al., Grand mal seizures temporally related to cocaine use: clinical and diagnostic features [see comments]. *Ann Emerg Med*, 1992. 21(7): p. 772–6.

208. Sarnquist, F. and C.P. Larson, Jr., Drug-induced heat stroke. *Anesthesiology*, 1973. 39(3): p. 348–50.

209. Rosenberg, J., et al., Hyperthermia associated with drug intoxication. *Crit Care Med*, 1986. 14(11): p. 964–9.

210. Sporer, K.A., The serotonin syndrome. Implicated drugs, pathophysiology and management. *Drug Saf*, 1995. 13(2): p. 94–104.

211. Walter, F.G., et al., Marijuana and hyperthermia. *J Toxicol Clin Toxicol*, 1996. 34(2): p. 217–21.

212. Ebadi, M., R.F. Pfeiffer, and L.C. Murrin, Pathogenesis and treatment of neuroleptic malignant syndrome. *Gen Pharmacol*, 1990. 21(4): p. 367–86.

213. Lecci, A., et al., Effect of psychotomimetics and some putative anxiolytics on stress-induced hyperthermia. *J Neural Transm Gen Sect*, 1991. 83(1–2): p. 67–76.

214. Halloran, L.L. and D.W. Bernard, Management of drug-induced hyperthermia. *Curr Opin Pediatr*, 2004. 16(2): p. 211–5.

215. Hadad, E., A.A. Weinbroum, and R. Ben-Abraham, Drug-induced hyperthermia and muscle rigidity: a practical approach. *Eur J Emerg Med*, 2003. 10(2): p. 149–54.

216. McGregor, I.S., et al., Increased anxiety and "depressive" symptoms months after MDMA ("ecstasy") in rats: drug-induced hyperthermia does not predict long-term outcomes. *Psychopharmacology* (Berlin), 2003. 168(4): p. 465–74.

217. Crandall, C.G., W. Vongpatanasin, and R.G. Victor, Mechanism of cocaine-induced hyperthermia in humans. *Ann Intern Med*, 2002. 136(11): p. 785–91.

218. Gordon, C.J., et al., Effects of 3,4-methylenedioxymethamphetamine on autonomic thermoregulatory responses of the rat. *Pharmacol Biochem Behav*, 1991. 38(2): p. 339–44.

219. Aniline, O. and F.N. Pitts, Jr., Phencyclidine (PCP): a review and perspectives. *Crit Rev Toxicol*, 1982. 10(2): p. 145–77.

220. Eastman, J.W. and S.N. Cohen, Hypertensive crisis and death associated with phencyclidine poisoning. *JAMA*, 1975. 231(12): p. 1270–1.

221. McCarron, M.M., et al., Acute phencyclidine intoxication: incidence of clinical findings in 1,000 cases. *Ann Emerg Med*, 1981. 10(5): p. 237–42.

222. Friedman, S.A. and S.E. Hirsch, Extreme hyperthermia after LSD ingestion. *JAMA*, 1971. 217(11): p. 1549–50.

223. Klock, J.C., U. Boerner, and C.E. Becker, Coma, hyperthermia and bleeding associated with massive LSD overdose. A report of eight cases. *West J Med*, 1974. 120(3): p. 183–8.

224. Mercieca, J. and E.A. Brown, Acute renal failure due to rhabdomyolysis associated with use of a straitjacket in lysergide intoxication. *Br Med J* (Clin Res Ed), 1984. 288(6435): p. 1949–50.

225. Armen, R., G. Kanel, and T. Reynolds, Phencyclidine-induced malignant hyperthermia causing submassive liver necrosis. *Am J Med*, 1984. 77(1): p. 167–72.

226. Loghmanee, F. and M. Tobak, Fatal malignant hyperthermia associated with recreational cocaine and ethanol abuse. *Am J Forensic Med Pathol*, 1986. 7(3): p. 246–8.

227. Zorzato, F., et al., Role of malignant hyperthermia domain in the regulation of Ca2+ release channel (ryanodine receptor) of skeletal muscle sarcoplasmic reticulum. *J Biol Chem*, 1996. 271(37): p. 22759–63.

228. Singarajah, C. and N.G. Lavies, An overdose of ecstasy. A role for dantrolene [see comments]. *Anaesthesia*, 1992. 47(8): p. 686–7.

229. Watson, J.D., et al., Exertional heat stroke induced by amphetamine analogues. Does dantrolene have a place? *Anaesthesia*, 1993. 48(12): p. 1057–60.

230. Behan, W., A.M.O. Bakheit, P.W. Hegan, and I.A.R. More, The muscle findings in the neuroleptic malignant syndrome associated with lysergic acid deithylamide. *J Neurol Neurosurg Psychiatry*, 1991. 54: p. 741–743.

231. Woodbury, M.M. and M.A. Woodbury, Neuroleptic-induced catatonia as a stage in the progression toward neuroleptic malignant syndrome. *J Am Acad Child Adolesc Psychiatry*, 1992. 31(6): p. 1161–4.

232. Totten, V.Y., E. Hirschenstein, and P. Hew, Neuroleptic malignant syndrome presenting without initial fever: a case report. *J Emerg Med*, 1994. 12(1): p. 43–7.

233. Daras, M., et al., Rhabdomyolysis and hyperthermia after cocaine abuse: a variant of the neuroleptic malignant syndrome? *Acta Neurol Scand*, 1995. 92(2): p. 161–5.

234. Wetli, C.V., D. Mash, and S.B. Karch, Cocaine-associated agitated delirium and the neuroleptic malignant syndrome. *Am J Emerg Med*, 1996. 14(4): p. 425–8.

235. SFPCC, *Poisoning & Drug Overdose. A Lange Clinical Manual*, K. Olson, Ed. 1994, Norwalk, CT: Appleton & Lange.

236. Zalis, E.G. and G. Kaplan, The effect of aggregation on amphetamine toxicity in the dog. *Arch Int Pharmacodyn Ther*, 1966. 159(1): p. 196–9.

237. Zalis, E.G., G.D. Lundberg, and R.A. Knutson, The pathophysiology of acute amphetamine poisoning with pathologic correlation. *J Pharmacol Exp Ther*, 1967. 158(1): p. 115–27.

238. Zalis, E.G., G.D. Lundberg, and R.A. Knutson, Acute lethality of the amphetamines in dogs and its antagonism by curare. *Proc Soc Exp Biol Med*, 1965: p. 557.

239. Davis, W.M., et al., Factors in the lethality of i.v. phencyclidine in conscious dogs. *Gen Pharmacol*, 1991. 22(4): p. 723–8.

240. Tek, D. and J.S. Olshaker, Heat illness. *Emerg Med Clin North Am*, 1992. 10(2): p. 299–310.

241. Callaham, M., Tricyclic antidepressant overdose. *JACEP*, 1979. 8(10): p. 413–25.

242. Sprung, C.L., Heat stroke; modern approach to an ancient disease. *Chest*, 1980. 77(4): p. 461–2.

243. Hamilton, D., Heat stroke. *Anaesthesia*, 1976. 32: p. 271.

244. Walker, J. and M.V. Vance, Heat emergencies, in *Emergency Medicine: A Comprehensive Study Guide*, J. Tintinalli, Ruiz, E, Krome, R.L., Eds. 1996, McGraw-Hill: New York. p. 850–856.

245. Rabinowitz, R.P., et al., Effects of anatomic site, oral stimulation, and body position on estimates of body temperature. *Arch Intern Med*, 1996. 156(7): p. 777–80.

246. Hooker, E.A., et al., Subjective assessment of fever by parents: comparison with measurement by noncontact tympanic thermometer and calibrated rectal glass mercury thermometer. *Ann Emerg Med*, 1996. 28(3): p. 313–7.

247. Yaron, M., S.R. Lowenstein, and J. Koziol-McLain, Measuring the accuracy of the infrared tympanic thermometer: correlation does not signify agreement. *J Emerg Med*, 1995. 13(5): p. 617–21.

248. Craig, J.V., et al., Infrared ear thermometry compared with rectal thermometry in children: a systematic review. *Lancet*, 2002. 360(9333): p. 603–9.

249. Selfridge, J. and S.S. Shea, The accuracy of the tympanic membrane thermometer in detecting fever in infants aged 3 months and younger in the emergency department setting. *J Emerg Nurs*, 1993. 19(2): p. 127–30.

250. White, N., S. Baird, and D.L. Anderson, A comparison of tympanic thermometer readings to pulmonary artery catheter core temperature recordings. *Appl Nurs Res*, 1994. 7(4): p. 165–9.

251. Doezema, D., M. Lunt, and D. Tandberg, Cerumen occlusion lowers infrared tympanic membrane temperature measurement. *Acad Emerg Med*, 1995. 2(1): p. 17–9.

252. Cabanac, M. and H. Brinnel, The pathology of human temperature regulation: thermiatrics. *Experientia*, 1987. 43(1): p. 19–27.

253. O'Donnell, T.F., Jr. and G.H. Clowes, Jr., The circulatory abnormalities of heat stroke. *N Engl J Med*, 1972. 287(15): p. 734–7.

254. O'Donnell, T.F., Jr. and G.H. Clowes, Jr., The circulatory requirements of heat stroke. *Surg Forum*, 1971. 22: p. 12–4.

255. Seraj, M.A., et al., Are heat stroke patients fluid depleted? Importance of monitoring central venous pressure as a simple guideline for fluid therapy. *Resuscitation*, 1991. 21(1): p. 33–9.

256. Zahger, D., A. Moses, and A.T. Weiss, Evidence of prolonged myocardial dysfunction in heat stroke. *Chest*, 1989. 95(5): p. 1089–91.

257. Clowes, G.H., Jr. and T.F. O'Donnell, Jr., Heat stroke. *N Engl J Med*, 1974. 291(11): p. 564–7.

258. Gottschalk, P.G. and J.E. Thomas, Heat stroke. *Mayo Clin Proc*, 1966. 41(7): p. 470–82.

259. Rockhold, R.W., et al., Dopamine receptors mediate cocaine-induced temperature responses in spontaneously hypertensive and Wistar-Kyoto rats. *Pharmacol Biochem Behav*, 1991. 40(1): p. 157–62.

260. Kosten, T.R. and H.D. Kleber, Rapid death during cocaine abuse: a variant of the neuroleptic malignant syndrome? *Am J Drug Alcohol Abuse*, 1988. 14(3): p. 335–46.

261. Fox, A.W., More on rhabdomyolysis associated with cocaine intoxication [letter]. *N Engl J Med*, 1989. 321(18): p. 1271.

262. Travis, S.P., Management of heat stroke. *J R Nav Med Serv*, 1988. 74(1): p. 39–43.

263. Rumack, B.H., Aspirin versus acetaminophen: a comparative view. *Pediatrics*, 1978. 62(5 Pt 2 Suppl): p. 943–6.

264. McFadden, S. and J.E. Haddow, Coma produced by topical application of isopropanol. *Pediatrics*, 1969. 43: p. 622.

265. Gabow, P.A., W.D. Kaehny, and S.P. Kelleher, The spectrum of rhabdomyolysis. *Medicine*, 1982. 61: p. 141–52.

266. Bogaerts, Y., N. Lameire, and S. Ringoir, The compartmental syndrome: a serious complication of acute rhabdomyolysis. *Clin Nephrol*, 1982. 17: p. 206–11.

267. Akisu, M., et al., Severe acute thinner intoxication. *Turk J Pediatr*, 1996. 38(2): p. 223–5.

268. Akmal, M., et al., Rhabdomyolysis with and without acute renal failure in patients with phencyclidine intoxication. *Am J Nephrol*, 1981. 1(2): p. 91–6.

269. Anand, V., G. Siami, and W.J. Stone, Cocaine-associated rhabdomyolysis and acute renal failure [see comments]. *South Med J*, 1989. 82(1): p. 67–9.

270. Bakir, A.A. and G. Dunea, Drugs of abuse and renal disease. *Curr Opin Nephrol Hypertens*, 1996. 5(2): p. 122–6.

271. Chan, P., et al., Acute heroin intoxication with complications of acute pulmonary edema, acute renal failure, rhabdomyolysis and lumbosacral plexitis: a case report. *Chung Hua I Hsueh Tsa Chih* (Taipei), 1995. 55(5): p. 397–400.

272. Chan, P., et al., Fatal and nonfatal methamphetamine intoxication in the intensive care unit. *J Toxicol Clin Toxicol*, 1994. 32(2): p. 147–55.

273. Cogen, F.C., et al., Phencyclidine-associated acute rhabdomyolysis. *Ann Intern Med*, 1978. 88(2): p. 210–2.

274. Henry, J.A., K.J. Jeffreys, and S. Dawling, Toxicity and deaths from 3,4-methylenedioxymethamphetamine ("ecstasy") [see comments]. *Lancet*, 1992. 340(8816): p. 384–7.

275. Melandri, R., et al., Myocardial damage and rhabdomyolysis associated with prolonged hypoxic coma following opiate overdose. *J Toxicol Clin Toxicol*, 1996. 34(2): p. 199–203.

276. Tehan, B., R. Hardern, and A. Bodenham, Hyperthermia associated with 3,4-methylenedioxyethamphetamine ("Eve"). *Anaesthesia*, 1993. 48(6): p. 507–10.

277. Curry, S.C., D. Chang, and D. Connor, Drug- and toxin-induced rhabdomyolysis. *Ann Emerg Med*, 1989. 18(10): p. 1068–84.

278. Welch, R.D., K. Todd, and G.S. Krause, Incidence of cocaine-associated rhabdomyolysis. *Ann Emerg Med*, 1991. 20(2): p. 154–7.

279. Knochel, J.P., Rhabdomyolysis and myoglobinuria. *Annu Rev Med*, 1982. 33: p. 435–443.

280. Koffler, A., R.M. Friedler, and S.G. Massry, Acute renal failure due to nontraumatic rhabdomyolysis. *Ann Intern Med*, 1976. 85: p. 23–28.

281. Grossman, R.A., et al., Nontraumatic rhabdomyolysis and acute renal failure. *N Engl J Med*, 1974. 291(16): p. 807–11.

282. Knochel, J.P., Rhabdomyolysis and myoglobinuria. *Semin Nephrol*, 1981. 1: p. 75–86.

283. Ron, D., et al., Prevention of acute renal failure in traumatic rhabdomyolysis. *Arch Intern Med*, 1984. 144(2): p. 277–80.

284. Knottenbelt, J.D., Traumatic rhabdomyolysis from severe beating — experience of volume diuresis in 200 patients. *J Trauma*, 1994. 37(2): p. 214–9.

285. Veenstra, J., et al., Relationship between elevated creatine phosphokinase and the clinical spectrum of rhabdomyolysis. *Nephrol Dial Transplant*, 1994. 9(6): p. 637–41.

286. Oda, J., et al., Analysis of 372 patients with crush syndrome caused by the Hanshin-Awaji earthquake. *J Trauma*, 1997. 42(3): p. 470–5; discussion 475–6.

287. Eneas, J.F., P.Y. Schoenfeld, and M.H. Humphreys, The effect of infusion of mannitol-sodium bicarbonate on the clinical course of myoglobinuria. *Arch Intern Med*, 1979. 139(7): p. 801–5.

288. Feinfeld, D.A., et al., A prospective study of urine and serum myoglobin levels in patients with acute rhabdomyolysis. *Clin Nephrol*, 1992. 38(4): p. 193–5.

289. Loun, B., et al., Adaptation of a quantitative immunoassay for urine myoglobin. Predictor in detecting renal dysfunction. *Am J Clin Pathol*, 1996. 105(4): p. 479–86.

290. Thomas, M.A. and L.S. Ibels, Rhabdomyolysis and acute renal failure. *Aust NZ J Med*, 1985. 15(5): p. 623–8.

291. Cadnapaphornchai, P., S. Taher, and F.D. McDonald, Acute drug-associated rhabdomyolysis: an examination of its diverse renal manifestations and complications. *Am J Med Sci*, 1980. 280(2): p. 66–72.

292. Knochel, J.P., Catastrophic medical events with exhaustive exercise: "white collar rhabdomyolysis." *Kidney Int*, 1990. 38(4): p. 709–19.

293. Kageyama, Y., Rhabdomyolysis: clinical analysis of 20 patients. *Nippon Jinzo Gakkai Shi*, 1989. 31(10): p. 1099–103.

294. Ellinas, P.A. and F. Rosner, Rhabdomyolysis: report of eleven cases. *J Natl Med Assoc*, 1992. 84(7): p. 617–24.

295. Ward, M.M., Factors predictive of acute renal failure in rhabdomyolysis. *Arch Intern Med*, 1988. 148(7): p. 1553–7.

296. Gardner, J.W. and J.A. Kark, Fatal rhabdomyolysis presenting as mild heat illness in military training. *Mil Med*, 1994. 159(2): p. 160–3.

297. Morocco, P.A., Atraumatic rhabdomyolysis in a 20-year-old bodybuilder. *J Emerg Nurs*, 1991. 17(6): p. 370–2.

298. Uberoi, H.S., et al., Acute renal failure in severe exertional rhabdomyolysis [see comments]. *J Assoc Physicians India*, 1991. 39(9): p. 677–9.

299. Zurovsky, Y., Effects of changes in plasma volume on fatal rhabdomyolysis in the rat induced by glycerol injections. *J Basic Clin Physiol Pharmacol*, 1992. 3(3): p. 223–37.

300. Sinert, R., et al., Exercise-induced rhabdomyolysis. *Ann Emerg Med*, 1994. 23(6): p. 1301–6.

301. Bunn, H.F. and J.H. Jandi, Exchange of heme analogue hemoglobin molecules. *Proc Natl Acad Sci USA*, 1977. 56: p. 974–8.

302. Paller, M.S., Hemoglobin- and myoglobin-induced acute renal failure in rats: role of iron in nephrotoxicity. *Am J Physiol*, 1988. 255(3 Pt 2): p. F539–44.

303. Anderson, W.A.D., D.B. Morrison, and E.F. Williams, Pathologic changes following injection of ferrihemate (hematin) in dogs. *Arch Pathol*, 1942. 33: p. 589–602.

304. Garcia, G., et al., Nephrotoxicity of myoglobin in the rat: Relative importance of urine pH and prior dehydration (abstract). *Kidney Int*, 1981. 19: p. 200.

305. Perri, G.C. and P. Gerini, Uraemia in the rabbit after injection of crystalline myoglobin. *Br J Exp Pathol*, 1952. 33: p. 440–4.

306. POISONDEX(R) Editorial Staff and K. Kulig, Rhabdomyolysis. 1992, POISONDEX(R): Treatment protocols.

307. Eneas, J.F., P.Y. Schoenfeld, and M.H. Humphreys, The effect of infusion of mannitol-sodium bicarbonate on the clinical course of myoglobinuria. *Arch Intern Med*, 1979. 139: p. 801–5.

308. Lameire, N., et al., Pathophysiology, causes, and prognosis of acute renal failure in the elderly. *Renal Fail*, 1996. 18(3): p. 333–46.

309. Druml, W., Prognosis of acute renal failure 1975–1995. *Nephron*, 1996. 73(1): p. 8–15.

310. Wilson, D.R., et al., Glycerol induced hemoglobinuric acute renal failure in the rat. 3. Micropuncture study of the effects of mannitol and isotonic saline on individual nephron function. *Nephron*, 1967. 4(6): p. 337–55.

311. Kjellmer, I., Potassium ion as a vasodilator during muscular exercise. *Acta Physiol Scand*, 1965: p. 466–8.

312. Knochel, J.P. and E.M. Schlein, On the mechanism of rhabdomyolysis in potassium depletion. *J Clin Invest*, 1972. 51(7): p. 1750–8.

313. Temple, A.R., Acute and chronic effects of aspirin toxicity and their treatment. *Arch Intern Med*, 1981. 141(3 Spec No): p. 364–9.

314. Javaheri, S., Effects of acetazolamide on cerebrospinal fluid ions in metabolic alkalosis in dogs. *J Appl Physiol*, 1987. 62(4): p. 1582–8.

315. Kaplan, S.A. and F.T. Del Carmen, Experimental salicylate poisoning. Observation on the effects of carbonic anhydrase inhibitor and bicarbonate. *Pediatrics*, 1958. 21: p. 762–70.

316. Lijnen, P., et al., Biochemical variables in plasma and urine before and after prolonged physical exercise. *Enzyme*, 1985. 33(3): p. 134–42.

317. Davis, A.M., Hypocalcemia in rhabdomyolysis [letter] [published erratum appears in *JAMA* 1987 Oct 9;258(14):1894]. *JAMA*, 1987. 257(5): p. 626.

318. Malinoski, D.J., M.S. Slater, and R.J. Mullins, Crush injury and rhabdomyolysis. *Crit Care Clin*, 2004. 20(1): p. 171–92.

319. Qureshi, A.I., et al., Cocaine use and hypertension are major risk factors for intracerebral hemorrhage in young African Americans. *Ethn Dis*, 2001. 11(2): p. 311–9.

320. Brecklin, C.S. and J.L. Bauman, Cardiovascular effects of cocaine: focus on hypertension. *J Clin Hypertens* (Greenwich), 1999. 1(3): p. 212–7.

321. Eagle, K.A., E.M. Isselbacher, and R.W. DeSanctis, Cocaine-related aortic dissection in perspective. *Circulation*, 2002. 105(13): p. 1529–30.

322. Brown, C., Phenylpropanolamine — an ongoing problem. *Clin Toxicol Update*, 1987. 9(2): p. 5–8.

323. Glick, R., et al., Phenylpropanolamine: an over-the-counter drug causing central nervous system vasculitis and intracerebral hemorrhage. Case report and review. *Neurosurgery*, 1987. 20(6): p. 969–74.

324. Jackson, C., A. Hart, and M.D. Robinson, Fatal intracranial hemorrhage associated with phenylpropanolamine, pentazocine, and tripelennamine overdose. *J Emerg Med*, 1985. 3(2): p. 127–32.

325. Nahas, G.G., R. Trouve, and W.M. Manger, Cocaine, catecholamines and cardiac toxicity. *Acta Anaesthesiol Scand Suppl*, 1990. 94: p. 77–81.

326. Rothman, R.B., et al., Amphetamine-type central nervous system stimulants release norepinephrine more potently than they release dopamine and serotonin. *Synapse*, 2001. 39(1): p. 32–41.

327. McDonald, A.J., D.M. Yealy, and S. Jacobson, Oral labetalol versus oral nifedipine in hypertensive urgencies in the ED. *Am J Emerg Med*, 1993. 11(5): p. 460–3.

328. Benowitz, N.L., Discussion over hypertension in drug abuse, 1996. Personal communication.

329. Rahn, K.H., How should we treat a hypertensive emergency? *Am J Cardiol*, 1989. 63(6): p. 48C–50C.

330. Somberg, J.C., The therapeutics of hypertensive emergency. *Am J Ther*, 1996. 3(11): p. 741.

331. Vidt, D.G., Emergency room management of hypertensive urgencies and emergencies. *J Clin Hypertens* (Greenwich), 2001. 3(3): p. 158–64.

332. Kumar, A.M., E.S. Nadel, and D.F. Brown, Case presentations of the Harvard Emergency Medicine Residency. Hypertensive crisis. *J Emerg Med*, 2000. 19(4): p. 369–73.

333. Haft, J.I., Use of the calcium-channel blocker nifedipine in the management of hypertensive emergency. *Am J Emerg Med*, 1985. 3(6 Suppl): p. 25–30.

334. Benowitz, N.L., Central nervous system manifestations of toxic disorders, in *Metabolic Brain Dysfunction in Systemic Disorders*, A.L. Arieff and R.C. Griggs, Ed. 1992, Boston: Little, Brown. p. 409–36.

335. Derlet, R.W. and T.E. Albertson, Acute cocaine toxicity: antagonism by agents interacting with adrenoceptors. *Pharmacol Biochem Behav*, 1990. 36(2): p. 225–31.

336. Trouve, R. and G.G. Nahas, Antidotes to lethal cocaine toxicity in the rat. *Arch Int Pharmacodyn Ther*, 1990. 305: p. 197–207.

337. Murphy, D.J., et al., Effects of adrenergic antagonists on cocaine-induced changes in respiratory function. *Pulm Pharmacol*, 1991. 4(3): p. 127–34.

338. Smith, M., D. Garner, and J.T. Niemann, Pharmacologic interventions after an LD_{50} cocaine insult in a chronically instrumented rat model: are beta-blockers contraindicated? *Ann Emerg Med*, 1991. 20(7): p. 768–71.

339. Hessler, R., Cardiovascular principles, in *Goldfrank's Toxicologic Emergencies*, L.R. Goldrank, N.E. Flomenbaum, and N.A. Lewin, Eds. 1992, Norwalk, CT: Appleton & Lange. p. 181–204.

340. Lange, R.A., et al., Potentiation of cocaine-induced coronary vasoconstriction by beta-adrenergic blockade [see comments]. *Ann Intern Med*, 1990. 112(12): p. 897–903.

341. Ramoska, E. and A.D. Sacchetti, Propranolol-induced hypertension in treatment of cocaine intoxication. *Ann Emerg Med*, 1985. 14(11): p. 1112–3.

342. Dusenberry, S.J., M.J. Hicks, and P.J. Mariani, Labetalol treatment of cocaine toxicity [letter]. *Ann Emerg Med*, 1987. 16(2): p. 235.

343. Sand, I.C., et al., Experience with esmolol for the treatment of cocaine-associated cardiovascular complications. *Am J Emerg Med*, 1991. 9(2): p. 161–3.

344. Darmansjah, I., et al., A dose-ranging study of labetalol in moderate to moderately severe hypertension. *Int J Clin Pharmacol Ther*, 1995. 33(4): p. 226–31.

345. Kenny, D., P.S. Pagel, and D.C. Warltier, Attenuation of the systemic and coronary hemodynamic effects of cocaine in conscious dogs: propranolol versus labetalol. *Basic Res Cardiol*, 1992. 87(5): p. 465–77.

346. Schindler, C.W., S.R. Tella, and S.R. Goldberg, Adrenoceptor mechanisms in the cardiovascular effects of cocaine in conscious squirrel monkeys. *Life Sci*, 1992. 51(9): p. 653–60.

347. Karch, S.B., Managing cocaine crisis [comment]. *Ann Emerg Med*, 1989. 18(2): p. 228–30.

348. Gay, G.R. and K.A. Loper, The use of labetalol in the management of cocaine crisis [see comments]. *Ann Emerg Med*, 1988. 17(3): p. 282–3.

349. Briggs, R.S., A.J. Birtwell, and J.E. Pohl, Hypertensive response to labetalol in phaeochromocytoma [letter]. *Lancet*, 1978. 1(8072): p. 1045–6.

350. Larsen, L.S. and A. Larsen, Labetalol in the treatment of epinephrine overdose. *Ann Emerg Med*, 1990. 19(6): p. 680–2.

351. Lange, R.A., et al., Cocaine-induced coronary-artery vasoconstriction [see comments]. *N Engl J Med*, 1989. 321(23): p. 1557–62.

352. Boehrer, J.D., et al., Influence of labetalol on cocaine-induced coronary vasoconstriction in humans. *Am J Med*, 1993. 94(6): p. 608–10.

353. Hamad, A., et al., Life-threatening hyperkalemia after intravenous labetolol injection for hypertensive emergency in a hemodialysis patient. *Am J Nephrol*, 2001. 21(3): p. 241–4.

354. Pollan, S. and M. Tadjziechy, Esmolol in the management of epinephrine- and cocaine-induced cardiovascular toxicity. *Anesth Analg*, 1989. 69(5): p. 663–4.

355. O'Connor, B. and J.B. Luntley, Acute dissection of the thoracic aorta. Esmolol is safer than and as effective as labetalol [letter; comment]. *BMJ*, 1995. 310(6983): p. 875.

356. Brogan, W.C.D., et al., Alleviation of cocaine-induced coronary vasoconstriction by nitroglycerin. *J Am Coll Cardiol*, 1991. 18(2): p. 581–6.

357. Gray, R.J., et al., Comparison of esmolol and nitroprusside for acute post-cardiac surgical hypertension. *Am J Cardiol*, 1987. 59(8): p. 887–91.

358. de Bruijn, N.P., et al., Pharmacokinetics of esmolol in anesthetized patients receiving chronic beta blocker therapy. *Anesthesiology*, 1987. 66(3): p. 323–6.

359. Bashour, T.T., Acute myocardial infarction resulting from amphetamine abuse: a spasm-thrombus interplay? *Am Heart J*, 1994. 128(6 Pt 1): p. 1237–9.

360. Ragland, A.S., Y. Ismail, and E.L. Arsura, Myocardial infarction after amphetamine use. *Am Heart J*, 1993. 125(1): p. 247–9.

361. Burton, B.T., M. Rice, and L.E. Schmertzler, Atrioventricular block following overdose of decongestant cold medication. *J Emerg Med*, 1985. 2(6): p. 415–9.

362. Pentel, P.R., J. Jentzen, and J. Sievert, Myocardial necrosis due to intraperitoneal administration of phenylpropanolamine in rats. *Fundam Appl Toxicol*, 1987. 9(1): p. 167–72.

363. Lucas, P.B., et al., Methylphenidate-induced cardiac arrhythmias [letter]. *N Engl J Med*, 1986. 315(23): p. 1485.

364. Jaffe, R.B., Cardiac and vascular involvement in drug abuse. *Semin Roentgenol*, 1983. 18(3): p. 207–12.

365. Lewin, N.G., L.R., and R.S. Hoffman, Cocaine, in *Goldfrank's Toxicologic Emergencies*, L. Goldfrank, Ed. 1994, Norwalk, CT: Appleton & Lange. p. 847–62.

366. Guidelines 2000 for Cardiopulmonary Resuscitation and Emergency Cardiovascular Care. Part 6: advanced cardiovascular life support: section 6: pharmacology II: agents to optimize cardiac output and blood pressure. The American Heart Association in collaboration with the International Liaison Committee on Resuscitation. *Circulation*, 2000. 102(8 Suppl): p. I129–35.

367. Hollander, J.E., The management of cocaine-associated myocardial ischemia. *N Engl J Med*, 1995. 333(19): p. 1267–72.

368. Benowitz, N.L., Clinical pharmacology and toxicology of cocaine [published erratum appears in *Pharmacol Toxicol* 1993 Jun;72(6):343]. *Pharmacol Toxicol*, 1993. 72(1): p. 3–12.

369. Catravas, J.D., et al., Acute cocaine intoxication in the conscious dog: pathophysiologic profile of acute lethality. *Arch Int Pharmacodyn Ther*, 1978. 235(2): p. 328–40.

370. Togna, G., et al., Platelet responsiveness and biosynthesis of thromboxane and prostacyclin in response to *in vitro* cocaine treatment. *Haemostasis*, 1985. 15(2): p. 100–7.

371. Schnetzer, G.W.D., Platelets and thrombogenesis — current concepts. *Am Heart J*, 1972. 83(4): p. 552–64.

372. Rezkalla, S.H., et al., Effects of cocaine on human platelets in healthy subjects. *Am J Cardiol*, 1993. 72(2): p. 243–6.

373. Hollander, J.E., et al., Nitroglycerin in the treatment of cocaine associated chest pain — clinical safety and efficacy. *J Toxicol Clin Toxicol*, 1994. 32(3): p. 243–56.

374. Billman, G.E., Effect of calcium channel antagonists on cocaine-induced malignant arrhythmias: protection against ventricular fibrillation. *J Pharmacol Exp Ther*, 1993. 266(1): p. 407–16.

375. Knuepfer, M.M. and C.A. Branch, Calcium channel antagonists reduce the cocaine-induced decrease in cardiac output in a subset of rats. *J Cardiovasc Pharmacol*, 1993. 21(3): p. 390–6.

376. Derlet, R.W. and T.E. Albertson, Potentiation of cocaine toxicity with calcium channel blockers. *Am J Emerg Med*, 1989. 7(5): p. 464–8.

377. Hoffman, R., Comment to calcium channel blockers may potentiate cocaine toxicity. AACT clinical toxicology update, 1990 (March).

378. Nahas, G., et al., A calcium-channel blocker as antidote to the cardiac effects of cocaine intoxication [letter]. *N Engl J Med*, 1985. 313(8): p. 519–20.

379. Negus, B.H., et al., Alleviation of cocaine-induced coronary vasoconstriction with intravenous verapamil. *Am J Cardiol*, 1994. 73(7): p. 510–3.

380. Hollander, J.E., W.A. Carter, and R.S. Hoffman, Use of phentolamine for cocaine-induced myocardial ischemia [letter]. *N Engl J Med*, 1992. 327(5): p. 361.

381. Bush, H.S., Cocaine-associated myocardial infarction. A word of caution about thrombolytic therapy [see comments]. *Chest*, 1988. 94(4): p. 878.

382. Hollander, J.E., et al., Cocaine-associated myocardial infarction. Clinical safety of thrombolytic therapy. Cocaine Associated Myocardial Infarction (CAMI) Study Group. *Chest*, 1995. 107(5): p. 1237–41.

383. Hollander, J.E., et al., Cocaine-associated myocardial infarction. Mortality and complications. Cocaine-Associated Myocardial Infarction Study Group. *Arch Intern Med*, 1995. 155(10): p. 1081–6.

384. Gitter, M.J., et al., Cocaine and chest pain: clinical features and outcome of patients hospitalized to rule out myocardial infarction [see comments]. *Ann Intern Med*, 1991. 115(4): p. 277–82.

385. Hollander, J.E., et al., "Abnormal" electrocardiograms in patients with cocaine-associated chest pain are due to "normal" variants. *J Emerg Med*, 1994. 12(2): p. 199–205.

386. Keller, K.B. and L. Lemberg, The cocaine-abused heart. *Am J Crit Care*, 2003. 12(6): p. 562–6.

387. Kontos, M.C., et al., Coronary angiographic findings in patients with cocaine-associated chest pain. *J Emerg Med*, 2003. 24(1): p. 9–13.

388. Derlet, R.W., T.E. Albertson, and R.S. Tharratt, Lidocaine potentiation of cocaine toxicity. *Ann Emerg Med*, 1991. 20(2): p. 135–8.

389. Liu, D., R.J. Hariman, and J.L. Bauman, Cocaine concentration-effect relationship in the presence and absence of lidocaine: evidence of competitive binding between cocaine and lidocaine. *J Pharmacol Exp Ther*, 1996. 276(2): p. 568–77.

390. Winecoff, A.P., et al., Reversal of the electrocardiographic effects of cocaine by lidocaine. Part 1. Comparison with sodium bicarbonate and quinidine. *Pharmacotherapy*, 1994. 14(6): p. 698–703.

391. Shih, R.D., et al., Clinical safety of lidocaine in patients with cocaine-associated myocardial infarction. *Ann Emerg Med*, 1995. 26(6): p. 702–6.

392. Beckman, K.J., et al., Hemodynamic and electrophysiological actions of cocaine. Effects of sodium bicarbonate as an antidote in dogs. *Circulation*, 1991. 83(5): p. 1799–807.

393. Goel, P. and G.C. Flaker, Cardiovascular complications of cocaine use. *N Engl J Med*, 2001. 345(21): p. 1575–6.

394. Barth, C.W.d., M. Bray, and W.C. Roberts, Rupture of the ascending aorta during cocaine intoxication. *Am J Cardiol*, 1986. 57(6): p. 496.

395. Brody, S.L., C.M. Slovis, and K.D. Wrenn, Cocaine-related medical problems: consecutive series of 233 patients [see comments]. *Am J Med*, 1990. 88(4): p. 325–31.

396. Derlet, R.W. and T.E. Albertson, Emergency department presentation of cocaine intoxication. *Ann Emerg Med*, 1989. 18(2): p. 182–6.

397. Rich, J.A. and D.E. Singer, Cocaine-related symptoms in patients presenting to an urban emergency department. *Ann Emerg Med*, 1991. 20(6): p. 616–21.

398. Silverstein, W., N.A. Lewin, and L. Goldfrank, Management of the cocaine-intoxicated patient [letter]. *Ann Emerg Med*, 1987. 16(2): p. 234–5.

399. Kloner, R.A., et al., The effects of acute and chronic cocaine use on the heart. *Circulation*, 1992. 85(2): p. 407–19.

400. Isner, J.M., et al., Acute cardiac events temporally related to cocaine abuse. *N Engl J Med*, 1986. 315(23): p. 1438–43.

401. Cregler, L.L. and H. Mark, Medical complications of cocaine abuse. *N Engl J Med*, 1986. 315(23): p. 1495–500.

402. Robin, E.D., R.J. Wong, and K.A. Ptashne, Increased lung water and ascites after massive cocaine overdosage in mice and improved survival related to beta-adrenergic blockage. *Ann Intern Med*, 1989. 110(3): p. 202–7.

403. Ouriel, K., Comparison of safety and efficacy of the various thrombolytic agents. *Rev Cardiovasc Med*, 2002. 3 Suppl 2: p. S17–24.

404. Baker, W.F., Jr., Thrombolytic therapy. *Clin Appl Thromb Hemost*, 2002. 8(4): p. 291–314.

405. Baker, W.F., Jr., Thrombolytic therapy: clinical applications. *Hematol Oncol Clin North Am*, 2003. 17(1): p. 283–311.

406. Nordt, T.K. and C. Bode, Thrombolysis: newer thrombolytic agents and their role in clinical medicine. *Heart*, 2003. 89(11): p. 1358–62.

407. Williams, M.L. and D.A. Tate, *Emergency Medicine: A Comprehensive Study Guide*. 4th ed, J. Tintinalli, E. Ruiz, and R.L. Krome, Eds. 1996, New York: McGraw-Hill. p. 344–54.

408. Grawe, J.J., et al., Reversal of the electrocardiographic effects of cocaine by lidocaine. Part 2. Concentration-effect relationships. *Pharmacotherapy*, 1994. 14(6): p. 704–11.

409. Tokarski, G.F., et al., An evaluation of cocaine-induced chest pain [see comments]. *Ann Emerg Med*, 1990. 19(10): p. 1088–92.

410. Hollander, J.E., et al., Prospective multicenter evaluation of cocaine-associated chest pain. Cocaine Associated Chest Pain (COCHPA) Study Group. *Acad Emerg Med*, 1994. 1(4): p. 330–9.

411. Adams, J.E., 3rd, et al., Cardiac troponin I. A marker with high specificity for cardiac injury. *Circulation*, 1993. 88(1): p. 101–6.

412. Kontos, M.C., et al., Utility of troponin I in patients with cocaine-associated chest pain. *Acad Emerg Med*, 2002. 9(10): p. 1007–13.

413. Wu, A.H., et al., Comparison of myoglobin, creatine kinase-MB, and cardiac troponin I for diagnosis of acute myocardial infarction. *Ann Clin Lab Sci*, 1996. 26(4): p. 291–300.

414. Graff, L., et al., American College of Emergency Physicians information paper: chest pain units in emergency departments — a report from the Short-Term Observation Services Section. *Am J Cardiol*, 1995. 76(14): p. 1036–9.

415. Lee, T.H., et al., Ruling out acute myocardial infarction. A prospective multicenter validation of a 12-hour strategy for patients at low risk. *N Engl J Med*, 1991. 324(18): p. 1239–46.

416. Weber, J.E., et al., Validation of a brief observation period for patients with cocaine-associated chest pain. *N Engl J Med*, 2003. 348(6): p. 510–7.

417. Hollander, J.E. and R.S. Hoffman, Cocaine-induced myocardial infarction: an analysis and review of the literature. *J Emerg Med*, 1992. 10(2): p. 169–77.

418. Zimmerman, J.L., R.P. Dellinger, and P.A. Majid, Cocaine-associated chest pain. *Ann Emerg Med*, 1991. 20(6): p. 611–5.

419. Kokkinos, J. and S. Levine, Stroke. *Neurol Clin*, 1993. 11(3): p. 577–90.

420. Petitti, D.B., et al., Stroke and cocaine or amphetamine use. *Epidemiology*, 1998. 9(6): p. 596–600.

421. Qureshi, A.I., et al., Cocaine use and the likelihood of nonfatal myocardial infarction and stroke: data from the Third National Health and Nutrition Examination Survey. *Circulation*, 2001. 103(4): p. 502–6.

422. Friedman, E.H., Cocaine-induced stroke. *Neurology*, 1993. 43(9): p. 1864–5.

423. Tolat, R.D., et al., Cocaine-associated stroke: three cases and rehabilitation considerations. *Brain Inj*, 2000. 14(4): p. 383–91.

424. Riggs, J.E. and L. Gutmann, Crack cocaine use and stroke in young patients. *Neurology*, 1997. 49(5): p. 1473–4.

425. Kaku, D. and D.H. Lowenstein, Emergence of recreational drug abuse as a major risk factor for stroke in young adults. *Ann Intern Med*, 1990. 113: p. 821.

426. Konzen, J.P., S.R. Levine, and J.H. Garcia, Vasospasm and thrombus formation as possible mechanisms of stroke related to alkaloidal cocaine. *Stroke*, 1995. 26(6): p. 1114–8.

427. Tardiff, K., et al., Analysis of cocaine-positive fatalities. *J Forensic Sci*, 1989. 34(1): p. 53–63.

428. Mueller, P.D., N.L. Benowitz, and K.R. Olson, Cocaine. *Emerg Med Clin North Am*, 1990. 8(3): p. 481–93.

429. Barsan, W.G. and M. Bain, Stroke, in *Emergency Medicine: Concepts and Clinical Practice*, P. Rosen and R.M. Barkin, Eds. 1992, St. Louis: Mosby Year Book. p. 1825–41.

430. Hacke, W., et al., Intravenous thrombolysis with recombinant tissue plasminogen activator for acute hemispheric stroke. The European Cooperative Acute Stroke Study (ECASS). *JAMA*, 1995. 274(13): p. 1017–25.

431. Randomised controlled trial of streptokinase, aspirin, and combination of both in treatment of acute ischaemic stroke. Multicentre Acute Stroke Trial — Italy (MAST-I) Group. *Lancet*, 1995. 346(8989): p. 1509–14.

432. Tissue plasminogen activator for acute ischemic stroke. The National Institute of Neurological Disorders and Stroke rt-PA Stroke Study Group. *N Engl J Med*, 1995. 333(24): p. 1581–7.

433. Thrombolytic therapy with streptokinase in acute ischemic stroke. The Multicenter Acute Stroke Trial — Europe Study Group. *N Engl J Med*, 1996. 335(3): p. 145–50.

434. Donnan, G.A., et al., Streptokinase for acute ischemic stroke with relationship to time of administration: Australian Streptokinase (ASK) Trial Study Group. *JAMA*, 1996. 276(12): p. 961–6.

434a. Hoffman, J.R., Should physicians give tPA to patients with acute ischemic stroke? *West J Med*, 2000. 173: p. 149–50.

435. Libman, R.B., et al., Conditions that mimic stroke in the emergency department. Implications for acute stroke trials. *Arch Neurol*, 1995. 52(11): p. 1119–22.

436. Turpie, A.G., R. Bloch, and R. Duke, Heparin in the treatment of thromboembolic stroke. *Ann NY Acad Sci*, 1989. 556: p. 406–15.

437. Sage, J.I., Stroke. The use and overuse of heparin in therapeutic trials. *Arch Neurol*, 1985. 42(4): p. 315–7.

438. Korczyn, A.D., Heparin in the treatment of acute stroke. *Neurol Clin*, 1992. 10(1): p. 209–17.

439. Salgado, A.V., et al., Neurologic complications of endocarditis: a 12-year experience. *Neurology*, 1989. 39(2 Pt 1): p. 173–8.

440. Hart, R.G., et al., Stroke in infective endocarditis. *Stroke*, 1990. 21(5): p. 695–700.

441. Showalter, C.V., T's and blues. Abuse of pentazocine and tripelennamine. *JAMA*, 1980. 244(11): p. 1224–5.

442. Caplan, L.R., C. Thomas, and G. Banks, Central nervous system complications of addiction to "T's and Blues." *Neurology*, 1982. 32(6): p. 623–8.

443. Lipton, R.B., M. Choy-Kwong, and S. Solomon, Headaches in hospitalized cocaine users. *Headache*, 1989. 29(4): p. 225–8.

444. Benowitz, N.L., How toxic is cocaine? *Ciba Found Symp*, 1992. 166: p. 125–43; discussion 143–8.

445. Satel, S.L. and F.H. Gawin, Migrainelike headache and cocaine use. *JAMA*, 1989. 261(20): p. 2995–6.

446. Rothrock, J.F., R. Rubenstein, and P.D. Lyden, Ischemic stroke associated with methamphetamine inhalation. *Neurology*, 1988. 38(4): p. 589–92.

447. Rumbaugh, C.L., et al., Cerebral vascular changes secondary to amphetamine abuse in the experimental animal. *Radiology*, 1971. 101(2): p. 345–51.

448. Wadworth, A.N. and D. McTavish, Nimodipine. A review of its pharmacological properties, and therapeutic efficacy in cerebral disorders. *Drugs Aging*, 1992. 2(4): p. 262–86.

449. Rickels, E. and M. Zumkeller, Vasospasm after experimentally induced subarachnoid haemorrhage and treatment with nimodipine. *Neurochirurgia* (Stuttgart), 1992. 35(4): p. 99–102.

450. Ansah, T.A., L.H. Wade, and D.C. Shockley, Effects of calcium channel entry blockers on cocaine and amphetamine-induced motor activities and toxicities. *Life Sci*, 1993. 53(26): p. 1947–56.

451. Derlet, R.W., C.C. Tseng, and T.E. Albertson, Cocaine toxicity and the calcium channel blockers nifedipine and nimodipine in rats. *J Emerg Med*, 1994. 12(1): p. 1–4.

452. Kaste, M., et al., A randomized, double-blind, placebo-controlled trial of nimodipine in acute ischemic hemispheric stroke. *Stroke*, 1994. 25(7): p. 1348–53.

453. Wooten, M.R., M.S. Khangure, and M.J. Murphy, Intracerebral hemorrhage and vasculitis related to ephedrine abuse. *Ann Neurol*, 1983. 13(3): p. 337–40.

454. Rumbaugh, C.L., et al., Cerebral microvascular injury in experimental drug abuse. *Invest Radiol*, 1976. 11(4): p. 282–94.

455. Citron, B.P., et al., Necrotizing angiitis associated with drug abuse. *N Engl J Med*, 1970. 283(19): p. 1003–11.

456. Loizou, L.A., J.G. Hamilton, and S.A. Tsementzis, Intracranial haemorrhage in association with pseudoephedrine overdose. *J Neurol Neurosurg Psychiatry*, 1982. 45(5): p. 471–2.

457. Brust, J.C. and R.W. Richter, Stroke associated with addiction to heroin. *J Neurol Neurosurg Psychiatry*, 1976. 39(2): p. 194–9.

458. Woods, B.T. and G.J. Strewler, Hemiparesis occurring six hours after intravenous heroin injection. *Neurology*, 1972. 22(8): p. 863–6.

459. Trugman, J.M., Cerebral arteritis and oral methylphenidate [letter]. *Lancet*, 1988. 1(8585): p. 584–5.

460. Fredericks, R.K., et al., Cerebral vasculitis associated with cocaine abuse. *Stroke*, 1991. 22(11): p. 1437–9.

461. Krendel, D.A., et al., Biopsy-proven cerebral vasculitis associated with cocaine abuse. *Neurology*, 1990. 40(7): p. 1092–4.

462. Kaye, B.R. and M. Fainstat, Cerebral vasculitis associated with cocaine abuse. *JAMA*, 1987. 258(15): p. 2104–6.

463. Nalls, G., et al., Subcortical cerebral hemorrhages associated with cocaine abuse: CT and MR findings. *J Comput Assist Tomogr*, 1989. 13(1): p. 1–5.

464. Salanova, V. and R. Taubner, Intracerebral haemorrhage and vasculitis secondary to amphetamine use. *Postgrad Med J*, 1984. 60(704): p. 429–30.

465. Cerebral vasculitis associated with cocaine abuse or subarachnoid hemorrhage? [letter]. *JAMA*, 1988. 259(11): p. 1648–9.

466. Powers, W.J., Acute hypertension after stroke: the scientific basis for treatment decisions. *Neurology*, 1993. 43(3 Pt 1): p. 461–7.

467. Kenton, E.J., III, Diagnosis and treatment of concomitant hypertension and stroke. *J Natl Med Assoc*, 1996. 88(6): p. 364–8.

468. Shephard, T.J. and S.W. Fox, Assessment and management of hypertension in the acute ischemic stroke patient. *J Neurosci Nurs*, 1996. 28(1): p. 5–12.

469. Brucia, J.J., D.C. Owen, and E.B. Rudy, The effects of lidocaine on intracranial hypertension. *J Neurosci Nurs*, 1992. 24(4): p. 205–14.

470. Lev, R. and P. Rosen, Prophylactic lidocaine use preintubation: a review. *J Emerg Med*, 1994. 12(4): p. 499–506.

471. Malouf, R. and J.C. Brust, Hypoglycemia: causes, neurological manifestations, and outcome. *Ann Neurol*, 1985. 17(5): p. 421–30.

472. Swartz, M.H., L.E. Teichholz, and E. Donoso, Mitral valve prolapse: a review of associated arrhythmias. *Am J Med*, 1977. 62(3): p. 377–89.

473. Savage, D.D., et al., Mitral valve prolapse in the general population. 3. Dysrhythmias: the Framingham Study. *Am Heart J*, 1983. 106(3): p. 582–6.

474. Washington, J.A.D., The role of the microbiology laboratory in the diagnosis and antimicrobial treatment of infective endocarditis. *Mayo Clin Proc*, 1982. 57(1): p. 22–32.

475. Hoffman, R.S., M.J. Smilkstein, and L.R. Goldfrank, Whole bowel irrigation and the cocaine body-packer: a new approach to a common problem. *Am J Emerg Med*, 1990. 8(6): p. 523–7.

476. Duenas-Laita, A., S. Nogue, and G. Burillo-Putze, Body packing. *N Engl J Med*, 2004. 350(12): p. 1260–1; author reply 1260–1.

477. Bulstrode, N., F. Banks, and S. Shrotria, The outcome of drug smuggling by 'body packers' — the British experience. *Ann R Coll Surg Engl*, 2002. 84(1): p. 35–8.

478. Traub, S.J., et al., Pediatric "body packing." *Arch Pediatr Adolesc Med*, 2003. 157(2): p. 174–7.

479. Roberts, J.R., et al., The bodystuffer syndrome: a clandestine form of drug overdose. *Am J Emerg Med*, 1986. 4(1): p. 24–7.

480. Olson, K.R., Is gut emptying all washed up? [editorial]. *Am J Emerg Med*, 1990. 8(6): p. 560–1.

481. Kulig, K., et al., Management of acutely poisoned patients without gastric emptying. *Ann Emerg Med*, 1985. 14(6): p. 562–7.

482. Albertson, T.E., et al., Superiority of activated charcoal alone compared with ipecac and activated charcoal in the treatment of acute toxic ingestions [see comments]. *Ann Emerg Med*, 1989. 18(1): p. 56–9.

483. Merigian, K.S., et al., Prospective evaluation of gastric emptying in the self-poisoned patient. *Am J Emerg Med*, 1990. 8(6): p. 479–83.

484. Pond, S.M., et al., Gastric emptying in acute overdose: a prospective randomised controlled trial [see comments]. *Med J Aust*, 1995. 163(7): p. 345–9.

485. Curtis, R.A., J. Barone, and N. Giacona, Efficacy of ipecac and activated charcoal/cathartic. Prevention of salicylate absorption in a simulated overdose. *Arch Intern Med*, 1984. 144(1): p. 48–52.

486. Tenenbein, M., S. Cohen, and D.S. Sitar, Efficacy of ipecac-induced emesis, orogastric lavage, and activated charcoal for acute drug overdose. *Ann Emerg Med*, 1987. 16(8): p. 838–41.

487. Olkkola, K.T., Effect of charcoal-drug ratio on antidotal efficacy of oral activated charcoal in man. *Br J Clin Pharmacol*, 1985. 19(6): p. 767–73.

488. Pollack, M.M., et al., Aspiration of activated charcoal and gastric contents. *Ann Emerg Med*, 1981. 10(10): p. 528–9.

489. Menzies, D.G., A. Busuttil, and L.F. Prescott, Fatal pulmonary aspiration of oral activated charcoal. *BMJ*, 1988. 297(6646): p. 459–60.

490. Givens, T., M. Holloway, and S. Wason, Pulmonary aspiration of activated charcoal: a complication of its misuse in overdose management. *Pediatr Emerg Care*, 1992. 8(3): p. 137–40.

491. Mariani, P.J. and N. Pook, Gastrointestinal tract perforation with charcoal peritoneum complicating orogastric intubation and lavage. *Ann Emerg Med*, 1993. 22(3): p. 606–9.

492. Ray, M.J., et al., Charcoal bezoar. Small-bowel obstruction secondary to amitriptyline overdose therapy [published erratum appears in *Dig Dis Sci* 1988 Oct;33(10):1344]. *Dig Dis Sci*, 1988. 33(1): p. 106–7.

493. Watson, W.A., K.F. Cremer, and J.A. Chapman, Gastrointestinal obstruction associated with multiple-dose activated charcoal. *J Emerg Med*, 1986. 4(5): p. 401–7.

494. Longdon, P. and A. Henderson, Intestinal pseudo-obstruction following the use of enteral charcoal and sorbitol and mechanical ventilation with papaveretum sedation for theophylline poisoning. *Drug Saf*, 1992. 7(1): p. 74–7.

495. Bradberry, S.M. and J.A. Vale, Multiple-dose activated charcoal: a review of relevant clinical studies. *J Toxicol Clin Toxicol*, 1995. 33(5): p. 407–16.

496. Pond, S.M., et al., Randomized study of the treatment of phenobarbital overdose with repeated doses of activated charcoal. *JAMA*, 1984. 251(23): p. 3104–8.

497. Boldy, D.A., J.A. Vale, and L.F. Prescott, Treatment of phenobarbitone poisoning with repeated oral administration of activated charcoal. *Q J Med*, 1986. 61(235): p. 997–1002.

498. Eroglu, A., et al., Multiple dose-activated charcoal as a cause of acute appendicitis. *J Toxicol Clin Toxicol*, 2003. 41(1): p. 71–3.

499. Everson, G.W., E.J. Bertaccini, and J. O'Leary, Use of whole bowel irrigation in an infant following iron overdose. *Am J Emerg Med*, 1991. 9(4): p. 366–9.

500. Turk, J., et al., Successful therapy of iron intoxication in pregnancy with intravenous deferoxamine and whole bowel irrigation. *Vet Hum Toxicol*, 1993. 35(5): p. 441–4.

501. Bock, G.W. and M. Tenenbein, Whole bowel irrigation for iron overdose [letter]. *Ann Emerg Med*, 1987. 16(1): p. 137–8.

502. Janss, G.J., Acute theophylline overdose treated with whole bowel irrigation. *S D J Med*, 1990. 43(6): p. 7–8.

503. Buckley, N., et al., Slow-release verapamil poisoning. Use of polyethylene glycol whole-bowel lavage and high-dose calcium. *Med J Aust*, 1993. 158(3): p. 202–4.

504. Burkhart, K.K., K.W. Kulig, and B. Rumack, Whole-bowel irrigation as treatment for zinc sulfate overdose. *Ann Emerg Med*, 1990. 19(10): p. 1167–70.

505. Melandri, R., et al., Whole bowel irrigation after delayed release fenfluramine overdose. *J Toxicol Clin Toxicol*, 1995. 33(2): p. 161–3.

506. Roberge, R.J. and T.G. Martin, Whole bowel irrigation in an acute oral lead intoxication. *Am J Emerg Med*, 1992. 10(6): p. 577–83.

507. Utecht, M.J., A.F. Stone, and M.M. McCarron, Heroin body packers. *J Emerg Med*, 1993. 11(1): p. 33–40.

508. Niazi, S., Effect of polyethylene glycol 4000 on dissolution properties of sulfathiazole polymorphs. *J Pharm Sci*, 1976. 65(2): p. 302–4.

509. Diacetylmorphine, in *Merck Index*. 1984, Rahway, NJ: Merck & Co, Inc. p. 429.

510. Rosenberg, P.J., D.J. Livingstone, and B.A. McLellan, Effect of whole-bowel irrigation on the antidotal efficacy of oral activated charcoal. *Ann Emerg Med*, 1988. 17(7): p. 681–3.

511. Tenenbein, M., Whole bowel irrigation and activated charcoal [letter]. *Ann Emerg Med*, 1989. 18(6): p. 707–8.

512. Ilkhanipour, K., D.M. Yealy, and E.P. Krenzelok, The comparative efficacy of various multiple-dose activated charcoal regimens. *Am J Emerg Med*, 1992. 10(4): p. 298–300.

513. Park, G.D., et al., Effects of size and frequency of oral doses of charcoal on theophylline clearance. *Clin Pharmacol Ther*, 1983. 34(5): p. 663–6.

514. Marc, B., et al., Managing drug dealers who swallow the evidence. *BMJ*, 1989. 299(6707): p. 1082.

515. Sporer, K., Cocaine body stuffers. 1997, unpublished data.

516. McCarron, M.M. and J.D. Wood, The cocaine 'body packer' syndrome. Diagnosis and treatment. *JAMA*, 1983. 250(11): p. 1417–20.

517. Caruana, D.S., et al., Cocaine-packet ingestion. Diagnosis, management, and natural history. *Ann Intern Med*, 1984. 100(1): p. 73–4.

518. Farmer, J.W. and S.B. Chan, Whole body irrigation for contraband bodypackers. *J Clin Gastroenterol*, 2003. 37(2): p. 147–50.

519. Jeanmarie, P., Cocaine, in *Emergency Medicine, A Comprehensive Study Guide*, J. Tintinalli, Ed. 1996, New York: McGraw-Hill. p. 777–778.

520. Weiner, J.S. and M. Khogali, A physiological body-cooling unit for treatment of heat stroke. *Lancet*, 1980. 1(8167): p. 507–9.

521. Barner, H.B., et al., Field evaluation of a new simplified method for cooling of heat casualties in the desert. *Mil Med*, 1984. 149(2): p. 95–7.

522. Al-Aska, A.K., et al., Simplified cooling bed for heatstroke. *Lancet*, 1987. 1(8529): p. 381.

523. Kielblock, A.J., J.P. Van Rensburg, and R.M. Franz, Body cooling as a method for reducing hyperthermia. An evaluation of techniques. *S Afr Med J*, 1986. 69(6): p. 378–80.

524. Wyndham, C.H., N.B. Strydom, and H.M. Cooke, Methods of cooling subjects with hyperpyrexia. *J Appl Physiol,* 1959. (14): p. 771.

525. White, J.D., et al., Evaporation versus iced gastric lavage treatment of heatstroke: comparative efficacy in a canine model. *Crit Care Med,* 1987. 15(8): p. 748–50.

526. Daily, W.M. and T.R. Harrison, A study of the mechanism and treatment of experimental heat pyrexia. *Am J Med Sci,* 1948. 215: p. 42.

527. Magazanik, A., et al., Tap water, an efficient method for cooling heatstroke victims — a model in dogs. *Aviat Space Environ Med,* 1980. 51(9 Pt 1): p. 864–6.

528. Bynum, G., et al., Peritoneal lavage cooling in an anesthetized dog heatstroke model. *Aviat Space Environ Med,* 1978. 49(6): p. 779–84.

529. Syverud, S.A., et al., Iced gastric lavage for treatment of heatstroke: efficacy in a canine model. *Ann Emerg Med,* 1985. 14(5): p. 424–32.

530. Chiulli, D.A., T.E. Terndrup, and R.K. Kaufer, The influence of diazepam or lorazepam on the frequency of endotracheal intubation in childhood status epilepticus. *J Emerg Med,* 1991. 9: p. 13–17.

Index